Chicago Sun-Times

20TH CENTURY CHICAGO

100 YEARS • 100 VOICES

Edited by Adrienne Drell

Sports Publishing Inc.
www.SportsPublishing.com

20TH CENTURY CHICAGO
100 YEARS · 100 VOICES

EDITED BY ADRIENNE DRELL

Chicago Sun-Times

Editor-in-Chief: **Nigel Wade**

Managing Editor: **Joycelyn Winnecke**

Coordinating News Editor: **Roger Flaherty**

Research Editor: **Lorraine V. Forte**

Design-News Editor: **James Wambold**

Design Editors: **Thomas Frisbie, Robert Oswald**

Photo Editor: **Nancy Stuenkel**

Sun-Times Photo Staff: **Bob Black, Richard A. Chapman, Tom Cruze, Robert A. Davis, Ellen Domke, Joe Erhardt, Jim Frost, Keith Hale, Rich Hein, Brian Jackson, Dom Najolia, Al Podgorski, Jon Sall, Scott Stewart, Ernie Torres and John H. White**

Artist: **Cliff Wirth**

Sports Publishing Inc.

Coordinating Editor: **Joseph J. Bannon, Jr.**

Book and Cover Design: **Terry Neutz Hayden**

Interior Layout: **Michelle A. Summers**

Photo Editors: **Scot Muncaster, Julie Denzer and Chuck Peters**

Developmental Editor: **Claudia Mitroi**

Research Editor: **Joanna Wright**

Copy Editor: **David Hamburg**

Production Assistant: **Crystal Gummere**

ISBN: 1-58261-239-0

Library of Congress Catalog Card Number: 99-68048

Printed in the United States

www.SportsPublishingInc.com

ACKNOWLEDGMENTS

Many people have been important to the development of this historical look at Chicago, starting with our 100 guest authors. But others also provided invaluable assistance.

They include the persistent research of the Chicago Sun-Times library staff: Terri Golembiewski, Judith Anne Halper, Virginia Davis, Theodore L. White, Herbert Ballard, Ronald W. Theel, Dale McCullough and Zigis Ulmanis; the constant vigilance of editorial assistants Jenny Fleishman, Jessica Fitch, Roy Smith, Richard J. Harris, Laura Castro, Steven Gohston and Albert Dickens; and the hard work of secretaries Karen Abee, Yolanda McCoy and Judy Rieke.

Shirlee DeSanti and Richard E. Harris deftly fielded hundreds of messages and visitors, and Photo Editor Nancy Stuenkel searched patiently for long-lost images. Editors Roger Flaherty and Michael Gillis shepherded the morass of text, and James G. Wambold was a design-news editor beyond compare. Robert Oswald and Thomas Frisbie created masterful layouts for the newspaper series, and Lorraine Forte checked often-obscure facts of city history.

The voices in our book ring loud and clear, thanks to insights from Sun-Times writers and editors such as Rosalind Rossi, Steve Neal, Scott Fornek, Neil Steinberg, Toni Ginnetti, Dan Haar, Don Hayner, Nancy Moffett, Lynn Sweet, Bill Adee and Thomas Frisbie, the man for all seasons and skills, who wrote, edited, critiqued, proofed, titled and beautifully presented so many years.

The book would not have been possible without the support of Nigel Wade, Joycelyn Winnecke, Larry Green and Emily Selene De Rotstein. It is impossible to list all of those who contributed to the project, but warm thanks are also due to Julia Sniderman Bachrach, Kristin Bagnato, Pat Bakunas, Mary Ann Bamberger, Russell Bath, Todd Behme, Bonnie Bellew, Lyle Benedict, Tracey Labovitz Berkowitz, Becky Beaupre, Jill Boba, Jeff Britt, Teresa Budasi, Jennifer Burklow, Margaret Burroughs, Rich Cahan, John Camper, Carmel Carrillo, Jennifer Ciminillo, Maureen Cotter, Gregory Couch, Patrick Deady, John Dodge, Pam Feigenbaum, Ercelle Feldman, Michael Flug, Stella Foster, Dana Kopp Franklin, Marlene Gelfond, Jennifer George, Gregory Good, Allen Harris, Diane Hawkins, Karen Huelsman, Dan Jedlicka, Jeff Johnson, James Kearney, Adam Krantz, Lisa Lenoir, Rebecca Little, Rosalie Lutzka, Mary McDonough, Margaret Maples, Kenneth Maluchnik, Ian Mitchell, Roy Moody, Archibald Motley, Bob Mutter, Angela Myers, Franklin Nitikman, Ellen O'Brien, Suzanne Ontiveros, Ken Price, Susan Randstrom, Stephanie Reynolds, Toby Roberts, David Roknic, Mary Rowitz, Norm Schaefer, Bob Shea, Kim Schulz, Char Searl, Frank Sugano, Dempsey Travis, Tom Travin, Charlotte Ulmanis, Rachel Webster, Cliff Wirth, Christopher Woldt, John Woolard and Rich Zamudio.

We also gratefully acknowledge the assistance of the Chicago Historical Society, the Chicago Park District, the University of Illinois at Chicago Library Special Collections, Robert M. Lightfoot III, Andrew Kopan, Richard Vachula, Chicago Symphony Orchestra Archives, the Vivian G. Harsh Collection of Woodson Regional Library, the Municipal Reference Collection and the Special Collections and Preservation Divisions of the Chicago Public Library and the South Side Art Center.

Adrienne Drell
Editor, *20th Century Chicago: 100 Years • 100 Voices*

THE 100 VOICES

EDITOR'S NOTE

The history of Chicago in the 20th century is a story of people building one of the greatest cities on earth, then moving ahead to rebuild, improve and make it even greater.

In our series "100 Years in 100 Days," the Chicago Sun-Times asked well-known writers and Chicago personalities to join us in recalling the city's story one year at a time. The chronicle unfolded neighborhood by neighborhood, one epic tale after another, over the last three and a half months of the 20th century.

Each day offered a different voice, another perspective, another drama or high achievement from the rambunctious history of this quintessentially American metropolis.

The series had not been running very long before readers began to write and call, asking whether the 100 installments could be collected and published as a book.

Here it is—the 20th century—as Chicagoans knew and lived it.

The Sun-Times is proud to help celebrate 100 years of the heritage, cultures and personalities of this wonderful town.

Nigel Wade

Editor-in-Chief

Chicago Sun-Times

CONTENTS

INTRODUCTION

BY ADRIENNE DRELL, EDITOR OF 100 YEARS • 100 VOICES

An amazing array of visionaries and rogues, artists and immigrants populated and built early 20th-century Chicago.

They included America's greatest architect, Frank Lloyd Wright, whose philosophy and contributions to design are unmatched to this day; merchant prince Marshall Field, whose store became a model for retail emporiums; and the likes of rascal aldermen Michael "Hinky Dink" Kenna and "Bathhouse" John Coughlin, who bribed anyone and everyone.

Although turn-of-the-century Chicago women did not have the vote, they still managed to wield power and influence—and enrich the lives of others in the modern city that rose from the rubble of the 1871 fire.

Bertha Honore Palmer, for example, lived in a splendid new Gold Coast mansion, where she amassed a breathtaking art collection and threw lavish parties for the social elite in a rooftop ballroom. But she also invited settlement workers, politicians and struggling artists to her soirees and was a driving force behind women's rights.

Ida B. Wells-Barnett was a journalist, teacher and civil rights activist who criticized President McKinley for his indifference to the rights of blacks. She served as a probation officer for the Chicago Municipal Court, helped found the National Association for the Advancement of Colored People and promoted suffrage for women. She worked with Jane Addams to block separate schools for blacks in Chicago.

Addams, who had a pampered childhood and was one of the first female college graduates in the country, rejected a privileged life to engage in altruistic work with Chicago's poor. Hull House, the renowned settlement community she founded, provided education, culture and help to thousands of immigrants in the Halsted Street area.

Others also shaped Chicago over the course of the 20th century. Enrico Fermi changed the world by splitting the atom. Ray Kroc revolutionized fast-food dining with his hamburger-franchise empire. William Wrigley built a fortune on chewing gum and left his name on perhaps the nation's most classic ballpark. And by century's end, Michael Jordan, the basketball whiz kid from North Carolina, finally supplanted hoodlum Al Capone as Chicago's best-known figure internationally.

To capture the unique flavor of the 20th century in this town, the Chicago Sun-Times invited 100 individuals who either created history here, lived it or reported on it to make the past come alive again.

Their accounts comprise *20th Century Chicago: One Hundred Years • One Hundred Voices,* the only year-by-year chronological history of 20th-century Chicago in either print or broadcast form.

Our authors include political power brokers, academics, theologians, sports figures, journalists, celebrities, scientists, authors, artists, historians and architects.

Some contributors bear the great names of Chicago. Potter Palmer recalls Bertha, his great grandmother and widow of the man who built the Palmer House. John Holabird writes about his father and grandfather's architectural works. Marshall Field V details how his grandfather started what became the Chicago Sun-Times, and Adlai Stevenson III writes about his dad's 1956 Democratic presidential nomination.

Other authors chronicle how immigrant groups were absorbed into the mainstream culture of Chicago. Cook County Treasurer Maria Pappas describes the early Greeks who got off the train and stayed here. Jan Lorys, curator of the Polish Museum, recalls the inspiring 1917 visit of Polish pianist and statesman Ignace Paderewski.

Potter Palmer Mansion

Mrs. Bertha Potter (center) at the Lake Forest Fair

North Wells Street in 1959, and the Rev. Martin E. Marty remembers marching in Selma, Ala., along with other Chicago religious leaders in 1965 to support Dr. Martin Luther King Jr.

Veteran newscaster John Callaway gives us a firsthand glimpse of 1968, which changed U.S. politics forever and deeply scarred Chicago. And Jane Byrne weighs in on becoming the first female mayor of Chicago in 1979. "It began in the snow," she writes. In a chapter written by former White House counsel Abner Mikva, renowned economist Milton Friedman gives a brief analysis of the causes of the Depression. Mike Ditka reveals surprising insights into the 1986 Bears Super Bowl victory. And Nobel Laureate Leon Lederman talks about the 1996 discovery of the "top quark."

Author Bill Brashler provides a raucous account of "Hinky Dink" and "Bathhouse's" antics at the 1908 "First Ward Ball," and Pulitzer Prize–winning author Studs Terkel recalls following the Depression and the St. Valentine's Day Massacre of 1929 from the small hotel run by his mother at Wells and Grand.

Elaine Sit interviews the 88-year-old daughter of Chicago's first Cantonese-American restaurant owner; and Irving Cutler, author of *The Jews of Chicago,* lists the famous figures who emerged from the bustling Maxwell Street area, such as actor Paul Muni, U.S. Supreme Court Justice Arthur Goldberg, CBS founder William Paley and U.S. District Court Senior Judge Abraham Lincoln Marovitz.

Some of the voices relive great moments in Chicago. We hear from Cardinal Francis George that his mother was among thousands of faithful enthralled by the 1926 Eucharistic Congress, and from Manhattan Project member John Simpson how Fermi and his team toasted the first nuclear chain reaction with Chianti. Press agent wizard Danny Newman describes how the Lyric Opera and Maria Callas both became stars in 1954, and historian Dempsey Travis writes about one of the city's deadliest race riots and the infamous Black Sox scandal—both in the year 1919.

Maria de los Angeles Torres remembers the Cuban children, herself included, who found refuge from Fidel Castro in Chicago, and Playboy founder Hugh Hefner recalls that because Nat "King" Cole and Ella Fitzgerald appeared on his 1960 television show, it was banned in the still-segregated south.

Bernard Sahlins recalls how American comedy changed forever when Second City opened in a converted Chinese laundry on

Literary favorite Harry Mark Petrakis evokes memories of his father's church in 1935, and Illinois Poet Laureate Gwendolyn

Ida B. Wells-Barnett

Brooks remembers the night in 1950 when she became the first black to win a Pulitzer Prize. Novelist-attorney Scott Turow recounts his 1978 return to Chicago, and playwright Vicki Quade relives the frightening pre-vaccine days of polio—the "silent disease" that stalked Chicago in 1953.

Of course, readers hear from Sun-Times staffers such as Mr. Chicago himself, the legendary Irv Kupcinet; Pulitzer Prize–winning movie seer Roger Ebert; critics Wynne Delacoma, Hedy Weiss, Lee Bey and Jim DeRogatis; and columnists Steve Neal, Neil Steinberg, Dave Hoekstra and Bill Zwecker.

Then, as a rousing finale, Chicago native and jazz great Ramsey Lewis presents both the "high" and "low" notes of 1999. And Mayor Richard M. Daley gives us a vision of the year 2000 and beyond.

May these and all 100 voices offer you an entertaining and enlightening journey through 100 years of Chicago history.

Enjoy.

SETTING THE STAGE: A NEW WORLD IN THE MAKING

BY PROF. DONALD L. MILLER

Every age brings forth cities that embody the spirit of its time. In industrial America during the last decade of the 19th century, it was Chicago.

As a French traveler at the time remarked: "In New York, business is the big word. In Chicago, it is the God, the first and last reason of every action and thought."

So it was fitting that as the 20th century approached, Chicago was the setting for an incredible spectacle that became the greatest tourist attraction in American history—the World's Columbian Exposition of 1893.

It was a fair to celebrate—one year late—the 400th anniversary of Columbus' discovery of the New World. And it drew 27 million people from every part of the globe.

The fair marked America's emergence from the Civil War as a reunified nation of unrivaled power and prosperity. But if this was America's fair, it was even more so Chicago's, a declaration that it had arrived as a city of global consequence. In 1830, Chicago barely existed. Sixty years later it was the second-largest city in America.

To make the fair truly spectacular, Chicago's master builder, Daniel Burnham, constructed a magnificent White city on former swampland along Lake Michigan. It was to be a vision of the urban future. But many Chicagoans saw their own city, the Black City of smoke and steel, as the true model of a new kind of industrial metropolis.

Chicago had won the right to hold the fair in a heated competition with New York that was decided in Congress. Windy City boosters managed to convince enough congressmen that their city, not New York, was the most American of the country's largest cities.

Like America itself, Chicago was young and brashly confident, a product of both frontier and technological expansion, a place of hustlers and visionaries disdainful of tradition and committed to the future. It was also a place that did things on a grand scale—rising bigger and better, in a mere 10 years, from the ashes of the Great Fire of 1871.

"Here of all her cities," wrote the novelist Frank Norris, "throbbed the true life—the true power and spirit of America."

Chicago was the Queen City of the Machine Age. The vast slaughtering mills of Philip Armour and Gustavus Swift and the mail-order houses of Richard Sears and A. Montgomery Ward were the incarnation of speed and efficiency. And Chicago's rebuilt downtown was a technological wonder, with streets lit by the wondrous new force, electricity, serviced by rapid-running streetcars and lined by solid rows of office skyscrapers.

The prairie colossus was a city unlike any other, yet soon all big industrial cities would be laid out much like it. It was, at the same time, a vertical and horizontal city, a city of steel-frame skyscrapers ringed by suburbs linked to the downtown by steel rails. Chicago's architecture mirrored the character of the place, a city built for business.

Yet, if Chicago got the fair for what it was, it used the occasion of the fair to try to remake its image and appearance, undertaking a building and beautification effort unprecedented in American history.

The business barons who had rebuilt Chicago after the Great Fire wanted to dispel the notion that their city was merely a center of pig killing and grain handling.

In preparation for the fair, they built several superb libraries, a world-class university—the University of Chicago—a new Art Institute on Paris-like Michigan Avenue and a magnificent center for the performing arts, Louis Sullivan and Dankmar Adler's Auditorium building. They also assembled an instantly renowned symphony orchestra under the direction of Theodore Thomas, whom they stole from New York.

By 1900 Chicago was a center of commerce and culture. But it was still its ferocious energy that most impressed out-of-towners. Visitors were overwhelmed by the velocity of Chicago because so much of its commercial activity was confined to its 1-square-kilometer Loop, named for the iron ring of transit lines that encircled it. The terrific crowding and noise there were shocking, even to New Yorkers, whose city's commercial activity was strung out for miles along its lengthy avenues.

They called it the city of Speed. Cable cars pushing through heavy traffic slammed into slow-moving drays, lifting them into the air and overturning wagons and teams. Signs hanging over office doors read, "Away for Lunch: Back in Five Minutes." And the movement of the crowds on the streets reminded one tourist of "an infantry attack."

Everything in the Loop was organized for the efficient conduct of capitalist enterprise. In the new, vertically organized skyscrapers, world-shaping deals could be sealed in a matter of minutes—to the amazement of European businessmen. And swift-running cable cars and electric trolleys brought shoppers from the city's far-flung suburbs right to the doors of fabulous State Street department stores such as Marshall Field's.

These new palaces of consumption helped to turn parts of the downtown into a woman's world. Traditionalists complained about the new vice of shopping. Yet the accepted place of Victorian women in a male-dominated society—in the home all day, taking care of children, sewing, cleaning, cooking, and entertaining—made shopping a liberating escape.

In its campaign to win the fair, Windy City boosters had portrayed their city as a community united by civic pride. But Chicago was a deeply divided, corrupt and violent city, a place of extreme contrasts, and it was this that gave it its character.

City of millionaires, in the 1890s it had some of the worst slums in the civilized world. The "most American of cities," more than three-quarters of its residents were of foreign parentage. Garden city of parks and tree-bordered boule-vards, most of its streets were filled with uncollected horse manure and swollen animal corpses. Temperance capital of the country, headquarters of Frances E. Willard's Women's Christian Temperance Union, it had one saloon for every 200 people, and its world-famous vice district—the Levee—operated around the clock with police protection.

Home of empire-building capitalists Philip Armour, George Pullman and Marshall Field, it was the center of the nations' trade-union and anarchist movements and the site of some of the most violent labor disturbances of the age,

including the Haymarket Riot of 1886 and the Pullman Strike of 1894. The most corrupt city in the country, it was rallying ground for urban reformers such as Jane Addams, founder of Hull House, the nation's most important center of labor and tenement-house reform.

Nowhere else in the world could there be found, in more dramatic display, such a combination of wealth and squalor, beauty and ugliness, corruption and reform. City of idealists and dissenters, it was the home of Ida B. Wells, one of the boldest African-American civil rights activists in the country, and of the sharp-dealing transportation king Charles Yerkes—the "goliath of Graft," people called him. And then there were the most legendary of all of Chicago's urban thieves: Michael "Hinky Dink" Kenna and "Bathhouse" John Coughlin, aldermen who gave one dollar to the needy for every two they stole.

Chicago in the 1890s was the birthplace of the first realistic American reportage and fiction about the big city, the haunt of Theodore Dreiser, Eugene Field, George Ade and Finley Peter Dunne, creator of the affable saloon-house philosopher, Mr. Dooley, who charmed millions of readers. And after the Great Fire, Chicago was rebuilt by the founders of modern American architecture, Sullivan and Adler, Daniel Burnham and John Wellborn Root, William Holabird and Martin Roche and two independent architects who helped revolutionize American building: William Le Baron Jenney and Frank Lloyd Wright.

Jenney pioneered metal-frame skyscraper construction, allowing vertical buildings to reach for the sky, while Wright became the high priest of horizontal construction.

In the time of these makers and dreamers, Chicago was the site of some of the greatest achievements and failures of American urban life. Theodore Dreiser thought Chicago a symbol of a "tremendous" American future. Rudyard Kipling said that having seen Chicago, he "urgently desired never to see it again." But no matter how observers differed in their reaction, Chicago, most agreed, was the city that typified rising America, with its enormous problems and promise.

The best place to rediscover this lost Chicago is in the work of Theodore Dreiser, his evocative autobiography as well as his novels. Dreiser took Chicago for what it was, the good and the bad, and brought it back to us in prose portraits that rival those of the outstanding urban interpreters of the age, Balzac and Dickens. And he caught the significance of the place. At the end of the last century, Chicago was an unequaled place to watch what he called "a new world in the making."

A CITY FULL OF NEWCOMERS

Irv Kupcinet
Sun-Times
columnist and
Chicago legend

Construction of the Sanitary
and Ship Canal was
instrumental in reversing the
flow of the Chicago River.

Immigrant children

KUP'S COLUMN
Irv Kupcinet

The **biggest snow storm** in 10 years couldn't keep Chicagoans from flocking to the **Columbia Theater** to see our favorite dramatic duo, **Henry Irving** and **Ellen Terry**, in "The Merchant of Venice." Terry pronounced our city "marvelous," as always. . . .

Not as noteworthy to the citizens of Chicago as the new year and century dawned in 1900, but certainly of vital importance to me—though I wasn't there to report on it—was a pair of humble Russian immigrants who lived above a grocery store at 16th and Kedzie. My father, Max Kupcinet, drove a bakery wagon, waking before the dawn to hitch up the horse. I wouldn't be born for a dozen years. But my older brothers, Ben, who would become a pressman, and Joe, who would become a football coach, were.

They were immigrants in a city of immigrants: 77 percent of Chicagoans in

---

JANUARY	FEBRUARY	MARCH	APRIL		MAY
Alexander Dowie announces he will build a Holy City of Zion north of Waukegan.	Seven thousand Chicago workmen in the building trades refuse to work on Saturday afternoons.	Columbia Theater burns. Susan Winans, last survivor of the Fort Dearborn massacre, dies.	The Chicago White Sox are born in a small wooden stadium at 39th and Wentworth when Charles A. Comiskey, an alderman's son who founded the team as the St. Paul Saints, moves it to Chicago.	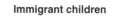 The Elevated train	The Northwestern Elevated Railroad opens.

1900 were either immigrants or their children. Ethnic allegiances were everything. It was the height of singing societies, dinner clubs and native pageants: A German group's canary-singing contest drew 106 entries and took two days to judge.

Perhaps the most important event of the year took place less than 48 hours after 1900 was ushered in.

Ada (left) and Minnie Everleigh ran the most notorious brothel in Chicago.

On the afternoon of Jan. 2, a steam shovel at Damen Avenue clawed away a dirt wall separating the Chicago River from the 28-mile-long Sanitary and Ship Canal. The canal, eight years in the making, required more soil to be moved than the Panama Canal did when it was dug over the next 14 years, using technology perfected here.

The river was reversed, which meant the end of washing the pollution and filth from city tenements, factories and slaughterhouses into Lake Michigan, a practice which had caused devastating outbreaks of diseases such as cholera.

Change in the river was almost immediate.

"Water in the Chicago River Now Resembles Liquid," announced a headline in the New York Times. "The impossible has now happened! The Chicago River is becoming clear."

Still, it would be nearly another century before the river would be clean enough to approach Mayor Richard J. Daley's fond dream that it would one day be a place where sportsmen angled for fish.

Downriver, St. Louis was less thrilled and rushed to reverse the reversal in the courts. To no avail. We sent St. Louis sewage, and in return they sent us ragtime, which was being played in the front parlors of the brothels that operated in broad daylight by the hundreds in Chicago.

Anyone who complains about low morals today doesn't understand the open vice in 1900 Chicago in places such as the Everleigh Club, an ornate palace, which opened its doors on February 1. Sisters Ada and Minnie Everleigh stood before their courtesans at the double brownstone at 2131-33 South Dearborn. "You have the whole night before you, and one $50 client is more desirable than five $10 ones. Less wear and tear," Minnie Everleigh said. The Everleigh was the most successful and notorious brothel in Chicago history, with its gold-trimmed fishbowls and $12 bottles of champagne in an era when a working man was lucky to earn $1 a day.

The mayor, Carter H. Harrison II, turned a blind eye to vice. That winter, the flamboyant mayor, often seen racing around town on his white mare, offered free city water and a permit to people who flooded their yards to build public ice skating rinks, and 60 Chicagoans complied. . . . Chicago got excited about the presidential election. William Wrigley Jr. sold campaign pepsin gum, in a red-white-and-blue wrapper, with celluloid buttons showing portraits of the candidates. . . . Jane Addams left Hull House for a European trip, thinking of the downtrodden back home as she listened to the Passion Play at Oberammergau. . . . The year was ushered out with songs and gunfire and ships' horns. At Potter Palmer's mansion at 100 Lake Shore Drive, a trumpet blared to announce the arrival of 1901. Robert Todd Lincoln, the president's son, was in attendance.

Jane Addams

JULY

Adlai E. Stevenson is nominated for vice president at the Democratic convention in Kansas City.

AUGUST

The Grand Army encampment of Civil War veterans opens in the new Chicago Coliseum.

Chicago City Hall and County Courthouse

ALSO IN 1900

Spitting in public is prohibited.

L. Frank Baum, a reporter for the Chicago Evening Post, publishes *The Wonderful Wizard of Oz*. The Emerald City of Oz was said to be inspired by the White City at the 1893 Columbian Exposition.

The Tin Man Statue in Oz Park on Chicago's North Side

CRUSADER HOGS SPOTLIGHT

Scott Fornek
Sun-Times staff reporter

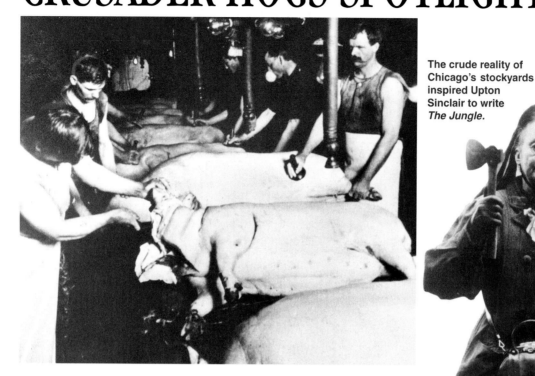

The crude reality of Chicago's stockyards inspired Upton Sinclair to write *The Jungle.*

Carry A. Nation

BY SCOTT FORNEK

The hog butcher for the world died in the opening days of 1901, but the sweat, slop and smell of the stockyards would linger for another 70 years.

Kansas saloon smasher Carry A. Nation bustled into town and received the same wary welcome Chicago would give Prohibition two decades later. And in a carpenter's cottage on the Northwest Side, Walter Disney was born, while 4,800 miles away an infant named Enrico Fermi cried his first in Rome.

One later left to build a magic kingdom on the back of a mouse. The other came here four decades later to harness an atom

and usher in the nuclear age. Just 64 years after a few shacks in a swamp incorporated as Chicago, the turn-of-the-century city was already a place that could rock the world.

No one better personified that spirit than Philip Danforth Armour, who helped build the meat-packing industry that would later prompt poet Carl Sandburg to dub the city "Hog butcher for the world."

Armour's recipe for success was less poetic. He built his empire by using all of the animal, pioneering refrigerated boxcars and working long hours.

JANUARY	FEBRUARY	APRIL		JUNE	JULY	OCTOBER
Just after midnight on Jan. 1, a policeman finds a terrorist's bomb in the La Salle and Randolph Street tunnel. It is safely detonated.	Chicago is dubbed "City of the Snows" when two storms in one week bring nearly 19 inches.	Pinkerton detectives confirm that a Gainsborough portrait of Georgiana Spencer, who became the Duchess of Devonshire, stolen 25 years earlier, had been found in Chicago in mint condition and returned to its owner in London.	Chicago stockyards	The temperature hits 93, beginning a monthlong series of heat waves marked by suicides, heat prostrations and weather-related insanity cases. A bull driven mad by the heat gores a cattleman at the stockyards.	The temperature hits 102 on July 10, the highest recorded in the city. The record is broken 11 days later at 103. The record stands for 33 years.	The South Park Commission changes the name of Lake Park, an eyesore once used as a garbage dump, to Grant Park in honor of former President Ulysses S. Grant. He was a state favorite because his Civil War headquarters was in Cairo, and he lived in Galena.

14

A bull-like man with a bald head and sandy side whiskers, Armour arrived at the Union Stockyards—or Packingtown as it was called—at 7 a.m. every day.

"I have no other interest in my life but business," Armour once said. "I do not love the money. What I do love is the getting of it, the making it."

When he died Jan. 6 at age 68 in his mansion at 2115 S. Prairie, Armour was exporting food all over the globe and had earned more than $45 million.

Famed anarchist Emma Goldman

His legacy is mixed. He helped put the city on the map and create what would become the Illinois Institute of Technology. But he also was a mover in an industry that muckraker Upton Sinclair would show treated many workers little better than the animals they slaughtered.

Carry Amelia Moore Nation demonstrated little love for money—or livestock for that matter. She was an intensely religious woman whose crusade against the demon rum helped bring about Prohibition nine years after her death in 1911.

A strong woman nearly 6 feet tall who dressed in funereal black, Nation went from praying outside taverns to destroying them with a hatchet.

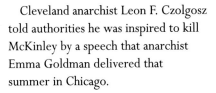

Carter H. Harrison II

When she announced she was planning to come to Chicago—where many aldermen owned saloons—Mayor Carter Harrison II warned her to leave her hatchet home.

"I have too much to do trying to run Chicago without tackling a Nation," he told reporters, after ducking out of City Hall to avoid meeting her.

Nation did not smash any gin mills when she arrived Feb. 12, but thousands flocked to catch a glimpse of her. She lectured, toured the notorious Levee district, pulled a cigar out of a man's mouth and shamed a Dearborn Street barkeep into covering a partially nude statue in his window.

"Oh, how I would like to do some smashing," she told a reporter.

Perhaps the greatest jolt that year came Sept. 6 when President William McKinley was shot by an assassin in Buffalo, N.Y. He died eight days later.

Chicagoans sang hymns, decorated their homes with portraits of the slain president and observed five minutes of silence during his funeral. And Harrison and his police tried to prove the assassination was a plot hatched here.

Cleveland anarchist Leon F. Czolgosz told authorities he was inspired to kill McKinley by a speech that anarchist Emma Goldman delivered that summer in Chicago.

"Her words set me on fire," Czolgosz said. He was later executed.

Goldman, then 32, and nine Chicago anarchists were arrested here but later released. Schoolboys threw stones and taunted Goldman when a horse-drawn carriage returned her to the home where she was staying on Carroll Avenue.

She steadfastly denied any role in McKinley's murder.

"He is the most insignificant president the United States ever had," Goldman said. "Still, I do not see what could come out of killing him."

Walter Elias Disney

DECEMBER

Walter Elias Disney is born in a two-story house at 2156 N. Tripp. His family moved to Missouri but later returned.

ALSO IN 1901

Poet Vachel Lindsay arrives from Springfield to study at the Art Institute. He lived on stale pastry until he got a job sorting boxes at Marshall Field's.

Meat baron Philip Danforth Armour dies, leaving a $31 million estate.

The American Bowling Congress holds its first national tournament on specially built lanes in the Welsbach Building on Wabash Avenue.

Sportswriters Fred Hayner and George Rice tag the north side baseball team with the nickname "Cubs" because there were so many young players on the roster. Hayner and Rice also designed a team logo with a bear cub, and in 1907 the "Cubs" nickname was officially adopted by the team.

Fred Hayner

HULL HOUSE LABOR MOVEMENT

Bernardine Dohrn

Director of the Children and Family Justice Center, Northwestern University Law School

Jane Addams is shown at her desk a few days before sailing for Europe to attend the World's Peace Conference at The Hague. She became international president, and it was her work with this organization that brought her the Nobel Prize in 1931.

In 1902, immigrant children often faced lives of toil, not school.

BY BERNARDINE DOHRN

At the first Hull House Christmas party, reformer Jane Addams tried giving candy to the children who came by. But a number of little girls refused it.

"They worked in a candy factory and could not bear the sight of it," Addams wrote in *Twenty Years at Hull House* of the exhausted girls, who put in 14-hour work days.

In 1902, children as young as 6 toiled in Chicago's stockyards, sweatshops, candy and cigar factories, department stores and on the streets as bootblacks and peddlers.

The injustices of an economic system that victimized the young led to significant labor and legislative movements that year. Children began organizing, and Hull House supporters secured pioneering child labor laws.

Owners and labor leaders alike feared the spread of strikes by such kids as messenger boys, who in 1902 demanded a 10-hour day, daily pay of 75 cents and overtime weekend pay. An army of 5,000 children working in factories took part in the 1902 Labor Day parade of union men.

By then the Hull House program was 13 years old. Addams, aghast by the misery

---

MARCH

George Ade's first comic musical, "The Sultan of Sulu," opens at the Studebaker Theater, introducing the phrase "cold gray dawn."

MAY

Richard J. Daley is born at 3602 S. Lowe, half a block from where he'll live for the rest of his life.

JUNE

Fire in the St. Luke's sanitarium kills 10, including blind alderman William E. Kent.

Benny Goodman, who grew up to be king of swing, paid a sentimental visit to Jane Addams' Hull House, where he received his first music lessons.

JULY

Forty children are arrested for begging and peddling.

Irish-born Patrick A. Feehan, the first Catholic archbishop of Chicago, dies.

child workers endured, agitated to abolish child labor and linked the effort to campaigns for compulsory education. With Hull House resident Florence Kelly, a Northwestern University law school graduate, she helped win Illinois' first law regulating sanitary work conditions and setting a minimum work age of 14.

Immigrants wait outside Hull House to see Jane Addams.

In 1889, Addams, the daughter of a wealthy downstate mill owner, and her friend Ellen Gates Starr established their great social service experiment in a decrepit mansion in the midst of the immigrant area on Halsted.

A majority of Chicagoans in 1902 were poor Italians, Greeks, Jews, Poles, Mexicans and Irish. All were welcomed at Hull House, where Chicago's first public gymnasium opened and its first women's basketball team was organized.

Its boys band boasted such graduates as Benny Goodman. And more than 1,000 people each week attended pottery, cooking, dressmaking, embroidery and language classes. They included my father, Bernard, and his five sisters, who walked to clubs at Hull House from my grandfather's plumbing store at 16th and Halsted.

Famed poet Carl Sandburg (left) and Bernard Dohrn, 1902

Determined and quietly observant, Addams created cures for the problems she saw firsthand. What she learned about delinquent children led to the first juvenile court in the country in 1899.

What she saw of children playing in the teeming streets became a program of school playgrounds, and her contact with child laborers wound up in landmark labor legislation.

An intellectual who in 1931 shared a Nobel Peace Prize, Addams wrote about how to cure social evils. In 1902, she published *Democracy and Social Ethics,* a series of lectures on public morality and social protest reviewed by philosopher William James as "one of the great books of the times."

The cause of Hull House became fashionable and drew famous people. Among those dining there were Carl Sandburg, Ida B. Wells, Frank Lloyd Wright, W.E.B. Dubois, Clarence Darrow and Prince Piotr Kropotkin. Gertrude Stein, scandalously dressed in black velvet pants and vest, entertained dinner guests by reciting, "Pigeons in the grass, Alas, Alas."

William Butler Yeats and John Galsworthy visited the Hull House Theater. Sears, Roebuck President Julius Rosenwald was inspired by the Hull House ethnic arts museum to build the Museum of Science and Industry. And in 1902, University of Chicago faculty member and Hull House resident John Dewey published his famous work, *The Child and The Curriculum.*

SEPTEMBER

The manager and president of the Masonic Temple are indicted, along with three other men, for conspiring to defraud the county out of taxes owed on the Temple and of forging tax receipts.

NOVEMBER

Thirteen men are killed in a boiler explosion at a refrigeration plant owned by meat packer Swift & Co. The force of the explosion sent a heavy valve flying onto the roof of a four-story building three blocks away.

DECEMBER

Apparently humiliated by being arrested for shoplifting, the wealthy widow of the publisher of the Swedish Tribune kills herself on Christmas Day. Lottie Chaiser had been arrested earlier in the month in a State Street store. She and her family were members of the Swedish royal family.

ALSO IN 1902

Packing House Teamsters strike when companies refuse to raise pay and shorten the work day.

Prisoners at the Cook County Jail publish the *Improvement Journal.*

A woman who ran a "baby farm" on Grand Avenue is charged with manslaughter in connection with the deaths of a number of the infants. Nellie Campbell's 12-year-old daughter testifies that her mother spanked, neglected and otherwise mistreated the babies.

Gilbert Jimenez
Sun-Times staff reporter

FIRE SPARKS NEW CODE

Interior of the Iroquois Theater after the fire

BY GILBERT JIMENEZ

Downtown 1903 Chicago was a raucous, happy mess—a hodgepodge of saloons, lunch counters, shops and offices.

Horse, wagon and motor traffic made street crossing difficult. Bandits and boodlers lurked at every turn looking for the easy mark. And there was music everywhere, echoing out of hundreds of theaters and music halls that served culture, both high and low, to the rough and tumble Midwest.

Chicago fire inspectors

By year's end, stunned silence would replace the gay songs as a shroud of grief befell the city with the loss of 602 people—mostly women and children—in a fire at the Iroquois Theater downtown.

Hundreds more were burned in what remains the deadliest blaze in city history, second in the nation and fourth world-wide.

It was bitter cold that Wednesday, Dec. 30, a harsh end to a harsh year fraught with strikes, economic depression and crime. Yet New Year's Eve was mere hours away, and Chicago was filled with the sound of children on holiday.

Iroquois Theater before the fire

MARCH

Gustavus F. Swift, of meat-packing fame, dies.

APRIL

President Theodore Roosevelt visits the Evanston Campus of Northwestern University and addresses a gathering of the faculty and students.

Theodore Roosevelt

MAY

The Illinois Legislature approves a bond act raising money to add 215 acres to Lincoln Park by filling in the lakefront from Fullerton to Cornelia.

Stock company players at the time of the fire

The five-week-old theater at 24-28 W. Randolph was crammed with 1,900 people who came to see popular vaudevillian Eddie Foy and a troupe of 500 in the musical "Mr. Blue Beard." The throng—300 over capacity—filled every inch of the six-story playhouse—main floor, box seats, balconies and all standing room.

Outside, people groused about the weather and the City Council's toy gun ban. Some buzzed around newsstand trash-can fires over the recent first flight of a couple of Ohio brothers or the declaration of University of Chicago head William R. Harper that the school was no longer a Baptist college.

Meanwhile inside, mirth reigned until 3:33 p.m. Within moments, merriment turned to horror, and the pleasure palace became a crematorium.

Foy had just walked onstage when an overhead light shorted and sparked, splashing rivulets of fire onto a velvet curtain and flammable props. Quickly, silently, the flames swelled. A panicked cast rushed a stage door but the whoosh of air when it opened fed the fire.

Foy tried to calm the crowd. A stagehand poured two cans of a fire-retardant chemical—all he had—on the blaze. They both failed.

Oddly, until that moment the crowd was "cool and collected," said witness Elvira Pinedo. Then "a great ball of fire rolled out and the panic began."

"A sort of cyclone came from behind," Foy reported. "And there seemed to be an explosion."

Lush upholstery had ignited tall curtains and two gas tanks erupted, spewing hellfire and poisonous gases into the faces of the audience. In darkness, the living clawed over bodies piled 10 high around doors and windows.

Firemen snuffed the blaze within 15 minutes, but hope did not survive. The fire doors were gated and locked; a fireproof curtain had stuck open; there were no hoses, sprinklers or emergency lights and only two fire extinguishers.

Hearings revealed that free tickets moved city inspectors to ignore the fire code and let the theater open, only to close in a disaster unmatched even by the Great Chicago Fire of 1871, which killed 250, or the 1942 Cocoanut Grove night club blaze in Boston, which claimed 490 lives.

Theater principals, building owners, Mayor Carter H. Harrison II and others were indicted, but nothing came of it. Harrison shut 170 theaters, halls and churches for a months-long reinspection that left 6,000 people unemployed. The fire code was changed to require theater doors to open outwards and fire curtains of steel, but sprinklers were not mandated.

The Iroquois, which sustained only light interior damage, was repaired and reopened as the Colonial Theater. In 1926, it was torn down to make way for the Oriental Theatre.

SEPTEMBER

Canadian James L. Kraft rents a horse and wagon and, with $65 capital, begins distributing bulk cheese to Chicago grocers.

NOVEMBER

Chicago police officer Joseph Driscoll is killed by the four so-called Car Barn Bandits. They are caught a week later; three are hanged the next year, one gets life in prison.

Henry Ford (right) and his son, Edsel

ALSO IN 1903

The first Ford automobile in America is sold to a Chicago dentist.

Flute-playing Chicago police chief Francis O'Neil publishes *O'Neil's Music of Ireland*.

The Chicago Hebrew Institute, the forerunner of today's Jewish community centers, starts in the Maxwell Street area in a rundown rented building on Roosevelt Road.

CHICAGO'S CULTURE TAKES ROOT

Wynne Delacoma
Sun-Times classical music critic

Theodore Thomas and Orchestra Hall

BY WYNNE DELACOMA

The concept of high and low culture probably didn't exist in 1904. Movies and recordings were in their infancy. TV was the stuff of science fiction.

But 1904 was a landmark year for both popular entertainment and high culture in Chicago. It was the birth year of Riverview Park, the beloved amusement park at Belmont and Western that attracted hundreds of thousands of visitors until its demise in 1967.

Another amusement park was born in 1904, in Ravinia, 25 miles north of Chicago, on a tract of woods and meadow bisected by railroad tracks. Railroad

officials built the park's baseball diamond, theater, dining pavilion and electric fountain in hopes of boosting their line's passenger revenues. Ravinia Park eventually became internationally renowned for its opera seasons and, since 1936, has been the Chicago Symphony Orchestra's summer home.

The year's most auspicious addition to Chicago's high culture scene was in downtown Chicago. On Dec. 14, 1904, Orchestra Hall opened, giving the Chicago Symphony Orchestra its first permanent home, one it has occupied ever since. The orchestra had been founded by German-born conductor Theodore Thomas, who had

Theodore Thomas at the conductor's stand

FEBRUARY

Fire breaks out at the Alhambra Hotel, killing three. The brick, L-shaped, three-story structure near State and Archer was destroyed and the adjacent Alhambra Theatre severely damaged.

Novelist James T. Farrell is born on the South Side. He will write 25 novels, including the Studs Lonigan trilogy, which chronicles a young man growing up among the Irish working class.

MAY

The Socialist Party holds its convention in Chicago, nominating Eugene V. Debs for president. An Indiana native who led the tumultuous Pullman strike in 1894, Debs ran for president five times—once from a prison cell, where he was serving a sentence for espionage that was later commuted.

Eugene Debs

JUNE

Theodore Roosevelt, who became president after William McKinley was assassinated, is nominated for president at the Republican National Convention at the Coliseum. This is the first major convention to allow women—four alternate delegates from Colorado, Utah and Idaho—to participate.

said he "would go to hell if they would give me a permanent orchestra." Thomas moved to Chicago in 1891, and the ensemble that would become the Chicago Symphony Orchestra gave its first concert Oct. 16 of that year.

Daniel Hudson Burnham, the vice president of the Chicago Symphony Orchestra board, hosts a luncheon for his business and city planning colleagues. Burnham is second from the left, upper row.

Until Orchestra Hall opened, orchestra and audience rattled around the 4,200-seat Auditorium Theatre, an acoustic marvel, but much too big for orchestral concerts. Built in 1899, it was perfect for the visiting opera companies that provided Chicago's only opera performances until 1910 when a succession of local resident companies began to appear. Ultimately, all disappeared until 1954 when the Lyric Opera of Chicago was established. Thomas had long agitated for a proper concert hall for his orchestra, and in 1904 he got his wish.

Daniel Burnham, vice president of the orchestra's governing board, as well as one of the city's leading architects, designed the building on the site of a livery stable where visitors to downtown parked their rigs during the day.

The 69-year-old Thomas had been ailing when he arrived in Chicago in October 1904. Worrying about the unfinished hall's

Riverview Park

acoustics and rehearsing amid cold drafts and damp cement and plaster didn't improve his health. But after a test rehearsal Dec. 6, he announced Orchestra Hall "a great success" and telegraphed Burnham that its "quality exceeds all expectations."

The glittering audience cheered the gala dedication concert, but doubts quickly set in. One newspaper critic denounced the acoustics, another added that the seats were too narrow with too little leg room.

Thomas, who had caught a cold in the opening concert, became sicker, but refused to stay away from Orchestra Hall. He knew that musicians need to get used to performing in new halls, and he worked feverishly to help the orchestra become familiar with its new home and make it work. On Dec. 30, for the first time in his career, he missed a concert because of illness. He died Jan. 4, 1905.

The Chicago Symphony Orchestra has gone on to become one of the world's great orchestras, and in 1997 Burnham's original building, built for $850,000, was updated, expanded and transformed into Symphony Center at a cost of $110 million.

JULY

Cattle butchers and other stockyard workers begin an 8 ½-week strike for better wages and hours. Before it's over, the packinghouses lose $10 million nationwide, fistfights break out and racial tensions flare when truckloads of African Americans are brought in to work.

Sixteen children and adults are killed and another 80 injured when a passenger train collides with a coal train in south suburban Glenwood. The train was returning South Side Sunday school students from a trip to Momence.

NOVEMBER

Oscar DePriest is elected Cook County commissioner. He will become the city's first black alderman in 1915 and the first African American to represent a northern state in Congress in 1928.

ALSO IN 1904

The first-ever gambling ship in America is established on Lake Michigan.

**Julia Sniderman
Bachrach**

Chicago Park
District historian

CITY TURNS NEW LEAF IN PARKS

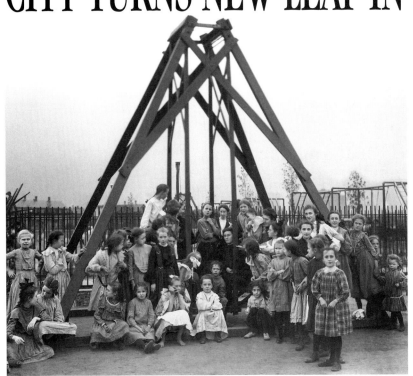

Children gather around the giant swing at Mark White Square (now McGuane Park). The swing was an innovative feature introduced by the South Park Commission in 1905.

BY JULIA SNIDERMAN BACHRACH

When lumber baron Benjamin Franklin Ferguson died April 10, 1905, he left $1 million to adorn Chicago's parks, boulevards and public areas.

The first sculpture commissioned with his bequest was Lorado Taft's Fountain of the Great Lakes, which still stands in the south garden of the Art Institute of Chicago.

Five years into the new century, Chicago had many parks, including the six major ones—Jackson, Washington, Humboldt, Garfield, Douglas and Lincoln—and an interlinking ribbon of green boulevards.

There were also several older Victorian parks including Jefferson (now Skinner) and

Union on the fashionable West Side. These were the backdrop for Theodore Dreiser's influential novel *Sister Carrie*. In this realistic work, considered immoral at the time, the married G.W. Hurstwood, waiting for his mistress, Carrie Meeber, "found a rustic bench beneath the green leaves of a lilac bush. At a little pond nearby some cleanly dressed children were sailing white canvas boats."

Unlike Dreiser's characters, though, many Chicagoans were not able to take full advantage of public parks in 1905. At the

Picnickers at Humboldt Park

FEBRUARY

Inga Hanson is convicted of perjury for pretending to be blind, deaf, dumb and paralyzed so she can sue Chicago City Railway Co. for an 1898 accident. The prosecutor calls her "a 200-pound giantess of fraud."

MAY

The Chicago Defender publishes its first edition. Publisher Robert S. Abbott uses it to encourage the great migration of African Americans from the South. It becomes one of the most influential black-oriented newspapers in the United States.

Robert S. Abbott

NOVEMBER

The Field Museum of Natural History gets its name. It was organized 12 years earlier in what is now the Museum of Science and Industry.

Legendary coach Amos Alonzo Stagg leads the University of Chicago football team to what is now called the Big Ten championship in an undefeated season. It is one of six gridiron titles the Maroons will win under Stagg.

Amos Alonzo Stagg

Newly conceived field houses offered year-round use of the parks.

time, parks were under the jurisdiction of three commissions established in 1869 when Chicago's population was 300,000. Thirty-six years later it had grown to 1.7 million, but new parkland did not keep pace.

By 1905, nearly 750,000 people lived more than a mile away from any park, and there were 846 city residents per acre of parkland.

To address this problem, the city had created the Special Park Commission. Members included Prairie School architect Dwight H. Perkins and landscape architect Jens Jensen. A Danish immigrant who had risen from laborer to Humboldt Park's superintendent, Jensen was ousted by a corrupt West Park Board in 1900 "because he was not a politician."

In 1905, Gov. Charles S. Deneen swept the board clean. Jensen became the West Park superintendent and chief designer for his expertise and "because he was not a politician."

Perkins and Jensen, in a seminal report, recommended an "outer belt" of natural forests and meadows, as well as additional inner-city playgrounds. The state Legislature authorized the outer belt, but politics delayed creation of the Cook County Forest Preserve until 1914.

In the tenement district, reformers in the 1890s established the city's first playground at Jane Addams' Hull House as an alternative for young boys who fished for rats in the street for recreation.

The Special Park Commission followed suit, creating its own playgrounds. Noting that existing playgrounds could be used only in warm weather, South Park Supt. J. Frank Foster conceived an innovative system of parks that would include a new type of building—the fieldhouse. Offering year-round recreational activities, the new parks also provided English lessons and other classes, plus inexpensive hot meals, free public bathing facilities and other health services.

Designed by D.H. Burnham and Co. architects and the Olmsted Brothers landscape architects, the first 10 of these revolutionary parks opened in 1905. They so impressed President Theodore Roosevelt that he declared them "the most important civic achievement in any American city."

The children's wading pool was another South Park Commission creation.

DECEMBER

The city's first motion picture theater opens on State Street near Adams. It seats 300 and costs a nickel. Early offerings include "The Great Train Robbery." Owner Aaron Jones eventually expands his empire to 36 movie theaters and playhouses, including the McVicker and Oriental.

Transit baron Charles Tyson Yerkes, a mixture of visionary and scoundrel, dies in New York. Before he left Chicago, Yerkes built the Loop L—some say with the help of $1 million in bribes to various aldermen.

Motion Picture Theatre

ALSO IN 1905

The Rotary Club is founded by Paul P. Harris, a lawyer, and four other businessmen. The first service club in the world, Rotary was the model for Kiwanis Clubs, which for 64 years was headquartered in Chicago, and for the Lions Clubs International, which has also been headquartered in Chicago or Oak Brook since 1917.

Dick Simpson
Former 44th Ward alderman, and now a professor of political science at the University of Illinois at Chicago

CHICAGO WASN'T READY FOR REFORM

Muckraking reporter Lincoln Steffens tagged city aldermen with the moniker "Grey Wolves" for "the color of their hair and the rapacious cunning and greed of their nature."

BY DICK SIMPSON

The Cubs and Sox were in the World Series in 1906. Who could say it was not a significant year?

Upton Sinclair published *The Jungle,* which would reform the meat-packing industry. Frank Lloyd Wright's Robie House opened. Joseph "Yellow Kid" Weil, charged with operating a confidence game, was freed by a jury. And Chicago was ruled by the City Council of the "Grey Wolves."

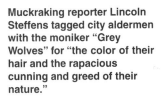

Frank Lloyd Wright (left) and "Bathhouse" John Coughlin

Aldermen were named Grey Wolves by Lincoln Steffens, a muckraking reporter for McClure's magazine, "for the color of their hair and the rapacious cunning and greed of their nature." Steffens said the government was the "most disreputable in the city's history," which for Chicago was a heady claim.

The council was filled with such colorful characters as "Bathhouse John" Coughlin, Michael "Hinky Dink" Kenna and Johnny

Upton Sinclair with his son, David, on the porch of their Princeton farm

William Rainey Harper

JANUARY

Marshall Field

Marshall Field, 70, Chicago's richest man and "the world's foremost merchant," dies of pneumonia. His fortune is estimated at $118 million. He leaves $8 million to the Field Museum.

William Rainey Harper, 49, first president of the University of Chicago, dies of cancer.

APRIL

The Division Street Russian Baths open for business at 1916 W. Division. It was not the first public bath in Chicago, but in 1999, it is the only one left.

"Da Pow" Powers. Aldermen were paid less than $200 a year at the turn of the century, yet crooked aldermen made the princely sum of $20,000 a year by taking bribes.

The Chicago Herald said an alderman is "in nine cases out of ten a bummer and a disreputable who can be bought and sold as hogs are bought and sold in the stockyards."

Ninth Ward Ald. Nathan Brenner said that of the 70 aldermen (two representing each of the 35 wards), perhaps only three were not able and willing to steal a red-hot stove.

Irishman Edward Dunne was elected and served as a reform mayor from 1905 to 1907 on a platform of establishing immediate municipal ownership of the transit system. For 50 years, transportation was by private horse railway and later trolley cars owned by separate companies. Service was bad, and there were no free transfers among the different systems. A former judge, Dunne campaigned for major social reforms and won election with the support of Machine Democratic ward committeemen, Democratic Party job holders and a grass-roots, populist campaign.

Party patronage workers such as James Quinn avowed: "I care nothing for municipal ownership. I'm for Judge Dunne. I have a good job in City Hall, and I'd be a fool to oppose him . . . and I'm for a [wide] open [drinking] town."

Upon his election in spring 1905, Dunne appointed labor leaders, radicals and social workers such as Jane Addams and Clarence Darrow to top positions in his administration. But he never gained control over the Council.

Despite previous referendums in favor of public ownership of the transit systems by votes as great as

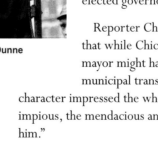

Edward Dunne

Inside the Chicago City Council chambers

142,826 to 27,998, he lost key City Council votes on the issue by a tally of 56-13. The aldermen instead proposed regulating transportation.

Voters didn't really care. They just wanted a better transit system, and they wanted it now. But creation of the CTA would wait until after World War II, 40 years later.

Dunne's real problem, like Harold Washington's in his first term 80 years later, was that he couldn't control the Grey Wolves. Although defeated in 1907 for re-election as mayor, Dunne would go on to be elected governor in 1913.

Reporter Charles N. Wheeler once said that while Chicago's great forgotten reform mayor might have failed in his goal for municipal transportation, "the fineness of his character impressed the whole community . . . [but] the impious, the mendacious and the shameless resented him."

MAY

Billiards ace Willie Hoppe, an 18-year-old "boy wonder" from New York, sets a world record by shooting 307 balls straight in at a tournament at Orchestra Hall.

White Sox owner Charles Comiskey (left) and Cubs owner William Wrigley

OCTOBER

The White Sox and the Cubs square off in the city's first and only "streetcar"—no subway yet—World Series. The Sox win, four games to two.

Considered a transit marvel in the late 1890s, the last cable cars are replaced by electric trolleys.

ALSO IN 1906

Chicago organizes its first mounted police unit.

The municipal court system goes into effect.

HOLLYWOOD BY THE LAKE

"His New Job" starred Charlie Chaplin (right) and Ben Turpin; it was the only movie Chaplin made in Chicago for Essanay studio.

Art Golab
Sun-Times staff reporter

The former Essanay Film Manufacturing Co. studio at 1345 W. Argyle is now part of St. Augustine College.

BY ART GOLAB

The country was in a financial panic, banks were closing and thousands were thrown out of work. But one new high-tech business was booming: motion pictures.

And Chicago, for a brief time, was to become the Silicon Valley of the new motion picture world.

It was 1907, and Chicago had 116 nickelodeons, 18 10-cent vaudeville houses and 19 penny arcades, all exhibiting the fledgling movie art form. There was no such thing as Hollywood, and most films were made on the East Coast. Businessman George K. Spoor wanted to change that.

Out of offices at 62 N. Clark, Spoor was renting all the film he could get his hands on to vaudeville houses, traveling shows and that new storefront phenomenon, the nickelodeons.

"These nickel theaters spread in the wildest expansion you could imagine," Spoor said in a 1943 interview. "Almost overnight I was swamped with orders for films."

The original construction gang of the old Essanay studio

MARCH	APRIL	MAY	JUNE	SEPTEMBER
The trial of the Standard Oil Company of Indiana on 1,903 counts of illegal conduct begins in the courtroom of Judge Kenesaw M. Landis in Chicago.	Postmaster Fred Busse, a Republican, defeats incumbent Democrat Edward Dunne in the mayoral election.	The Ravenswood L opens.	Architect William LeBaron Jenney, designer of the first steel skeleton skyscraper, dies.	The Loop's underground freight tunnel system, begun in 1899, is completed.

Essanay churned out several 20-minute shorts a week, which each cost about $1,000 to produce but brought in $20,000.

At first, actors like Turpin, who was paid $50 a week, did not share in the bonanza. But Spoor helped change that in 1915 by luring Chaplin to Chicago from Keystone Studios in Los Angeles for $1,250 a week, a salary at the time second only to Mary Pickford's.

Chaplin commuted to Argyle Street from the Brewster Apartments at Diversey and Pine Grove. His first movie for Essanay, the aptly titled "His New Job," featured Gloria Swanson in a small role. In the film Chaplin gets a behind-the-scenes job at a movie studio and wreaks slapstick havoc.

But "The Little Tramp" soon tired of Chicago's weather and, after that one film, decamped to Essanay's West Coast studios to finish his contract.

In the teens many other studios had the same idea and followed the sunshine to Hollywood. Chaplin, Essanay's biggest star, left the studio for a higher salary of $670,000 a year. That was the beginning of the end for Essanay.

By 1918, production at the Argyle Street studios slowed to a trickle. Other Chicago studios had either called it quits or left for the coast. Spoor, who was being clobbered by West Coast studios willing to pay higher salaries for stars, closed the doors that year, leaving the motion picture business with an estimated $4 million fortune.

He died at 81 in his daughter's home at 908 W. Argyle in 1953, only a few blocks away from the studio he founded.

The building, now part of St. Augustine College, remains, the Indian-head logo still visible above the door, a reminder of when Chicago was Hollywood by the Lake.

Charlie Chaplin

So in 1907 he started to make his own movies, organizing the Essanay Film Manufacturing Co., whose name came from the initials of Spoor and his partner, cowboy movie actor and director G. M. "Bronco Billy" Anderson.

The pair built studios at 1345 W. Argyle, and their films, emblazoned with an Indian-head logo, eventually featured Gloria Swanson, Wallace Beery, Francis X. Bushman and Charlie Chaplin.

Cross-eyed comedian Ben Turpin was Essanay's first star. With Anderson behind the camera, Turpin would skate down Wells Street, bumping into bystanders. People who chased him unwittingly wound up as extras.

OCTOBER
The Cubs beat Detroit in four games straight to capture the World Series.

Albert Michelson

NOVEMBER
The Nobel Prize in science goes to University of Chicago physicist Albert Michelson for measuring the speed of light. He won $40,000, and he was the first of many U of C faculty to win a Nobel.

DECEMBER
Chicago's police chief issues an order to enforce the ordinance banning women from smoking in public during New Year's Eve celebrations.

ALSO IN 1907
The Cliff Dwellers Club is organized by writers and artists.

Citizens of west suburban Harlem vote to change their town's name to Forest Park.

CUBS WIN, SO DO CROOKS

Bill Brashler
Chicago writer and novelist

1908 was a time for hedonism—Chicago style. First Ward aldermen kept the houses of ill repute open, the Grand Ball was the best party ever and the Cubs won the World Series again.

BY BILL BRASHLER

For the Chicago debaucher, hedonist and baseball fan, times would never be so sweet. Two doubles and a triple: Michael "Hinky Dink" Kenna and "Bathhouse John" Coughlin; Ada and Minnie Everleigh; Tinker to Evers to Chance.

1908 was a bustle and spat year, horse-and-buggy, still genteel. Central city streets were largely free of automobiles, entirely devoid of traffic lights (the latter only existed on the waterways), but jammed with every type of trolley and horse-drawn conveyance.

A gentleman did not glimpse a lady's bare ankle. Teddy Roosevelt was in his last year in the White House; a decent sort named Fred Busse was mayor. Two cents sent a letter first class.

In March, an "anarchist" named Lazarus Averbuch stabbed Police Chief George Shippy and shot Shippy's young son during a home invasion before he was shot and killed. Hamlin Garland was a heavyweight

MARCH	MAY	JUNE	OCTOBER
A collision between L cars at State and Van Buren injures 25 people.	A census of the Chicago public schools finds 602 children over the age of 12 who cannot read or write in any language.	The end of the fiscal year finds that 183 men were killed in Illinois mine accidents, leaving 223 orphans and 90 widows.	The Cubs win their second World Series in a row, playing at a West Side field near where Cook County Hospital now stands. Near the left-field line was a mental hospital where patients used to hang out the windows to watch the games, giving birth to the expression "You're out in left field."
			Louis D. Taylor, 86, of Glencoe dies. He had arrived in Chicago as a child in 1827, six years before it was declared a city.

Johnny Evers

writer; Jack Johnson was heavyweight champion of the world.

The city decided to number streets starting at State and Madison. Population: 2,049,185.

More important, Chicago's National League Cubs, residents of the West Side Grounds, played superb baseball due mostly to shortstop Joe Tinker, who scooped up grounders and flipped them to second baseman Johnny Evers, a character so irascible they called him the Crab, who tossed to Frank Chance, the Peerless Leader, at first.

They beat the New York Giants in a playoff game to win the pennant, then smacked the Detroit Tigers in five games to win the World Series. Evers had a nervous breakdown three years later. The Cubs have yet to win another Series, giving rise to the saw, "Any team can have a bad century."

Victory, among other excuses, was cause for celebration at the Everleigh Club, an exquisite brothel run by sisters Minnie and Ada Everleigh in the raunchy Levee District of the near South Side. Protected by corrupt police and even more corrupt 1st Ward Aldermen Kenna and Coughlin, the club offered refined ladies, soundproof rooms, silk curtains, mahogany staircases and dinner, all for a whopping-but-worth-it $50 a night.

To celebrate and enhance their graft, Hinky Dink and Bathhouse annually threw a 1st Ward Ball, and none was bigger or more of a drunken mess than that of Dec. 15. A seedy crowd of 15,000—revelers, pimps, prostitutes, pickpockets, bartenders, politicians and cops—crammed the Coliseum, swigged 35,000 quarts of beer and 10,000 quarts of champagne and turned the Ball into a riot.

Fights, smashed glasses, overturned tables and drunks pawing women who fought back with hatpins.

1st Ward Aldermen Michael "Hinky Dink" Kenna and "Bathhouse" John Coughlin (front) protected—and patronized—the brothels in their ward.

The orgy was interrupted at midnight when Coughlin and Kenna, with Minnie and Ada Everleigh on their arms, made their grand entrance.

All were dressed to the nines, especially Bathhouse John in his pink gloves, lavender trousers, yellow pumps and silk top hat.

Said Hinky Dink of the Ball: "It's great! It's a lollapalooza! All my friends are out! Chicago ain't no sissy town!"

The 1908 bash proved to be too much, and city fathers were pushed to dismantle the Levee. Subsequent balls were tame, then defunct; the Everleigh sisters closed their joint, pooled a cool $1 million and left town.

The Levee was shut down, but its lords, Kenna and Coughlin, stayed on in City Hall and collected boodle for years.

Frank Chance

Joe Tinker

 ALSO IN 1908

The Chicago Police Department purchases three motorized cars to replace horse-drawn patrol wagons.

Edward K. Uhlir
Architect and
project director of
the Millennium Park

CITY MAKES BIG PLANS

The Burnham plan

BY EDWARD K. UHLIR

When architect Daniel Burnham's master plan for Chicago was unveiled on July 4, 1909, it created an immediate sensation. Its later impact was to reach far beyond Chicago and influence city planning across the nation and the world.

Burnham's ideas began developing when he was director of the World's Columbian Exposition of 1893 in Jackson Park. He wanted Chicago to match the glory of the exposition's splendid neoclassical "White City" buildings, pastoral green space and lagoons.

In his plan, the creative designer (responsible for the Marshall Field's store and the Reliance Building) envisioned a lakefront park linked to the fair site by beaches, seven islands and a chain of Venice-like canals and lagoons.

He saw a downtown Chicago in the style of central Paris, with a vast civic center and a widened Michigan Avenue. Burnham also proposed a huge neoclassical museum for the center of Grant Park, where

Daniel Burnham

The making of Grant Park

JANUARY	FEBRUARY	AUGUST	SEPTEMBER
Forty-seven men die when a fire breaks out in a wood-lined shaft of a water crib under construction in Lake Michigan at 71st St.	Nine spitters were fined $1 plus $1 in court costs for spitting. The acting police chief orders his men to go after every spitter.	Leroy T. Stewart, former postmaster of Chicago, is named chief of police.	A new grid street-numbering system takes effect, assigning 800 numbers to the mile, based on a starting zero axis point at State and Madison.

Buckingham Fountain now stands.

Newspapers applauded the museum, but mail-order king Aaron Montgomery Ward did not. To keep the lakefront "forever open, clear and free," he filed the latest in a series of lawsuits.

Ward, whose mail-order business was on Michigan Avenue, invoked a state law that said neighboring property owners could object to proposed buildings in Grant Park. He had earlier agreed to the Art Institute, but later regretted it.

Because of his opposition, Ward became one of the most hated men in Chicago, reviled and ridiculed by city officials, civic and business leaders, the press and Burnham.

Aaron Montgomery Ward

However, Ward was not dissuaded and won a final court victory in 1911. The Field Museum was located at its present site across from the southern end of Grant Park in a new park ironically named to honor Burnham.

In spite of obstacles, much of Burnham's plan was carried out.

Turn-of-the-century ladies' baseball team

Features included the enhancement of Michigan Avenue into a swank shopping street, construction of a two-tiered Wacker Drive, the building of the Congress Street Gateway and the straightening of the Chicago River. The only lagoon is now Burnham Harbor.

Burnham believed that parks should be the great unifying element of a city that all citizens could enjoy, regardless of their economic or social status.

Most of his dream for a continuous lakefront park system extending from Indiana to Wilmette has been realized, with 26 miles of shoreline creating 3,000 acres of new parks.

At the end of the 20th century, 90 years after his Chicago Plan was released, many of Burnham's ideas were still alive and to be incorporated in the Millennium Park under construction as a 24-acre addition to Grant Park.

The park will provide year-round programs and include an outdoor music theater, an ice skating rink, a terrace for shows and festivals, gardens, a new fountain and, under the park, a 1,500-seat indoor music and dance theater.

Burnham's ideas are also thriving elsewhere, with the conversion of the former U.S. Steel South Works site to a lakefront park, the proposal to turn Meigs Field into a 70-acre environmental park and the eight-mile shoreline reconstruction.

Unfortunately, Daniel Burnham died in 1912, before much of his plan could be implemented. But as we approached the turn of the century, his ideas and words were still valid.

"Make no little plans. They have no magic to stir men's blood, and probably themselves will not be realized. Make big plans; aim high in hope and work," he said.

GREEKS VOYAGE TO "DELTA"

Maria Pappas
Sociologist, lawyer and Cook County treasurer

Many pioneering Chicago Greeks began as peddlers selling fruit, candy and vegetables. But they changed course in 1910, a year after the city increased the annual peddler's license fee from $25 to $200.

BY MARIA PAPPAS

By 1910 Chicago had the largest Greek community in the nation. It was just north of the famed Hull House settlement near Halsted, Harrison and Blue Island and was known as "the Delta."

In this transplanted section of Greece could be found small family restaurants, fresh produce stands, Greek-language newspapers, coffeehouses, barbershops, doctors' and lawyers' offices and churches catering to an estimated 15,000 first- and second-generation Greek Americans.

"Halsted Street wasn't like it is today with the row of large Greek restaurants and speciality stores. It was just a few places,

very small snack shops located near Madison Street," said Louis Pappas, 95, a dear friend who is not related but shares my last name and heritage.

Young Greek men in Chicago

In the late 19th century, driven by Balkan wars and poverty, Greeks such as my grandfather John Papadakis emigrated to this country seeking jobs on the railroad and in coal and copper mines out West. Many Greeks, however, came directly to Chicago.

MARCH
Moderates rebel against U.S. House Speaker Joseph G. Cannon, the tyrant from Downstate Danville known as "Uncle Joe." They establish the seniority system for committee chairmanships.

MAY
Earth passes through the tail of Halley's Comet, but "in the smoke-obscured atmospheres of large cities like Chicago . . . the view was not satisfactory," the Chicago Daily News Almanac reported.

JULY
Comiskey Park opens at 35th and Shields. The White Sox lose to the St. Louis Browns, 2-0.

Holy Trinity, the first permanent Greek Orthodox church in Chicago

(I didn't make it until 1972, though!)

DePaul Professor Emeritus Andrew Kopan, a Greek-American history scholar, recalls, "My father got off the train in 1910 and decided to stay here because it was the end of the line, because it was a big city and because there were jobs."

Some Greeks returned to Chicago after stints in the mines.

"My aunt and uncle went to Utah in 1910, where my uncle worked in the copper mines, and my aunt was the chef and laundress for all the Greek miners. After they had a nest egg, they came to Chicago to join their fellow islanders from Crete and opened the Pantheon Restaurant on Halsted," said George Zimbrakos, a north side liquor store owner.

The first Greek communities were near Clark and Kinzie and then around the Randolph Street produce market, where most worked. But by 1910, the largest concentration of Greeks was in the near West Side Delta. Here, with Hull House as their cultural home and Jane Addams as their spiritual mother, they formed mutual aid and various interest organizations.

Kopan describes a visit to Hull House by former President Theodore Roosevelt, who addressed a group of young Greek men from the Hellenic League.

"Roosevelt urged them to preserve their incomparable heritage because it was the basis for Western civilization," Kopan said.

Ladies' Greek sisterhood at Hull House

The first Greek family in Chicago

Anchoring the Greek community was the church, with Holy Trinity in the Delta as the first permanent Greek Orthodox church in the Midwest. Communal day schools were also vital in reinforcing Greek culture and pride.

Holy Trinity's Socrates School was established in 1908, followed in 1910 by the Koraes School of Saints Constantine and Helen Church in a newer Greek community in Lawndale.

Many pioneering Chicago Greeks began as peddlers selling fruit, candy and vegetables. But they changed course in 1910, a year after surrounding City Hall with their fruit carts to protest an increase in the annual peddler's license fee from $25 to $200.

Finally, they agreed to abandon their street vehicles and become established businessmen. All those who could scrape together enough money rented stores, opened restaurants and started shoeshine and shoe repair shops, florists, confectionary and fruit stores, hotel concessions and ice cream businesses.

Kopan reports the first soda fountain was in a Greektown ice cream parlor. Eventually, the Greek entrepreneurs were so successful, they gained control of the retail and wholesale food industry in Chicago. The Delta flourished as the center of Chicago Greek life until the 1960s construction of the University of Illinois at Chicago campus.

SEPTEMBER

The downtown area is added to the new city street-numbering system, making State and Madison zero. The system went into effect April 1, 1911.

Ten officials at Armour, Swift and Morris meat-packing firms are indicted under antitrust laws. They are later acquitted.

Aviator Walter R. Brookins flies an "aeroplane" from Washington Park to Springfield.

OCTOBER

The Philadelphia Athletics beat the Cubs in the World Series, four games to one.

DECEMBER

Seven African-American baseball teams form the National League of Colored Baseball Clubs at 5324 S. State.

ALSO IN 1910

Sixteen women protesting working conditions, hours and a cut in the piece rate for seaming pants launch the great garment strike in Chicago. About 40,000 workers pour out of sweatshops in a strike that lasts 17 weeks.

CHICAGO GROWS BY DESIGN

John Holabird
Retired partner in the architectural firm of Holabird & Root

Notable buildings by the Holabird firm include (from left) the Old Colony Building, Soldier Field, the Gage Building, the Chicago Board of Trade and City Hall, which was under way in 1911.

BY JOHN HOLABIRD

In 1911, my grandfather William Holabird's architectural office had just completed City Hall to adjoin the County building finished by Holabird & Roche a few years earlier.

The imposing City-County Building filled an entire city block.

City Hall alone used 100,000 cubic feet of granite and 4 million bricks. Huge columns girded the exterior, and massive arches were built along the ground-floor corridors of the entire building.

From the start, critics called the edifice monumental. It was a very different kind of building than the simple "Chicago School" style the firm had done in its 30 years of practice up to that time.

City Hall (which I think looks like a Roman Bath) was what the general public and the politicians thought a civic building should be—big, powerful and classical.

William Holabird met Martin Roche when both were working as draftsmen for skyscraper pioneer William LeBaron Jenney. Grandfather started his own office in 1880. As Holabird & Roche, they

William Holabird

JANUARY	MAY	JULY	AUGUST
Federal Judge Kenesaw Mountain Landis impanels a grand jury to investigate Chicago meat packers for price collusion.	The Chicago and North Western depot opens. It took five years to build and cost $23 million.	The Great Lakes Naval Training Center at North Chicago is commissioned.	Matt McGrath sets a world's record in Chicago, throwing a 56-pound weight 16 feet, 6 1/4 inches.

Federal Judge Kenesaw Mountain Landis

Holabird & Roche was to build more than 80 downtown buildings and in 1911 was designing more hotel and department stores than any other architectural office. The Sherman Hotel (now the site of the Thompson Center) was under construction, and the firm was designing the LaSalle, Morrison, Congress and Stevens hotels, as well as the Palmer House.

Robert Bruegmann, Professor of Architectural History at the University of Illinois at Chicago, who has cataloged the firm's work, called these hotels the most advanced buildings of their time. They provided for the interaction of guests at restaurants, and elegant ballrooms were serviced by elaborate kitchens with extensive ventilation, ductwork and electric wiring.

By 1911, the firm's department stores were lining State Street. There was Mandel Brothers at 1 N. State and across the street The Boston Store and Rothschild & Co. at 333 S. State. All were clad in terra cotta.

Ginger Rogers, Robert Taylor and Merle Oberon were born in 1911, but I was minus 9. My mother, Dorothy Hackett, daughter of Chicago Evening Post music critic Karleton Hackett, was a sophomore at the University of Chicago High School and had not yet met my father, John, then studying architecture at the Ecole des Beaux Arts in Paris.

Marquette Building

designed the Marquette Building, 140 S. Dearborn, the McNeil Building at Jackson and Franklin and the Gage Building on Michigan Avenue.

In addition, the firm designed the Old Colony Building at 407 S. Dearborn with rounded corners and pioneering wind bracing.

These buildings all rejected classical forms to emphasize functional needs of light and ventilation. With structural steel frames, the outer walls no longer bore the weight of the floors above, and the buildings featured so-called "Chicago Style" windows, a large fixed center panel of glass with double hung windows on either side.

Old Palmer House

In the future, my father would return to Chicago and the architectural firm, which became Holabird & Root in 1928. The firm was responsible for 333 N. Michigan, the Board of Trade, Soldier Field and the Palmolive Building.

I am the third generation of Holabird architects. None of my five daughters has chosen architecture as a profession. Holabird & Root, however, is still a viable firm that continues to design quality buildings.

SEPTEMBER

Fifteen Chicago police assigned to the outside of Comiskey Park are arrested and charged with taking $50 bribes from bookmakers working the sidewalk on Labor Day.

NOVEMBER

Northwestern University's football team loses to the University of Illinois 27-0.

ALSO IN 1911

The City Council votes to widen 12th Street from Michigan to Ashland, the first step in the Chicago Plan.

The Federated Jewish Charities of Chicago is formed. Among its founding members is Maimonides Hospital, which closes within three years because of financial difficulties. It later was reorganized as Mt. Sinai Hospital.

DePaul University becomes the first Catholic University in the United States to go coed.

CHINESE PUT DOWN ROOTS

Yokelund Wong and Chin Foin were wed in an arranged marriage.

Elaine Sit
Lawyer, writer and Chinese-American historian

BY ELAINE SIT

Gladys Wang was one year old in 1912 when her family moved to a new home on fashionable Calumet Avenue. The neighborhood was miles from the city's first Chinatown on Clark between Van Buren and Harrison streets.

But Wang's father, prosperous restaurateur Chin Foin, felt "no resident section of Chicago should be beyond the reach of a modern-day Chinese gentleman . . . there is room . . . for those who reach the top, be they Caucasian or Mongolian."

Chinatown

Foin got rich catering to Chicagoans. His advertised "high-class oriental" restaurant, the Mandarin-Inn, 414-16 S. Wabash, was probably the first in the city to offer American-style Chinese food.

Chicagoans flocked to the modern, large eatery to dine on such "exotic" foods as egg foo young and chop suey, along with roast turkey, frog legs, steaks and rounds of beef.

"The opera people with their top hats and limousines would go there. We had a dance

Yokelund Wong and Chin Foin's daughter, Gladys Wang, displays a picture of her father's Mandarin-Inn restaurant on South Wabash.

JANUARY

Chicago lawyer Clarence Darrow is indicted on charges he bribed a jury in a Los Angeles bombing case. He is acquitted Aug. 17, prompting the judge to remark, "Hundreds of thousands of Hallelujahs will go up from as many throats when they hear of this."

Clarence Darrow

FEBRUARY

Thomas Jennings is executed at the old Cook County Jail. He is the first person ever convicted and sentenced to death with fingerprints as the only evidence.

APRIL

The Titanic sinks, sending 1,513 to their deaths. Before he drowns, millionaire John Jacob Astor secures lifeboat seats for Chicagoans Ida Hippach, 44, and her daughter, Jean, 17. Nine years earlier, Ida Hippach lost two children in the Iroquois Theater fire.

Her father was among the lucky few to have a family in America. In 1882, to limit the thousands of Chinese who migrated here to pan for gold or work on the railroads, Congress passed the Chinese Exclusion Act. It barred women from entering the country. As a result, the ratio of Chinese women to men in 1912 was approximately 1 to 10.

Wang's father and San Francisco-born mother Yokelund Wong wed in an arranged marriage. Foin then sent his 15-year-old bride to Wisconsin to be educated. "He wanted her to be up to the lifestyle they would lead," said Wang.

Chinese began settling in Chicago after the Great Fire, fleeing lynchings, beatings and discrimination in Western states. By 1912 the community of approximately 2,000 Chinese in Chicago—mostly from the province of Canton—included 110 children enrolled in public schools. Of these, 99 were American-born of foreign parents, many of whom toiled in the 300 Chinese laundries scattered throughout the city.

In August 1912, plans were announced to build a new Chinatown near Wentworth and 22nd streets, considered a slum and vice district. Anchoring the area was a (still-standing) two-block-long building with 15 storefronts, two large restaurants, 30 apartments and a club room for the Chinese Merchants Association now know as the On Leong Tong.

Gladys Wang attended public schools here until 1925, when she and her sister were sent to China to be exposed to their cultural heritage. She married career diplomat Gung Hsing Wang after her return to Chicago in 1938.

The Wangs lived many years in Chicago, where Mr. Wang created the Chinese American Civic Council and was director for the Chicago Dwellings Association, which helped develop more than 70 building projects. He died in March 1999.

Restaurateur Chin Foin got rich catering to Chicagoans on South Wabash.

floor, and sometimes movie stars performed in the floor show," recalls Wang, now an 88-year-old South Shore grandmother.

When her father—known as the "prince of Chicago's Chinese merchantdom"—purchased the large brick home on Calumet, it made news. "Rich Chinese Merchant Champions Cause of His Race," read the headline in the August 29, 1912, Chicago Record-Herald.

"We were pioneers to move into an area where we weren't accepted," said Gladys Wang.

JUNE

President William H. Taft wins the nomination at the Republican Convention at the Coliseum on the South Side.

President William H. Taft

AUGUST

The progressive "Bull Moose" Party holds a convention at the Coliseum, nominating former GOP President Theodore Roosevelt. Jane Addams seconds the nomination. Roosevelt and Taft both lose to Woodrow Wilson in November.

DECEMBER

Chicago physician James Bryan Herrick, 51, is the first to identify and diagnose blood clots as a cause of heart attacks.

1913

JEWS STAND UP TO BIAS

Brenda Warner Rotzoll

Sun-Times staff reporter

Bernice Katz, second from the left in the lineup, circa 1913, and in the inset, remembers job and housing discrimination against Jews.

BY BRENDA WARNER ROTZOLL

If you wanted to ride those newfangled elevated trains from one side of Chicago to another in the early days, you had to take one company's car to the Loop, get off, walk to another train and pay another fare.

That changed in 1913, when the City Council agreed to allow longer station platforms in exchange for the four private L operators granting through routing and free transfers. On Nov. 1 a crosstown train ran from Stony Island Avenue on the South Side to Linden in Wilmette, the first step of a decades-long process of consolidation that led to today's CTA.

View of Alley "L" locomotive

That agreement meant nothing to eight-year-old Bernice Katz, then living in the Maxwell Street neighborhood.

"When we were little, we didn't ride the L. Everything was horse and buggy at that time. I think most people were a little leery about the L at first," said Bernice Katz Mendelsohn, now 94 and a Lincolnwood resident.

What she remembers is that Jewish immigrants "had difficult times finding

JANUARY	FEBRUARY	MARCH	JUNE
Edward C. Waller and Oscar J. Friedman buy the land at 60th and Cottage Grove on which they commission Frank Lloyd Wright to build Midway Gardens.	The local orchestra founded in 1891 by Theodore Thomas officially takes the name Chicago Symphony Orchestra.	The New York "Armory Show," America's first showcase of European modern art, arrives for a 24-day run at the Art Institute. It drew numerous protests and 188,650 spectators.	The federal government refuses Chicago's request to more than double the flow of Lake Michigan water to 10,000 cubic feet per second. Today only 3,200 is allowed.

William A. Stewart, who came to town from Kalamazoo, Mich., opened a tiny coffee roasting plant that he made into a multimillion-dollar food operation serving hotels, clubs and restaurants—Stewart's Private Blend.

places to live and finding jobs. If you said you were Jewish, they would not hire you."

Worse, she said, was that many of the men selling fruit and vegetables door-to-door in the alleys around Hastings and Laflin "were killed because they were Jewish peddlers."

That ended when a Jewish boy named Davy Miller got together a gang that beat up the groups attacking his people's peddlers. Miller went on to become a prominent 1920s gambler and bootlegger hooked up with the Dion O'Banion mob.

A far better known and ultimately world-reaching effort for Jewish rights began that year in Chicago. Working in one small room in the Loop, lawyer Sigmund Livingston founded the Anti-Defamation League "to stop, by appeals to reason and conscience, and if necessary, by appeals to law, the defamation of the Jewish people... and put an end forever to unjust and unfair discrimination against and ridicule of any sect or body of citizens."

Authur Andersen

At another Loop office, a young man named Arthur Andersen set up in business as a certified public accountant. One of his first customers demanded that Andersen cook the books to show inflated earnings for an interurban line. Andersen refused, then set about convincing all his clients it was in their best interests to become open and honest about their bookkeeping. Today Arthur Andersen consulting and accounting firms employ 130,000 people in 81 countries and have revenues of more than $10 billion a year.

William A. Stewart came to town from Kalamazoo, Mich., looking for opportunity. He found it in a tiny coffee roasting plant that in his first 15 years in Chicago he made into a multimillion-dollar food operation providing high-quality coffee to hotels, clubs and restaurants. Today Stewart's Private Blend is a household word nationwide.

It was a big year for building. The Shriners built Medinah Temple on North Wabash, topped with twin copper domes of Moorish shape. Back then they could be seen from Michigan Avenue.

Four miles south, the Wabash Avenue YMCA opened to become a major social and educational center in what then was called the Black Metropolis, center of Chicago's African-American culture in the early part of the century. Frank Lloyd Wright started construction of Midway Gardens, his short-lived version of a German concert garden, at 60th and Cottage Grove. And the city Parks Commission started work on Clarendon Beach in Uptown. The beach later disappeared under a landfill on which the Outer Drive was built.

JULY	**AUGUST**	**SEPTEMBER**	**DECEMBER**
Oak Park High School wins the national interscholastic track and field meet at the international athletic games in Chicago.	Chicago changes many street designations, replacing numbered courts and avenues with names on both the South and North sides.	Lorado Taft's Fountain of the Great Lakes sculpture is installed on the south wing of the Art Institute.	A. Montgomery Ward, founder of the first mail-order business, and known locally as the "protector of the lakeshore," dies.

CHICAGO GETS WRITERS' BLOC

Frank Sullivan
Public relations consultant and author of a book about 1914 in Chicago

Harriet Monroe used her journal, "Poetry, a Magazine of Verse," to nurture many great Chicago writers, including Carl Sandburg.

BY FRANK SULLIVAN

On a March night in 1914 at the private Cliff Dwellers club then atop Orchestra Hall, Harriet Monroe brought together a group that felt the way she did about poetry.

Carl Sandburg was there. The part-time poet of the people and full-time newspaper reporter was still exuberant over the premiere of his newest poem in the current issue of Monroe's publication, "Poetry, a Magazine of Verse."

Carl Sandburg

In it, Sandburg hailed the "Stormy, husky, brawling City of the Big Shoulders ... " from his famous poem "Chicago." His free verse, as well as other poetic forms, received Monroe's encouragement.

Monroe, a newspaper literary critic and poet in her own right, asked why there was such great support for the Art Institute and liberal endowments for painters and sculptors, but "general

William Butler Yeats (left) and Ring Lardner

In May 1914, Edgar Lee Masters' *Spoon River Anthology* was published.

contemptuous indifference toward the poet and the beautiful art he practices?"

Indifference would end, she believed, if she could succeed with her magazine. "Poetry," after a year of publication, was having its first awards banquet that night.

The principal speaker, who traveled across the Atlantic to receive the $250 first prize for the best poem of the previous year, was Irishman William Butler Yeats.

Said Yeats in his acceptance speech, quoting Francis Bacon, "There is no excellent beauty without strangeness."

Monroe had prevailed upon one of the magazine's guarantors, Albert Loeb (father of the man who later murdered Bobby Franks), to donate a second prize of $50 for another poem which she deemed especially meritorious, "General William Booth Enters Into Heaven."

The 35-year-old, relatively unknown creator of the poem, Vachel Lindsay, traveled from Springfield to accept the award. He did more than respond with gratitude. He recited his newest poem still in manuscript:

" . . . with a boomlay, boomlay boom. Then I saw the Congo, creeping through the black, cutting through the forest with a golden track."

Chicago in 1914 was a magnet attracting crafters of words from throughout the mid-continent. In addition to

Ben Hecht

Edna Ferber (left) and Vachel Lindsay

Sandburg from Galesburg, there was his walking companion Edgar Lee Masters from downstate Lewiston. In May, his *Spoon River Anthology* was published.

From Niles, Mich., had come sports reporter Ring Lardner, whose beat included the new ballpark at Clark and Addison, which opened in April. In March, Sherwood Anderson of Elyria, Ohio, was living in a room on Wabash near Superior, at work on a novel about a town he would call Winesburg.

Edna Ferber, from Appleton, Wis., had been living in Hyde Park and writing excitedly about her new home: as " . . . one of the most vital, unformed, fascinating, horrible, brutal, civilized and beautiful cities in the world."

And the newspapers? In 1914, there were eight dailies in English. Ben Hecht from Racine, Wis., on his way to making himself the exemplar of all reporters of his era, received his first byline in May in the Chicago Daily Journal.

"It is a fine thing," he wrote, "to be a reporter, and young and working in Chicago."

A month later there were new words for writers to deal with—Bosnia, Sarajevo, Serbian nationalism and world war. An epoch had ended. The other 1914 was to begin.

CHICAGO'S WORST DISASTER

Andrew Herrmann
Sun-Times columnist

Celebration turned to chaos when the Eastland went over in the Chicago River.

BY ANDREW HERRMANN

What a wonderful day July 24, 1915, was to have been. For that year's company picnic, Western Electric had arranged for a cruise on Lake Michigan.

Employees gathered early on the south side of the Chicago River near the Clark Street Bridge. Workers, spouses and children found they had a choice of six ships: the Theodore Roosevelt, the Petroskey, the Maywood, the Racine, the Rochester.

And the Eastland—the clear favorite.

Built of steel and four decks high, the ship went by the nickname "Speed Queen of the Lakes." Its 22-mile-an-hour slice through water was due to its unusually narrow width of 36 feet. Sure, there had been rumors of its instability, but there had been that dare offered by one of the ship's owners: a $5,000 reward for the man who could prove that the Eastland was unsafe. No one took the bait.

Besides, the federal government had just that very summer inspected the 2,500-passenger ship and determined it to be safe.

By 6:30 a.m. about 5,000 people were already on the docks. As the Eastland's gangplank was lowered at 6:40 a.m., people rushed onto the ship. One minute later, the Eastland began to lean.

FEBRUARY

Roswell C.F. Smith, who killed an 8-year-old girl, is hanged at the Cook County Jail at 10:14 a.m. The Daily News reports that Smith died "game," repeating the words of a psalm before his execution.

"Big Bill" Thompson

APRIL

The first black alderman, Oscar DePriest, and the first Latino alderman, William E. Rodriguez, are elected. William "Big Bill" Thompson wins the mayor's seat.

JUNE

Cubs win! In the year's longest major league game, the Cubs beat Brooklyn in 19 innings.

JULY

Archbishop James E. Quigley dies at his brother's home in Rochester, N.Y. Thousands of children escort Quigley's body from his home on North State to Holy Name Cathedral for the funeral mass.

Streetcar motormen and conductors win a 3-cent-an-hour pay increase—to a maximum 36 cents—in a labor dispute with the Chicago Surface Lines that is mediated by Mayor Thompson.

Years later, bridge-tender Fred Hornburg views the scene of the Eastland disaster from his window of the tower.

"I shall never be able to forget what I saw," one eyewitness said. "People … were clustered so thickly that they literally covered the surface of the water." People clutched "at anything they could reach—at bits of wood, at each other, grabbing each other, pulling each other down, and screaming! The screaming was the most horrible of all."

On shore, bystanders threw wooden planks and crates into the river to help the floundering Western Electric employees stay afloat. Alerted by screams coming from inside the Eastland, workmen cut holes in the ship's exposed side in an effort to free those trapped. By 8 a.m.—just an hour and a half after the laughter of anticipation had filled the air—it was over.

Eight hundred and forty-four people had drowned in 20 feet of water, the worst disaster in Chicago history.

After many years, the courts blamed a by-then deceased engineer who, it was charged, neglected to fill the ballast tanks properly. Few were convinced, and in the years since then, historical sleuths have sought to spread the blame. They note that just before the 1915 season, 2 inches of concrete—14 tons— had been laid between decks to keep the ship's wooden floors from rotting, contributing to its instability. George W. Hilton, writing in *Eastland: Legacy of the Titanic,* says that in the aftermath of the Titanic, public pressure required ships to add additional lifeboats. Did the extra weight of the boats help tip the Eastland?

As the crew frantically tried to adjust the ballasts, there was no worry among the passengers. The women, garbed in ankle-length dresses and knee-high boots, were more concerned with a light rain, and they scurried to find shelter in the ship's inner cabins.

Those remaining topside laughed at the ship's unstableness. A Chicago fire boat went by, blew its whistle, and folks rushed over to see it, unbalancing the Eastland further. Chairs, picnic baskets and bottles began to slide across the decks.

Laughter was replaced by panic. Then, still dockside, the ship tipped.

An Eastland victim's funeral

The disaster was, said Karl Sup, co-founder of the Eastland Memorial Society and the grandson of two Eastland survivors, "a dark chapter in Chicago history."

James E. Quigley

REVOLUTION PROMPTS INFLUX

Laura Emerick
Sun-Times
assistant features
editor

Francisco "Pancho" Villa (left) and General John J. "Black Jack" Pershing meet at the Mexican-U.S. border in early 1916, before Pershing began his 11-month pursuit of Villa.

The 1916 U.S. pursuit into Mexico of revolutionary Francisco "Pancho" Villa and the decline of European immigration during World War I brought many Mexicans to Chicago.

BY LAURA EMERICK

Chicago's Latin community owes its existence, in part, to the Mexican Revolution and one of its generals, Francisco "Pancho" Villa.

When revolution broke out in 1910, many Mexicans fled their homeland for safe havens in the United States, including Chicago. Here they found jobs in the steel mills, railroad yards and meat-packing plants.

In March 1916, the revolution crossed the border when Villa raided Columbus, N.M., and killed 17 Americans. That attack led Gen. John J. "Black Jack" Pershing to pursue Villa into Mexico for an 11-month cam-

paign. Pershing never captured his target; Villa instead became a hero.

But not to all Mexicans, including my grandfather. He was already thinking of leaving for greater work opportunities. The Villa chase of 1916 sealed his decision. Making sure he had the proper entry documents, he scouted out several possible places to relocate, including northern California and Chicago.

When he finally settled here in Chicago, he had to change his name. Due to Pancho Villa's

General John J. Pershing

Antonio Mendez

notoriety, he met frequent prejudice during his first trip north. His given name, Antonio Jesus Avila, prompted many to ask if he were somehow related to the infamous revolutionary.

"If he would have stayed in Mexico, he would have had to join the revolution, which he didn't really support," recalls his daughter (and my mother) Rosalie Emerick. "When he came back to Chicago with his wife, he decided to adopt his mother's maiden name [Mendez]."

Like many Mexican immigrants, they settled in South Chicago, in the 95th Street area. "The Southeast Side settlement is the oldest Mexican community in the city and one of the more important," said Dominic Pacyga, a Columbia College professor who specializes in immigration history.

The steel mills on the Southeast Side drew many immigrants, who put down roots. The oldest Mexican parish, established in 1923 by the Rev. William Kane,

with Cardinal George Mundelein's blessing, is Our Lady of Guadalupe on East 91st Street. St. Kevin's parish on Torrence Avenue in South Deering is another.

Though early Mexican immigration to Chicago was fueled by political unrest back home, the outbreak of World War I also helped to spur the exodus. The war curtailed European immigration, so heavy industry turned to other sources of labor, including recent arrivals from Mexico.

Not everyone was consigned to toiling in the factories, though. "My father had skills which spared him working as a laborer, especially in steel mills," recalls my aunt Elizabeth Postal.

"He taught himself how to repair shoes and learned how to make dress patterns so that he could sew clothes for his seven children. He worked all his life, his kids were never on welfare. He always had a job, even during the Depression, because of the skills he acquired by working at a hotel."

Within a few years of arrival, my grandfather learned English fluently. Adapting to life in Chicago was much easier for him than it was for my grandmother, who never became fluent.

"It's very hard to come from a foreign country, not knowing the language," recalls another aunt, Mary Medina. "My mother would cut out labels from food packages and show them to store clerks, because she didn't know the words in English."

Like many immigrants, my grandparents became U.S. citizens and put down roots in their adopted community. They did not return to Mexico, not even for a visit, until the early '60s. Though they moved to different neighborhoods, including Lawndale and Humboldt Park, they never left. Chicago was their home.

JUNE		**JULY**	**NOVEMBER**	**DECEMBER**	**ALSO IN 1916**
Two presidential conventions come to Chicago: the Republicans at the Coliseum and the National Progressives at the Auditorium Theatre. The GOP nominates U.S. Supreme Court Justice Charles E. Hughes, while the "Moose" slate Teddy Roosevelt.	 **Navy Pier**	Thousands of Chicagoans show up at the newly built Navy Pier—then called Municipal Pier—forcing officials to hold an impromptu dedication of the facility, even though it wasn't scheduled to open until mid-month. The pier was part of Daniel Burnham's 1909 plan for the city.	Bishop Charles Edward Cheney, a national figure in the Reformed Episcopal church, dies at 80. Cheney had been rector of Christ Church since 1860.	Many of the city's poor lose their only means of bathing when the health commissioner orders all 18 public baths closed. Budget cuts are blamed for the shutdown.	Carl Sandburg publishes the poem "Chicago," containing the lines "hog butcher for the world" and "City of the Big Shoulders."

POLONIA RICH IN HISTORY

Jan Lorys
Director of the
Polish Museum of
America

Polish immigrants on the Northwest Side are sworn in to Poland's army in 1917. More than 2,500 Polish immigrants in Chicago enlisted in Poland's armed forces during World War I.

BY JAN LORYS

More than 40,000 Polish Americans jammed the Dexter Pavilion of the stockyards on a fall Sunday in 1917 to hear Polish statesman and concert pianist Ignace Paderewski speak on behalf of a free Poland.

The crowd had earlier attended a mass at St. Joseph's Church at 48th and Paulina and then marched to the hall singing Polish and American anthems.

The date was Oct. 14, the 100th anniversary of the death of Thaddeus Kosciuszko, a Polish volunteer in the American Revolution who returned to his homeland to organize a revolt against the Russians.

Paderewski, who had visited Chicago many times since 1891, when he played a Chopin concert at the newly built Auditorium Theatre, urged listeners to follow Kosciuszko's example and join the battle to free Poland, then partitioned by Russia, Germany and the Austro-Hungarians.

"The situation in Poland is desperate," said Paderewski, praising U.S. President Woodrow Wilson, who had once received him in the White House, and, in turn, received a huge electoral vote of confidence from Chicago's Poles.

In 1917, Chicago's Polish community, or Polonia, was 50 years old and numbered

Ignace Paderewski—pianist, activist, first premier of Poland

FEBRUARY	APRIL	JUNE	JULY
Fourteen die in a gas explosion at a tenement house at 14th and Newberry.	The City Council adopts the official Chicago flag. It has three horizontal white stripes, two light blue ones and two red stars—symbolizing the World's Fair in 1893 and the Great Fire of 1871.	At a prison riot in Joliet, one convict is killed, more than 20 prisoners and guards are injured and the warden narrowly escapes death. The disturbance ends as three companies of the 1st Illinois infantry are about to fire into the mob.	Many African Americans are shot and hanged in race riots in East St. Louis that leave 20 to 75 dead.

350,000. The predominantly Roman Catholic Poles lived near 50 parishes in several neighborhoods: on the Northwest Side around the "Polish Triangle" of Milwaukee, Division and Ashland, in what is now the Pilsen neighborhood, near the stockyards and near the steel mills in South Chicago.

The first Polish church, St. Stanislaus Kostka Parish, was established by 150 families in 1867 on Noble Street. By the turn of the century, it had become the largest Catholic parish in the world, with 5,438 families.

And by 1908, Chicago's Poles finally achieved representation in the Irish- and German-controlled Catholic Church in Chicago when Southeast Sider Paul Rhode was named the first American bishop of Polish descent.

Before the United States' entrance into World War I in 1917, most Americans had been reluctant to become involved in Europe's struggle.

But Polonia's sons, brothers and fathers saw the war as an opportunity to regain independence for their native land. An editorial in the April 14, 1917, issue of the Polish newspaper Narod Polski urged them to join the U.S. Army.

"Do not wait and do not say, 'Let the others go first.' Your country calls. It is

Jan Kostrubala, a 17-year-old Chicagoan from Poland, lied about his age to enlist in the army in 1917.

General Thaddeus Kosciuszko

time to go and defend our new Fatherland. Long live the United States of America."

The same month Paderewski was in Chicago, the U.S. War Department authorized Polish immigrants who still held foreign passports to enlist in the Polish army in France. More than 2,500 signed up from Chicago, trained in Canada, fought in France and eventually returned to an independent Poland in 1919. Some later came back to Chicago.

In his 1917 speech, Paderewski stirred youths such as Jan Kostrubala, a 17-year-old Polish immigrant who lived in the Back of the Yards neighborhood, lied about his age to enlist in the Polish army, fought in France and later in Poland.

He returned to Chicago in 1921, became a shoe salesman, sold insurance and then began working as a reporter for the daily newspaper Dziennik Chicagosk. He was executive editor when he died in 1958.

Kostrubala's grandson Dr. Paul Valasek, president of the Polish Genealogical Society of America, says his grandfather "was motivated by patriotism to help liberate Poland, but was always proud to be an American."

OCTOBER

The White Sox win the World Series, beating the New York Giants four games to two.

James Colosimo and Johnny Torrio open the Speedway Inn in Cicero, one of the first mob-run suburban roadhouses.

NOVEMBER

Plan Commission Chairman Charles H. Wacker reports on a plan to move South Water Street, and its market, outside the Loop to create a "modern, high-class business thoroughfare" (which now bears his name).

Charles H. Wacker

ALSO IN 1917

Jazz pioneer Joseph "King" Oliver, 32, a cornetist, moves to Chicago after military authorities shut down New Orleans red-light district sporting houses.

GREAT WAR ENDS

Potter Palmer

President of Palmer-Florida Corp., a Lake Forest-based investment management company

Chicago celebrates the end of WWI.

BY POTTER PALMER

On the day the Great War ended, Chicagoans began celebrating early.

At 2 a.m., a parade formed at Madison and State, as workers left their posts to join soldiers, sailors and hotel guests.

"Every conceivable sort of noise-making device—dishpans, horns, revolvers, whistles, the whole category of ear-splitting paraphernalia—

Potter Palmer Mansion

appeared as by magic," the Daily News reported.

World War I, known then as the Great War, had lasted more than four years and claimed nearly 10 million lives, including 116,516 Americans. On the Western Front, guns went silent on the 11th hour of the 11th day of the 11th month of 1918.

Chicago's celebration continued into the night. Crowds lit bonfires and held mock

Bertha Honore Palmer

 JANUARY

A blizzard and 14-below-zero temperatures kill seven Chicagoans and cut train and telegraph service from the city to the outside world for two days.

 FEBRUARY

President Wilson fixes a minimum price of $2.20 per bushel for 1918 wheat at Chicago.

MARCH

The New National Party, led by breakaway Socialists and Progressives, is formed in Chicago. It endorses Prohibitition, women's suffrage, and government ownership of some utilities and industries.

 MAY

A $50,000 statue of the Republic, a bronze reproduction of the Daniel Chester French sculpture from the 1893 World's Fair, is unveiled in Jackson Park on the former site of the fair's administration building.

Masked against the flu, Chicago sanitation workers are inspected before going on duty in October 1919, during the height of the epidemic.

funeral processions for Kaiser Wilhelm II, Germany's defeated emperor. Steam whistles blew, church bells clanged, ticker tape fluttered, schools closed, workers played hooky and county jail prisoners sang in chorus.

Chicagoans had been pinched by war shortages throughout 1918. In January, the government ordered "coaless" days every Monday, forcing Chicago schools to close, but not taverns—raising angry protests from reformers. Washington also declared "meatless" and "wheatless" days so food could be shipped to Europe. And citizens were urged to buy war bonds to "Beat back the Hun."

The baseball season ended early in deference to the war effort. The Cubs won the pennant. But, ever the Cubs, they blew it in the World Series to Boston, four games to two. A Boston pitcher named Babe Ruth won two games. The Cubs' home games were played in Comiskey Park because it had more seats.

Besides the war, the year's other big story was the worldwide flu epidemic that killed 51 million people,

including 550,000 in the United States. Nearly three in 10 Americans caught the flu, and two percent of those who got sick died. In Chicago, the epidemic peaked on Oct. 17, when 520 people died.

Hotels were converted to hospitals. Indian Hill Golf Club also became a temporary hospital, with society ladies serving as nurses. So many telephone operators called in sick, the phone company asked the public to make fewer calls.

Street cleaners wore white paper masks. The Board of Health ordered police to arrest anyone who spit in the street or sneezed without covering his mouth. North suburban schools, churches and theaters closed, and only close relatives were allowed at funerals.

But Chicago schools remained open. Kids attended class in their coats, with the windows open to admit fresh air. On streetcars, doors and windows also were kept open.

On a personal note, 1918 was a momentous year for my family. My great-grandmother, philanthropist Bertha Honore Palmer, died at age 68, leaving the Art Institute her magnificent art collection. Her gift forms the core of the museum's impressionist paintings, including works by Renoir, Degas and Monet.

Bertha Palmer was the widow of Potter Palmer, who made his fortune in retailing, built the Palmer House and made State Street great. Her art "had decorated her mansion and demonstrated her sophisticated taste," School of the Art Institute student Margo Hobbs wrote in her thesis. "Upon her death, Palmer had no need for either, and she could graciously disperse it."

JUNE

Sixty-eight circus performers are killed when a Hagenbeck-Wallace Circus train stops on the tracks near Hammond, Ind., and another train plows into it. Funeral services a few days later draw 1,500 mourners.

AUGUST

William D. Haywood and more than 100 other WWI leaders are indicted in Chicago for conspiracy against prosecution of the war. All later receive heavy sentences and fines.

SEPTEMBER

Postal aviator E.V. Gardner completes the first one-day trip from Chicago to New York, spending 10 hours in the air.

DECEMBER

The City Council votes 62-2 to ban the display of the red flag, a symbol of anarchism. Two Socialist aldermen cast the "no" votes.

SHAME AND SCANDAL

Dempsey Travis
Real estate
developer and
author

Raymond Elementary School 8th-grade class photo. Eugene Williams, the initial riot victim of Chicago's "blood red summer," is seated at the far right of the third row.

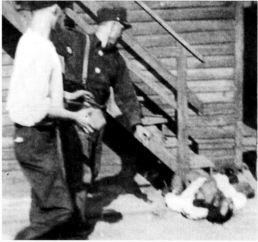

Members of a white mob stone a black youth to death during the 1919 race riots that left 38 dead.

BY DEMPSEY TRAVIS

The year 1919 saw Chicago's summer of shame. Thirty-eight people were killed in the deadliest episode of racial violence in the city. And a fixed World Series between the White Sox and Cincinnati Reds created the biggest scandal in the history of baseball.

Troubles began on a hot Sunday in July when Eugene Williams, a recent Raymond Elementary School graduate, decided to cool his ebony body in Lake Michigan off the 27th Street Beach.

Floating on a homemade Huckleberry Finn raft constructed of two wooden railroad ties, Williams accidentally drifted south of the invisible line at the 29th Street Beach reserved—by unwritten understanding—"for whites only."

Angered by the black boy's intrusion into their territory, several young whites began throwing bricks at Williams, who fell off the raft and drowned.

The lad became a footnote in Chicago's political history as the first murder victim of five days of rioting. The racist spirits fueling this violence were an outgrowth of competition for jobs and housing between black

JANUARY
The Republican National Committee, meeting in Chicago, advocates women's suffrage.

The Great Lakes Navy team wins the Rose Bowl, beating the Mare Island (Calif.) Marines 17-0.

FEBRUARY
James B. Herrick of the Rush Medical College publishes the first electrocardiogram of heart malfunction.

MAY
Author Frank Baum, who lived on the Northwest Side while writing *The Wizard of Oz*, dies at age 62.

Susan B. Anthony

JUNE
Illinois Legislature votes to ratify the 19th Amendment, which extends full suffrage to women. The so-called Susan B. Anthony Amendment took effect Aug. 26, 1920, after three-quarters of the states approved it.

1919

1919 White Sox

random from the windows of their automobiles as they raced a mile a minute up and down State Street. Throughout the night, groups of whites in auto caravans kept shooting gangster-style out of both sides of their cars," Grinnell recalled.

It took four white National Guard regiments and a thunderstorm to restore order. (Gov. Len Small did not enlist the services of the black Eighth Regiment, although it was located at 35th and Giles in the heart of the riot area.)

When the rain stopped and the smoke cleared, 38 men and boys, including 23 blacks, had been killed. And 537 people were wounded, 342 of them black.

and white World War I veterans and the growing number of blacks moving here from the South.

Within two hours, word of Williams' murder circulated through the South Side's "Black Belt." When the 29th and Wabash gang heard one of the many versions of his death, they sprang into action. White men who were unfortunate enough to come in contact with that bunch of hoodlums were beaten to a pulp. Five men were stabbed, and one was shot.

Retaliatory action came quickly. Between 9 p.m., Sunday, July 27, and 3 a.m. the next day, the white gangs and athletic clubs west of the stockyard district bricked, bat whipped, stomped, stabbed and shot 27 African Americans.

In 1977, I interviewed Anna Mary Grinnell, a 96-year-old woman, who, at the time of the riot, lived with her husband and 18-month-old daughter in an apartment above their bakery at 3308 S. State.

"We spent most of Monday night, July 28, lying on the floor of our apartment dodging bullets being fired by whites at

"Shoeless" Joe Jackson

The blood from the riot had barely dried when newspaper headlines were screaming about the Chicago White Sox baseball scandal. Eight Sox players (later dubbed the "Black Sox") agreed to throw games during the World Series for a promised $20,000 apiece from New York gamblers.

Sox owner Charles A. Comiskey, who paid his star players $6,000 a year, suspected a fix. He was right. The players were indicted for conspiracy to commit fraud. They were acquitted, but suspended from baseball for life.

Strolling out of the courthouse after testifying, one of their number, outfielder "Shoeless" Joe Jackson, was grabbed by a tearful 10-year-old paperboy. "Say it ain't so, Joe! Say it ain't so!" he pleaded. "It's so, kid," Jackson replied.

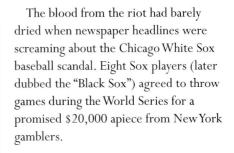

JULY

In its first day of operation between Grant Park and the White City amusement park, the dirigible Wing Foot Express bursts into flames and falls through the skylight of the Illinois Trust & Savings Bank. Thirteen people, including 10 bank employees, are killed and more than 20 are hurt.

OCTOBER

Federal troops take control of Gary, Ind., to quell riots by striking steelworkers. The rioting broke out after strikers left a mass meeting and came upon a streetcar carrying 50 strikebreakers hired by the U.S. Steel Corp. Troops were called in after 2,000 strikers, led by former soldiers in uniform, held a rally in defiance of city officials' orders.

ALSO IN 1919

Chicago Daily News reporter Carl Sandburg wins the Pulitzer Prize for "Cornhuskers."

Daily airmail service begins between Chicago and New York.

FROM BROTHELS TO BOOZE

Neil Steinberg
Sun-Times
columnist

Cook County prosecutors dump the contents of an illegal still during Prohibition, as officials pursued the war against bootleggers.

Archbishop Mundelein

BY NEIL STEINBERG

Big Jim Colosimo's May 15 funeral was a pageant of power as well as a celebration of the mutually profitable union of organized crime and city government.

The First Ward Democratic Club alone sent 1,000 marchers. Three judges, a congressman, a state representative, an assistant state's attorney, nine aldermen and 4,000 or so other, ordinary people followed the body of the notorious pimp, murderer and thug to its final home at Oak Woods Cemetery. One of his pallbearers was the infamous Ald. "Bathhouse" John Coughlin.

Archbishop George Mundelein refused to allow use of a Catholic Church or let Colosimo be buried on consecrated ground—not for any of his crimes, but because he had divorced his wife to marry a showgirl. Pleas from Chicago's powerful to the pope for intervention fell on deaf ears.

It was the nation's first grand, ceremonial gangster funeral. Many more would follow, as Chicago became the center of organized crime in the United States. Before the decade was out, there would be 20,000 speakeasies in the city, and hundreds of mob-related murders as bands of criminals gunned each other down, competing for the chance to supply those speakeasies.

FEBRUARY

The Air Board of Chicago is formed, with Col. Bion J. Arnold as president.

MAY

There is a public celebration to mark the widening of Michigan Avenue and the opening of the new double-leaf bascule bridge across it.

JUNE

Appearing before a Congressional committee, U.S. Attorney General Palmer accuses Chicago's Louis F. Post, the assistant secretary of labor, of showing a "perverted sympathy" for anarchists he should be deporting.

A young pregnant woman named Ruth Wanderer is shot at her door by a "ragged stranger" and dies in the arms of her husband, Carl, a decorated war hero. Chicago police soon learn that Wanderer had a woman on the side and had hired a skid row bum to pose as a hold up man. Wanderer later was hanged for the crime.

Johnny Torrio

While Colosimo is considered the first Prohibition mob boss, he was killed, most likely, because he was slow to truly recognize the lucrative nature of the booze trade. And why would he? He was earning $50,000 a month from brothels and opium dens in an era when a clerk earned a dollar or two a day.

The young hotheads working for Colosimo couldn't wait. After presiding over the Chicago crime world for most of the first two decades of the century, Colosimo lasted only five months under Prohibition. The 18th Amendment, which made every thirsty American a potential criminal, began on Jan. 17—Al Capone's 21st birthday, ironically enough. On May 11, someone— police never figured out who—stepped up to Colosimo in his restaurant at 2126 S. Wabash, put a .38 pistol to his head and pulled the trigger twice.

The primary beneficiary of the killing was Colosimo's second-in-command, Johnny Torrio, his wife's cousin, who wasted no time gearing up for the illegal liquor trade. That trade was quickly taken over by his lieutenant, who was brought to Chicago to stand in the street and ballyhoo a brothel. His name was Al Capone.

Colosimo's funeral was big, but it wasn't the biggest story as spring gave way to summer in 1920. That was the Republican National Convention, which put elements of the city into a frenzy. Thousands of people mobbed the Coliseum, trying to get in with streetcar transfers, skating medals and letters from their postmaster.

The real action wasn't on the floor, though. That took place in suite 4046, on the 13th floor of the Blackstone Hotel, in a late-night meeting that created the phrase "smoke-filled room."

Ohio's bland, inoffensive Warren G. Harding was offered up as a compromise candidate with no enemies. Harding was called to the Blackstone at 2 a.m. to answer one crucial question: Did he have any dark secrets? No,

Blackstone Hotel

Harding lied, ignoring his mistresses and his illegitimate child, less than a year old. He was on his way to the presidency.

That, of course, was not all. The fads and fevers that defined the 1920s were also taking hold. Chicago women took a sudden, mad passion for overalls, so much so that one manufacturer took out a full-page newspaper ad, asking the fashion-addled not to strip the shelves and "deprive the working man of an article of clothing which *he must wear daily.*"

Warren G. Harding

OCTOBER

Two Russian anarchists, Nicolai John Jazzinski and John Holoeny, are arrested and charged with possessing literature urging the murder of police and the seizing of wealth.

NOVEMBER

The cornerstone of the Wrigley Building is laid. Inside are samples of every type of chewing gum the company sells.

The Wrigley Building

DECEMBER

Kenesaw Mountain Landis, a federal judge in Chicago, is named baseball's first commissioner, a post he holds until his death in 1944.

ALSO IN 1920

The $10 million Drake Hotel opens at Michigan and East Lake Shore Drive with a lavish New Year's Eve party for 1,000 people. Designed by self-taught architect Ben Marshall, the 13-story Drake contains details copied from Italian Renaissance palaces. Guests have included Queen Elizabeth, Prince Philip and Princess Diana, King Hussein, Jawaharlal Nehru, Winston Churchill, Eleanor Roosevelt, Charles Lindbergh and Walt Disney.

COLEMAN TAKES TO THE AIR

Chicago Theatre interior (left) and exterior (below)

Father and Son Duo
Robert J. Herguth (left)
Sun-Times columnist
Robert C. Herguth (right)
Sun-Times reporter

BY ROBERT J. HERGUTH AND ROBERT C. HERGUTH

It was a high-flying year for Chicagoans, and Bessie Coleman was the highest flier of all.

In 1921 she became the world's first African-American woman to earn an international pilot's license.

The young 35th Street manicurist, fascinated by flying, went to Europe to get that license, recalls niece Marion Coleman, because she couldn't find a flight instructor in the United States who would train her. "She was

BLACK HERITAGE

USA 00

BESSIE COLEMAN

what I would call different," remembers Marion, now 83, who was instrumental in having the Postal Service issue a Bessie Coleman stamp.

Bessie died in a Florida plane crash in 1926 after daredevil flying in air shows everywhere. She had hoped to open a flight school for African Americans but perished before her dream was realized.

MAY	JUNE		JULY	SEPTEMBER
A University of Chicago study shows that male college graduates average $5,762 a year after 10 years of work.	The trial of the eight White Sox accused of throwing the 1919 World Series ends in their acquittal. The grand jury records, including the confessions of "Shoeless" Joe Jackson and Eddie Cicotte, are missing. They will show up four years later in the hands of team owner Charles Comiskey's lawyer.	 William A. Wieboldt	Department store owner William A. Wieboldt gives 14 pieces of real estate, valued at $4.5 million, to a charitable corporation. Income from the properties will go to Chicago charities.	The play "Tarzan of the Apes," from the book by Oak Park resident Edgar Rice Burroughs, opens on Broadway with lions, apes and other jungle animals onstage. Chicago railroad officials are arrested for failing to give workers two hours off to vote.

It was a golden year for many Chicago kids. "Streetcars every-where!" marvels Dorothy Otis, now 92. Margaret Whitesides, then a fifth grader at St. Ita's, recalls, "We rode streetcars and Ls, and we used to play a lot of softball in the street and mark up the sidewalk with chalk" in Edgewater.

"People's palaces" were coming in. The magnificent 4,307-seat Chicago Theatre opened Oct. 26 on State Street in the Loop. Buster Keaton was its first star.

Civic leader and attorney Marshall Holleb, born in 1916, fondly remembers the theater. "I went there as a kid. My dad took me. Two movies and a stage show! It was THE place to go, particularly in summer: It had its own air-conditioning system." In the mid-1980s, Holleb headed the successful effort to save the theater from demolition. It reopened in 1986 with Frank Sinatra.

It was an era of heavy-duty philanthropists. Chicagoans such as Julius Rosenwald of Sears, Roebuck had made millions and then gave lots of them back in the form of muse-ums, foundations and schools.

Rosenwald helped found the Museum of Science and Industry later in the 1920s and gave mightily to the University of Chicago. His Julius Rosenwald Fund was established mainly to improve the education of African Americans. It helped build more than 5,000 schools in 15 southern states.

Mr. and Mrs. Julius Rosenwald

Double-decker bus

Merchandiser Marshall Field had given land as a site for the new University of Chicago, and $8 million to launch the Field Museum of Natural History. The museum began in 1893 but opened at its current site May 2, 1921.

The south tower of the Wrigley Building was completed in 1921, and Wrigley's PK chewing gum was introduced. A Wrigley spokesman says PK stood for "packed tight," not for P.K. Wrigley.

It was a time of striving for young writer Ernest Hemingway, raised in Oak Park. He lived on the Near North Side and had difficulty finding a job. Then Oak Park's Tubby Williams hired him to do piecework ad copy for Firestone Tires.

Meanwhile, Carl Sandburg reviewed for the Chicago Daily News. He wrote that "One Arabian Night" with Pola Negri was "decid-edly a movie worth seeing."

Newfangled radio met big-time culture in Chicago for the first time: On Nov. 11 the Chicago Grand Opera Company opened its season at the Auditorium Theatre with "Madame Butterfly" being broadcast on a microphone.

Double-decker buses were beginning to grip the city's imagination—you could ride on top in the open. Nego-tiations started in 1921 to supplement the crowded transit system by adding double-decker bus service on the boulevards.

JAZZING UP THE TOWN

Don Rose
Political consultant,
food buff, and jazz
aficionado

Louis Armstrong

BY DON ROSE

At City Hall, it was business as usual: Mayor William Hale "Big Bill" Thompson's pal Fred Lundin was indicted for defrauding the school system of a cool million dollars. He was acquitted—as were other Thompson cronies—by the brilliant legal tactics of a local lawyer named Clarence Darrow.

The Chicago Literary Renaissance was in full blossom that year.

Clarence Darrow (left) gained an acquittal for Fred Lundin.

Chicago Daily News columnist Ben Hecht published his collection of sketches, "A Thousand and One Afternoons in Chicago."

Theodore Dreiser published his autobiography, *Newspaper Days.* Poet Carl Sandburg brought out his collection, *Slabs of the Sunburnt West.*

At Orchestra Hall, Frederick Stock conducted the world premieres of works by

In the 1920s, the Ercelle Sisters, a Chicago-born duo, performed on Broadway and in local theaters and nightclubs.

APRIL	**MAY**		**JUNE**

Radio station WMAQ, owned by the Chicago Daily News, goes on the air. The following month, WDAP begins broadcasting; in 1924 its owner, the Chicago Tribune, changes the call letters to WGN, short for "World's Greatest Newspaper."

An agreement between the Amalgamated Clothing Workers Association and Chicago employers cuts the wages of an estimated 50,000 workers by about 10 percent.

Governor Len Small

Gov. Len Small is acquitted in Waukegan on state charges of pocketing interest earned on public funds while he was state treasurer. Small died in 1933 during an effort to reopen criminal charges against him. The effort was led by future governor Otto Kerner's father, then Illinois attorney general.

Guards kill two strikers trying to persuade strikebreakers to leave a coal mine, precipitating an attack by an armed mob of miners in downstate Herrin, killing 19 non-union miners and injuring 30. Defeated strikers return to work in September. Murder trials in November end in acquittals.

two Chicago composers, Eric DeLamarter and Leo Sowerby, while on the South Side, another epic-making musical premiere was in the works.

Joe "King" Oliver's Creole Jazz Band was holding forth at Lincoln Gardens dance hall, perfecting what would become America's most significant contribution to world art and making Chicago its center.

With Oliver on cornet, Johnny Dodds on clarinet, Honore Dutrey on trombone, Lil Hardin on piano, Bill Jackson on banjo and Baby Dodds on drums, the band brought New Orleans-style collective improvisation to its highest moment.

In July, Oliver decided to add another horn and summoned from New Orleans an unknown 21-year-old who would become the Crescent City's most famous expatriate: Louis Armstrong.

Armstrong's playing began to crack the New Orleans mold. Instead of improvising only in counterpoint to the other band members, he leaped forward to create the jazz solo and the rhythmic concept of swinging—the fundamentals for music during the rest of the century. He also created the jazz vocal.

The same year Armstrong's residency began, a group of aspiring young musicians from Austin High School—tenor

Benny Goodman

Nat "King" Cole

saxophonist Bud Freeman, cornetist Jimmy McPartland and clarinetist Frank Teschemacher—started meeting at a soda shop and listening to New Orleans jazz records.

They went to Lincoln Gardens to hear the new trumpet phenomenon, inspiring them further. The Austin High Gang laid the foundation of what the world came to know as Chicago jazz. It featured drummer Davey Tough, and later his protégé, Gene Krupa.

Occasionally, a clarinetist from nearby Harrison High School played with them. By 1938, Benny Goodman was "the King of Swing."

Years later, an inventive young Chicago pianist named Nat Cole crowned himself "King," as Oliver did.

Then came an unending chain of jazz innovators: pianist Lennie Tristano, composer-leader William Russo, tenor sax men Gene Ammons and Johnny Griffin, instrumentalist Ira Sullivan and avant-garde bandleader Sun Ra.

In the '60s, the Association for the Advancement of Creative Musicians founded the second great Chicago school of jazz. The chain continues today with saxophonist Ken Vandermark—a chain whose first link was forged that hot summer when the King called Satch up here from New Orleans.

AUGUST

Inventor Alexander Graham Bell dies, 46 years after patenting the telephone and 30 years after making the first telephone call from New York City to Chicago.

NOVEMBER

In a nonbinding referendum, Cook County residents vote 552,003-138,109 to modify Prohibition to allow the manufacture, sale and transportation of less-than-4-percent beer and wine for home consumption.

The cornerstone of the Chicago Temple is laid at Washington and Clark. The $3.5 million building, designed by Holabird & Roche, will be 21 stories, the maximum number of stories allowable.

ALSO IN 1922

An 8-hour day and pay raise to 70 cents an hour is won by striking streetcar workers as they settle their strike.

REFORM IN THE BIG CITY

Douglas Bukowski
Chicago writer and historian

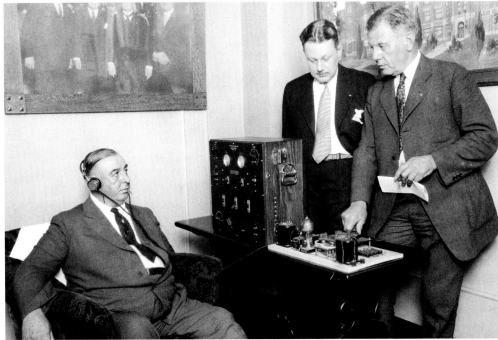

Mayor "Big Bill" Thompson (left) listening in on a television-like device that transmitted his image by radio

BY DOUGLAS BUKOWSKI

"Who's Sorry Now." "That Old Gang of Mine." "There'll Be Some Changes Made."

In Chicago the hit songs of 1923 did double-duty as entertainment and political commentary. That spring Mayor William Hale "Big Bill" Thompson was feeling pretty sorry about the changes taking place around City Hall.

After two terms (1915-1923) in office, Thompson and his gang were out because Chicagoans opted for a little reform. They got it, and then some, to the point that four years later they sang, "Gee, but I'd give the world to see that old gang of mine" in returning Thompson for a third term.

Big Bill had the uncanny ability to embrace and then discard issues without suffering any long-term backlash. He entered office as a self-proclaimed reformer who enforced the Sunday closing of saloons, tried to break the teachers' union and championed business concerns over labor.

Mayor Thompson throws out the first ball.

JANUARY

George F. Morse Jr. is hired as the director for the Chicago Zoological Park, later the Brookfield Zoo, at an annual salary of $5,000. Morse was the first salaried manager to run the affairs of the Zoological Society and eventually, the zoo.

APRIL

WBBM radio takes to the airwaves. In 1929 it moved into the Wrigley Building. The same month, 60 station heads met in Chicago to fight for the right to broadcast copyrighted music.

The City of Chicago can't sue newspapers for defamation, the Illinois Supreme Court rules. The city sued the Daily News and Tribune for libel after they criticized administration support of Gov. Len Small in the 1920 election.

JUNE

The Illinois Legislature prohibits ticket scalping by owners of baseball parks, circuses, theaters and other places of amusement. Punishment is $500 per offense and revocation of operating license, and victims are entitled to compensation of $20.

The General Assembly repeals a law barring divorced people from remarrying within one year.

A federal judge grants a government injunction against the Metropolitan Sanitary District to prevent it from taking more than 4,167 cubic feet of water a minute from Lake Michigan. It had been taking 10,000 cubic feet.

Mary Bartelme, first woman judge

All the ribbon-cutting ceremonies earned him the nickname "Big Bill the Builder."

But in 1923 Thompson was down on his luck. He had been dogged by a series of corruption scandals, including the indictment of his police chief. When a school scandal broke in early 1923, Thompson opted for retirement.

"Chicago was not worthy of him," mocked the New York Times in an editorial. As ever, though, New York misread Chicago, and Big Bill returned for a third term in 1927, courtesy of the Democrat William Dever. An honest-to-goodness reformer, Dever actually tried to enforce Prohibition while acting like a good-government Republican.

In January 1923, an aldermanic committee investigated claims that the city payroll was providing refuge to members of the Ku Klux Klan. The Klan stories faded with spring; the Cubs and White Sox followed suit in summer.

Then the unexpected happened in November: Mary Bartelme won election to the Circuit Court as the first woman judge in Illinois history and the second nationwide.

By the time he left City Hall in 1931, Thompson had become the working man's friend and sworn enemy of King George, a mayor who kept his promise to give Chicago enough alcohol to make the city wetter than "the middle of the Atlantic."

As to the exact nature of his relationship with Al Capone, not even the Justice Department knew for sure.

The only real constant in Thompson's career was his love of public works, including the Michigan Avenue Bridge.

Michigan Avenue Bridge

Born in 1866, Bartelme remembered the Chicago Fire. As a judge, she stocked her courtroom with white hankies for defendants who broke into tears. Her passion was the plight of juveniles. Bartelme donated her own home as a shelter for homeless girls.

And she earned the nickname of "Suitcase Mary" for raising funds to provide girls with a new suitcase filled with clothes when they went to a foster home.

As the song said, there were some changes made in the Chicago of 1923.

AUGUST

A city count of traffic over the Michigan Avenue Bridge on Aug. 11 shows that 53,014 cars crossed the bridge from 7 a.m. to midnight, including 4,360 during the rush hour of 5:15-6:15 p.m.

DECEMBER

Officials report that since Jan. 1, 721 people in Cook County have died after being struck by automobiles.

ALSO IN 1923

Charles Comiskey hires former Cubs star, Frank Chance, as manager of the White Sox.

CRIME AND COMPULSION

William J. Helmer
A crime writer

Al Capone (above) rose to power shortly after the funeral of his brother Frank (left).

BY WILLIAM J. HELMER

Despite a flurry of ceremonial saloon closings four years earlier, by 1924 few Chicagoans found themselves greatly inconvenienced by Prohibition.

Drunkenness among workers predictably diminished, as did minor crime. And the growing number of car accidents could be blamed on the proliferation of automobiles, just as the increase in police and political corruption could be blamed on Mayor William "Big Bill" Thompson.

Mayor William E. Dever

His unvarnished venality prompted formation of the Chicago Crime Commission (the first in the country) and paved the way for the election of the honest, if naive, reform mayor, William E. Dever.

While not a Prohibitionist, Dever decided the best way to repeal or modify the unpopular Volstead Act was enforcement with a vengeance against bootleggers, proliferating speakeasies, underground brewers and even the major

JUNE	JULY	AUGUST	SEPTEMBER	OCTOBER
The first board of directors of the American Heart Association is elected in Chicago.	Johnny Weissmuller, former altar boy at St. Michael's Church, 458 W. Eugenie, sets the world swimming record for both the 100- and 400-meter freestyle at the Paris Olympics. At their convention in Chicago, Farmer-Laborites reject Robert M. La Follette in favor of Communist William Z. Foster.	Ku Klux Klan violence kills 30 in downstate Herrin.	Army Air Service planes "Chicago" and "New Orleans" reach Seattle to complete the first around-the-world flight. The trip, which started with four planes, took 175 days and 57 stops. The College of Jewish Studies, which later became the Spertus Institute of Jewish Studies, is founded.	A Chicago court orders convicted speeders to visit a home for crippled children.

Johnny Weissmuller

breweries skilled at circumventing "near-beer" licensing restrictions.

His crackdown dismayed Chicago's thriving nightlife community, whose police and political protection had been simply part of the overhead.

Over the dead body of longtime vice lord Big Jim Colosimo stepped John Torrio, ably assisted by a young "Scarface" Al Capone, who helped parcel out the city to street gangs and hoodlums filling the vacuum left by previously legal booze distributors.

Not counting a few unauthorized shootings, this Pax Torrio functioned quietly and harmoniously, serving a complacent public—until Dever's reform efforts widened cracks in the underworld infrastructure.

The decline in street crime reflected new job opportunities for young hoods—driving or escorting beer trucks—on the condition they abandon burglary and the molestation of citizens.

While Torrio tried to hold together the coalition of brewers and bootleggers, Capone dogged the do-gooders by boldly taking over Cicero during an election so violent that Dever invaded with Chicago police.

Frank Capone was killed in the melee, and it was his garish funeral that ended the obscurity of brother Al, who relocated from the Metropole Hotel to Cicero and

Dion O'Banion   **Johnny Torrio**

quickly transformed that town and other suburbs with thinly disguised taverns, gambling parlors and whorehouses.

Other events in 1924 included the kidnap-murder of young Bobby Franks by Richard Loeb and Nathan Leopold, two thrill-seeking University of Chicago students, and the first killing of a prominent gangland chieftain.

Dion O'Banion was greeted at noon on Nov. 10 with friendly smiles and six bullets in a memorable "handshake murder" at his flower shop across from Holy Name Cathedral.

O'Banion had sold Torrio his interest in a North Side brewery targeted by Dever, and Torrio's arrest at the scene would cost him jail time for a second conviction.

O'Banion's death led to the shooting of Torrio, plunging Chicago into five years of beer wars that introduced Americans to the Thompson submachine gun and culminated in the 1929 St. Valentine's Day Massacre.

Ironically, it was O'Banion himself who discovered the little known "tommy gun" while vacationing in Colorado, where mining companies were using it to intimidate strikers. He included the gun (named after its inventor, John Thompson) in weaponry purchased in Denver shortly before he was killed.

Capone and company soon put the gun to such good use, it became known as the "Chicago typewriter."

Famed attorney Clarence Darrow argues for the lives of his clients, Leopold and Loeb.

GALLOPING INTO THE BIG LEAGUE

Jim Ritter
Sun-Times staff reporter

Clarence Darrow (left) and William Jennings Bryan

BY JIM RITTER

On Thanksgiving Day 1925, professional football came of age at Wrigley Field.

The Chicago Bears opened a 19-game postseason barnstorming tour that would transform pro football from a struggling enterprise into a major sport.

The Bears filled stadiums from New York to Los Angeles, playing, in one brutal stretch, eight games in 12 days. The sport's sudden popularity was due to Wheaton native Harold "Red" Grange, who signed with the Bears after three spectacular years at the University of Illinois.

He was called Red for his flaming hair, and the Galloping Ghost for his elusive running style. The three-time All-American once scored four touchdowns in 12 minutes on runs of 95, 67, 56 and 44 yards.

"There had never been such evidence of public interest since our professional league began," Bears owner George Halas later recalled. "I knew then and there that pro football was destined to be a big-time sport."

In the Golden Age of sports, Red Grange dominated football as much as Babe Ruth, boxer Jack Dempsey, golfer Bobby Jones and tennis star Bill Tilden dominated their sports.

Harold "Red" Grange

JANUARY

Knute Rockne's Notre Dame team, coming off a perfect nine-victory season with its "Four Horsemen" backfield, trounces Stanford 27-10 in the Rose Bowl.

Knute Rockne

FEBRUARY

Robert Wood opens the first Sears retail store on the first floor of the firm's mail-order plant. Seven more stores open by the end of the year.

MARCH

The crossword puzzle craze prompts a Chicago Board of Health report that "crossworditis" improves health.

The Chicago epidemic of grippe (now called influenza) kills 279.

AUGUST

Victor Fremont Lawson, 74, owner (since 1876) and editor of the Daily News and a founder of the Associated Press, dies and leaves a $20 million estate.

A $1 million produce market opens at Morgan and West 15th Street with 166 buildings, replacing commission houses demolished to make way for the new Wacker Drive.

Victor F. Lawson

Goodman Theatre Center of the Art Institute

Mrs. Dalloway by Virginia Woolf and *An American Tragedy* by Theodore Dreiser were published, and Sinclair Lewis' *Arrowsmith* won the Pulitizer Prize.

Chicago's cultural life was enriched by the opening of the Goodman Theatre. Howard Van Doren Shaw designed it, and Mr. and Mrs. William Goodman paid for it as a memorial to their son Kenneth, who was killed in World War I.

Another Chicagoan, Clarence Darrow, made headlines in 1925. The liberal attorney and social reformer spent a sweltering summer in Tennessee, defending high school teacher John Scopes' right to teach evolution.

Darrow became famous defending labor leaders and other unpopular clients. "He was a fighter for the underdog, no matter who the underdog was," said Tracy Baim, Darrow's great-grandniece. Baim is the publisher of Outlines, a gay and lesbian newspaper in Chicago.

But not everyone was a fan. When Grange was introduced to Calvin Coolidge, the president was told Grange played for the Bears. "Young man," Coolidge said, "I always liked animal acts."

Coolidge was a tight-lipped, tax-cutting Republican, who proclaimed, "The business of America is business." But despite a booming economy—the gross national product increased 10 percent in 1925—Coolidge was a skinflint. He cut the White House budget by $12,500, replacing paper cups with glasses, reducing the number of bathroom towels and ordering that manila envelopes be reused.

It was a grand year for literature as well as football. *The Great Gatsby* by F. Scott Fitzgerald,

Jack Dempsey

Chicagoans listened to WGN radio as Darrow sparred with prosecuting counsel William Jennings Bryan, the populist three-time presidential candidate and fundamentalist Christian. Darrow called Bryan to the stand, and in the trial's most memorable exchange, asked Bryan if he believed the story of Jonah being swallowed by a whale.

"Yes sir . . . " Bryan said. "If the Bible said so."

Seventy-four years later, the debate still raged. Kansas' decision to drop evolution from the high school curriculum outraged scientists. But no one with the passion and eloquence of Clarence Darrow has stepped forward to champion their cause.

OCTOBER   **Field Museum**

Theodore Roosevelt Jr. and his brother Kermit cable the Field Museum, for which they are collecting specimens in Central Asia, that they have bagged ovis poli rams, ibex, roe, rare birds and goitered gazelles.

The Art Institute of Chicago declares American art standards are superior to Europe's and that Cubism and post-Impressionism are fading.

DECEMBER

Cost of a city license is set at $5 a year for bowling alleys. Also: pool tables $7.50 each; horse-drawn coupes, $1; fireworks dealers, $10; bakeries, $15; beauty parlors, $10; fishing (hook and line), 50 cents.

CATHOLICS CELEBRATE FAITH

Cardinal Francis George, O.M.I.
Archbishop of Chicago

Newspaper accounts of the International Eucharistic Congress reported crowds so massive that they overstrained the three lines of steam railroads connecting Mundelein to the city, as well as electric transport facilities.

BY CARDINAL FRANCIS GEORGE, O.M.I.

A few years ago, a University of Illinois doctoral student came upon a 1926 documentary that was so intriguing, he made the film's topic the subject of his dissertation.

The film did not seek to document that year's first airmail drop by Charles Lindbergh between Chicago and St. Louis. Neither did it follow the Prohibition-era exploits of Al Capone or the local organizing efforts of the Brotherhood of Sleeping Car Porters.

It did not reveal how Oak Park's Ernest Hemingway came to publish *The Sun Also Rises* that year—and it never mentioned that "Cubs Park" was renamed "Wrigley Field"!

What fascinated the student was perhaps one of the most humanizing events in Chicago's history. Over five June days, more than 500,000 devout Catholics, from native Chicagoans to hundreds of bishops from around the world, came together by bus, streetcar and train to celebrate their faith.

The documentary film showed huge crowds gathered at open-air Masses in Soldier Field and at the recently completed St. Mary of the Lake Seminary in Mundelein attending the International Eucharistic Congress held for the first time ever in the United States.

Ernest Hemingway published
The Sun Also Rises.

APRIL	MAY	AUGUST	SEPTEMBER
Boxing and wrestling matches are permitted by a referendum vote of 366,860-96,166.	The Municipal Airport, Chicago's first public airfield, begins operating and is being described within a few years as the world's busiest. It will lose that distinction to O'Hare Airport—and be renamed Midway Airport—after World War II.	The name of Grant Park Stadium, which opened the previous year, is changed to Soldier Field.	Jelly Roll Morton and his Red Hot Peppers cut their first record here with RCA.

It's hard to record something as invisible as faith, yet its influence in the life of great cities can't be ignored. Daily newspaper accounts from that time reported the crowds were so massive, they over-strained the three lines of steam railroads connecting Mundelein to the city as well as electric transport facilities. Other reports depicted the event's grandeur:

Parishioners cross a stream on their way to the Eucharistic Congress.

"Seldom has modern civilization attempted such a triumph of emotion, spiritual or material, chromatic and vibrant," waxed the Chicago Daily Journal.

"The greatest religious spectacle witnessed by the western world, the most colossal prayer meeting in the authentic annals of Christendom," reported another daily paper.

Just what had Chicago come together to celebrate? According to New York Archbishop Cardinal Patrick Hayes, our metropolitan community did no less than "prepare for our Eucharistic King . . . an 'upper room' where Christ and His disciples have assembled," where believers "profess[ed their] unchanging belief in the real presence of Christ in the Eucharist."

Prominent civic leaders were no less enthusiastic. Then-U.S. Supreme Court Justice Pierce Butler, who addressed the Congress, called it his "privilege to

Eucharistic Congress in Mundelein

speak of the Holy Eucharist, the sacrament of peace."

I remember my own mother, Julia McCarthy George, recalling the beauty of a choir comprising 62,000 children who sang at Soldier Field, the downpour of rain and hail that drenched her and my grandmother and hundreds of thousands of other pilgrims as they walked around the grounds of the seminary in procession with the Blessed Sacrament and the excitement of using the new railroad connection between Chicago and Mundelein.

I wasn't there in 1926, but—God willing—I'll be there on June 24, 2000, on the eve of the Feast of Corpus Christi, when thousands of Chicagoland Catholics will again return to Soldier Field to celebrate the Great Jubilee Year. I also plan to take part in a grand gathering at St. Mary of the Lake Seminary that the Archdiocese is planning for September 2000 to celebrate the history of the Catholic faith in Cook and Lake counties.

I pray that when some future graduate student comes across a videotaped account of our gathering in the year 2000, he or she will see how we were moved— as Chicago was in 1926—to express our faith and to worship a God who is the same yesterday, today and forever.

Eugene V. Debs

OCTOBER

Eugene V. Debs, 70, former Socialist candidate for president, dies in Elmhurst.

NOVEMBER

U.S. Route 66 opens, linking Chicago to Los Angeles. The "Mother Road," as John Steinbeck called it, will later be romanticized in song, literature and a TV show before it is decommissioned in 1985.

The seven-car Chief starts daily train service between Chicago and Los Angeles.

Chicagoans vote 385,636-200,781 to continue daylight saving time.

ALSO IN 1926

Architect Howard Van Doren Shaw, who designed the Goodman Theatre and many North Shore mansions, dies at age 57.

JEWS MAKE CHICAGO HOME

Irving Cutler
Professor emeritus at Chicago State University and author of *The Jews of Chicago*

Maxwell Street was a bustling center of commerce in Chicago for Jewish immigrants.

Matzoh in boxes at the Wittenberg Matzoh Company

BY IRVING CUTLER

In 1927, almost 30 percent of Chicago's population was European born, and the city resembled an ethnic checkerboard. Aligned along Halsted Street, for example, were about a dozen different communities, starting with the Swedes in the north and the Dutch in the south.

The most colorful area was around Maxwell and Halsted, home of thousands of poor Eastern European Jewish immigrants. There they re-created a bustling, crowded Old World-style market complete with open stands, live chickens, spirited haggling and a store that boldly advertised "We Cheat You Fair."

Despite the help of the earlier-arriving, more affluent German Jews living on the South Side, Maxwell Street remained a physical ghetto.

An unusual number of prominent people had their roots there. They included musician Benny Goodman, Admiral Hyman Rickover, CBS founder William Paley, U.S. Supreme Court Justice Arthur Goldberg, author Meyer Levin, community organizer Saul Alinsky, political power broker Jacob Arvey, Paramount Pictures president Barney Balaban, Oscar winner Paul Muni and U.S. Judge Abraham Lincoln Marovitz.

FEBRUARY
Chicago gets long-distance telephone service to London, two weeks before San Francisco.

MARCH
Three commissioners of the city's South Park System return from a seven-city European museum tour to report $5 million more will be needed for the industrial museum planned for Jackson Park. The facility, later named the Museum of Science and Industry, is supported by a $3 million bequest from merchant Julius Rosenwald and a $5 million bond issue.

APRIL
Mayor William Hale "Big Bill" Thompson wins a third term.

Charles Lindbergh

AUGUST
Three months after crossing the Atlantic, Charles Lindbergh speaks at Soldier Field on developing Chicago as the nation's center of aviation.

Wheaton native Judge Elbert H. Gary, head of U.S. Steel and namesake of Gary, Ind., dies at 80.

Also coming from the neighborhood were Jake "Greasy Thumb" Guzik, who was bookkeeper for Al Capone, and con artist Joseph "Yellow Kid" Weil.

Marovitz, now 94, said his Maxwell Street childhood "helped make me a more understanding and compassionate judge and human being."

With approximately 275,000 Jews, Chicago in 1927 had the third-largest Jewish population in the world. By then, the Jews of Maxwell street (including my family) had begun dispersing, with the vast majority moving westward to Lawndale. Smaller numbers went northward to Rogers Park, Albany Park and Humboldt Park-West Town.

Humboldt Park and its environs were home to movie impresario Michael Todd, comedian Jackie Leonard, Broadway composer Jule Styne, Nobel Prize-winning novelist Saul Bellow and industrialist/philanthropists Henry Crown and A.N. Pritzker.

The year was marked athletically by the legendary "long count" Dempsey-Tunney fight in the new Soldier Field before a crowd of 105,000 and by the founding of the Harlem Globetrotters comic basketball team by 5-foot, 3-inch Chicagoan Abe Saperstein, who drew laughs whenever he subbed for one of his towering players.

Maxwell Street merchants bring their wares to market.

Abe Saperstein's Harlem Globetrotters became one of sport's greatest attractions. Saperstein is shown with basketball legend and former Globetrotter, the late Wilt Chamberlain.

In 1927, when Charles Lindbergh flew the Atlantic, Chicago officially opened Municipal (Midway) Airport on the Southwest Side. Grant Park saw Buckingham Fountain dedicated by Kate Sturges Buckingham, in memory of her brother, Clarence, and the opening of the 3,000-room Stevens Hotel (now Chicago Hilton and Towers).

Chicago Jews in 1927 welcomed Zionist leader Chaim Weizmann, later to become the first president of Israel. They enjoyed Yiddish theater in the neighborhoods and traveled downtown to see cantor's son Al Jolson in the first major sound movie, "The Jazz Singer," debuting in Loop movie theaters. Those who could afford it boarded the S.S. Theodore Roosevelt at $1.50 for an excursion across the lake to the Jewish summer resorts of South Haven, Mich.

Jews, like most immigrants, opposed the federal law then becoming effective that restricted immigration and foreshadowed the decline of Chicago's inner-city European ethnic communities.

As immigrants worked their way economically upward and outward, increasing numbers of migrants from the South filled their neighborhoods and the labor market. Today, the European-born population of Chicago has dwindled to less than 5 percent, and ethnic communities such as Maxwell Street are just a memory.

SEPTEMBER

The dedication of Leif Ericson Drive between 23rd and 57th streets—a road eventually to become part of Lake Shore Drive—attracts a crowd of 25,000, mostly of Norwegian birth or ancestry.

NOVEMBER

Ground is broken for the $3 million Shedd Aquarium, named for the late benefactor John G. Shedd. Its exterior is to be in harmony with the nearby Field Museum.

John G. Shedd

ALSO IN 1927

Belmont Community Hospital (now called Vencor Hospital-Chicago Central) opens in 1927 to serve the North West Side European community. An early graduate of its training school for nurses (right) holds a newborn child.

Chicagoans O.E. Barnhart and W.W. Wilson finish first and second in the American Roque League tourney in Winona Lake, Ind. Roque is a form of croquet played on a hard-surfaced court with a raised border for bank shots.

LITTLE ITALY BLOSSOMS

Miriam Di Nunzio
Sun-Times
Weekend Plus
editor

The spiritual center of Little Italy was the church. Children took first communion in churches where masses were offered in Italian.

BY MIRIAM DI NUNZIO

In 1928, Anthony Sorrentino was 14 years old and graduating from Andrew Jackson Grammar School in the heart of Chicago's Little Italy.

The near West Side neighborhood was rich in Italian culture—from the food to the customs to the language. It was settled by immigrants from southern and central Italy who had come to the city by the lake in search of a better life.

In the 1920s, nearly 5 percent of the city's population, or approximately 128,000 people, were Italians. Most worked in Loop factories, for the railroad, as laborers or as shop owners along Taylor, Maxwell and

Halsted streets. Italians also settled in neighborhoods on the north and south sides, such as the Bridgeport area, and in industrial suburbs like Chicago Heights.

In Little Italy in the Taylor Street area, the immigrant families fashioned a lifestyle reminiscent of their native towns, complete with Italian language newspapers, bakeries and social clubs.

"It was a hardworking community," said Sorrentino, 85. "We were blue-collar workers. The streets were our piazzas where

Anthony Sorrentino

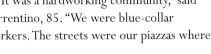

MAY
Louis Armstrong begins recording "Hot Fives and Sevens, Vol. 3," considered one of the greatest jazz albums of all time.

AUGUST
Chicago's Johnny Weissmuller swims to victory in the 400-meter race at the summer Olympics in Amsterdam and retires, having set 67 world records and captured three Olympic gold medals.

Chicago utilities broker Samuel Insull starts a flood on the market with more than $650 million in public securities, which would fuel the market crash in October 1929.

SEPTEMBER
The cornerstone is laid for the Daily News Building at 400 W. Madison.

1928 THE CHICAGO DAILY NEWS AN INDEPENDENT NEWSPAPER FOUNDED IN 1875

NOVEMBER
Oscar DePriest becomes the first black U.S. Congressman from a northern state, after having served as the first black alderman on the City Council.

the people would gather to talk. The men would play bocci ball."

Monday morning was laundry day.

"You would just see it fluttering in the breeze on porch lines everywhere," recalled Sorrentino, who also remembers hanging out on street corners and playing handball and stickball with buddies.

"Everybody shopped every day for fish, bread, milk and meat. Peddlers, some with horse-drawn carts, would sell everything from vegetables to nuts. . . . People would make bread dough at home, then take it to one of the local bakeries who would bake it for you for a few pennies. There was a real sense of community and sharing. Everybody looked out for every-body else."

The spiritual center of this part of Little Italy was the church. Sorrentino's family attended Our Lady of Pompeii Church on Lexington, which offered Italian masses.

"Family and church—those were the two most important things to us. And everybody knew every-body—by name," said Sorrentino, now a retired State of Illinois worker.

Sorrentino's father died shortly after his son's 8th-grade graduation, and the young Sorrentino went to work as a $12-a-week office boy for a LaSalle Street stockbroker. He walked to the office to save the seven-cent streetcar

Italian immigrants created a community with Italian-owned businesses like this butcher shop.

Amos 'n' Andy

fare. The job gave him a unique perspective on Chicago's varying economic lifestyles.

"I'd have to deliver packages to the rich people up along Michigan Avenue or to Oak Park and see all the mansions of the upper class," Sorrentino said. "I became acutely aware of the social class structure of the city, because at the end of the day I went home to a working-class neighborhood. It was like night and day."

The Sorrentinos did not own a radio, but the young boy would listen to popular music and variety shows at the homes of friends and relatives. He eagerly followed the stories of boyhood heroes Babe Ruth and Charles Lindbergh. He was also fond of "Amos 'n' Andy," the No. 1 radio show in the country.

Then originating from the WMAQ studios, Raymond Freeman Gosden and Charles Correll—who were both white—created two black characters who humorously re-counted tales of life's ups and downs.

"It was a 10-minute show, 6 nights a week," said Chuck Schaden, host of "Those Were the Days" every Saturday afternoon on WNIB radio. "And everything stopped when it was on. You could walk down the street in the summer-time and literally hear the entire program as you strolled past homes that had their doors and windows open."

Sorrentino, who now lives in suburban Hinsdale, recalls the year of his graduation fondly. "Life was simple, but it was good. *Molto bene.*"

ALSO IN 1928

The Front Page, a witty send-up on Chicago newspaper life by Ben Hecht and Charles MacArthur, opens on Broadway.

Construction begins on the Civic Opera House.

Amelia Earhart becomes the first woman to fly across the Atlantic.

Carl Sandburg publishes an optimistic volume of poetry called "Good Morning America."

Mahalia Jackson moves to Chicago where she becomes a soloist with the Greater Salem Baptist Church. In the 1940s, Chicagoans were among the first whites to hear Jackson sing as her records were played on local radio. When she died in 1972, 50,000 people attended her funeral.

Ben Hecht

Amelia Earhart

CRASH BRINGS ON HARD TIMES

Studs Terkel
Author and Pulitzer
Prize winner

Pandemonium
reigned on the New
York Stock Exchange
as collapsing prices
set the stage for the
Great Depression.

BY STUDS TERKEL

I don't really recall that bleak October Tuesday in 1929 when the Crash took place. But I knew something had happened by the headlines. "Wall Street Lays An Egg," yelled Variety.

My father leased and ran a men's hotel called the Wells-Grand. When he died, my mother, Annie, took over. In the 1920s all 50 rooms were usually occupied.

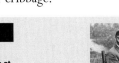
The jobless wait for work.

Our guests were various workmen, retired railroad engi-neers, a hard-of-hearing coppersmith and a number of other well-educated persons. I was 17 years old and still going to Crane Junior College before attending the University of Chicago.

Most of our guests paid their rent on Saturdays. I would then walk the money over to the neighbor-hood Cosmopolitan Bank. The hotel would be empty during the days, just a few old guys playing pinochle or cribbage.

No work, no money and nowhere
to go for thousands of Chicagoans
during the Great Depression

MAY	JUNE	JULY		
Senn High School wins the Class A championship of a national band contest in Denver.	Two suburban airports open: Curtiss Flying Service Corp.'s $1 million field on 430 acres in Glenview and United Aviation Corp.'s $350,000 Sky Harbor in Northbrook.	President Hoover starts the presses at the Daily News' new $12 million building, designed by Holabird & Root, at 400 W. Madison.		Herbert Hoover (left), then the Republican nominee for president, visits with Vice President Charles G. Dawes at the latter's home in Evanston.

Cubs catcher Gabby Hartnett asked Al Capone for his autograph, and then returned the favor, signing a ball for Capone.

We knew guys were losing their jobs. Al Capone even had a soup line.

I went to school and was a big baseball fan. I knew the lineups of every team, but liked the Giants best, since I was born in New York.

I knew the names of all the announcers—Hal Totten, Pat Flanagan and Bert Wilson. I went to games sometimes, sat in the bleachers. I preferred the Sox to the Cubs, but remember one where Cubs catcher Gabby Hartnett ran toward Al Capone for his autograph, and then Hartnett autographed a ball for Capone.

A few of my McKinley High School classmates became members of a farm club for the mob known as the 42's. A mob soldier named Upsadaisy Connors lived at the hotel. They found him floating face down in a drainage canal. He owed us six months' rent.

But after the Depression, you saw a change. There were men in the lobby during the day. They were idle, frustrated. They drank. Tempers grew short, and the men fought over nothing. The card decks wore out faster, and then there were fewer and fewer men. Guests handed us relief checks where before it was a paycheck or cash.

Bit by bit the rooms grew empty. We posted a vacancy sign on the hotel door. A lot of people who lived through the Depression carry baggage the rest of their lives. Some horde money. In my case, it's seeing a neon vacancy sign outside a ma and pa motel. It brings back memories of the Wells-Grand and of the hard times.

Samuel Insull

So I opened a frayed steamer trunk in Upsadaisy's room, and there's this silk dressing gown. It was maroon with black stripes. I wore it for years. When I looked in a mirror, I imagined I was Clark Gable in "A Free Soul" playing gangster Ace Wolfgang, who seduced Norma Shearer.

Or I imagined I was "Machine Gun" Jack McGurn, suspected head of the Capone hit team who killed some of Bugs Moran's boys in a brick garage in the 1929 St. Valentine's Day Massacre. Jack had a blonde alibi, Louise Rolfe.

But as fate would have it, a few years later on St. Valentine's Day, McGurn received a love token back in the form of lead: mowed down in a bowling alley just as he was about to make a strike. All he made was a bloody spare!

My mother was pretty clever when it came to money. She withdrew savings from Reliance State Bank the day before it closed. She lost money, though, investing with Samuel Insull, president of Commonwealth Edison, who built the Opera House which opened that year. A lot of opera singers lost money with him too. He later went to jail.

SEPTEMBER

The cornerstone is laid for the $22 million Board of Trade Building.

OCTOBER

Manager Joe McCarthy's Cubs, starring Rogers Hornsby, Hack Wilson and Gabby Hartnett, lose the World Series to Connie Mack's Philadelphia Athletics, with Jimmie Foxx, four games to one. The Cubs set the record for highest batting average of a series loser (.235) and most strikeouts (50).

Twelve die and 60 are rescued when the passenger steamer Wisconsin, bound from Chicago to Milwaukee, goes down in a storm off Kenosha, Wis.

NOVEMBER

The $20 million Civic Opera House opens with a performance of Verdi's "Aida."

ALSO IN 1929

Senn High School graduate Herbert Lawrence Block begins his career as a political cartoonist at the Chicago Daily News. Better known as Herblock, he will go on to join the Washington Post, be syndicated in more than 300 newspapers and win three Pulitzer Prizes and share in a fourth.

Herbert Lawrence Block

1930

A LOT OF MERCHANDISE

Christopher G. Kennedy
Executive President of the Merchandise Mart

The Merchandise Mart, under construction during the early 1930s, provided badly needed construction jobs to thousands of workers during the Great Depression.

BY CHRISTOPHER KENNEDY

By 1930, the Great Depression had touched the lives of every American. Banks failed. Life savings disappeared. Families were evicted from their homes and jobs were scarce.

In Chicago, however, 5,700 men found work as riggers, carpenters, plumbers and bricklayers trying to complete the world's largest commercial building.

The Chicago Board of Trade and the Adler Planetarium were also nearing completion that year. But no other endeavor

Robert F. Kennedy

symbolized the transition from boom to bust and the eventual postwar renewal like the colossus of marketplaces being erected on the Chicago River's north bank. It was the Merchandise Mart.

Conceived during the roaring '20s as a national wholesale center for Marshall Field & Co, the building was not completed until the middle of the Depression. Another two decades would elapse before tradesmen on the project would find this kind of work again. Chicagoans would not see the construction

Joseph P. Kennedy

of another major building for 20 years.

But the Mart's show-rooms, distributed over some 4.2 million square feet and 7 ½ miles of corridors, would later attract thousands of visitors each year, helping lay the foundation for Chicago's eventual dominance of the convention and tourism industry. International visitors to its frequent trade shows also helped the Mart make a massive economic impact on the city.

Completed Merchandise Mart

The Merchandise Mart was the first building here to be built on air rights. They were purchased from the North Western railway, which operated a 30-track freight car yard even as the massive structure was being built overhead.

Two new bridges—on Orleans and Wells—were built to provide access to the Mart, the gateway to River North. The Mart's visitors fueled growth in art galleries and specialty shops as Chicago moved from a center of industry into the country's most livable city.

R. Sargent Shriver (left) and Mayor Richard J. Daley

The Wells Street bridge is one of the few spots in the world where a plane can fly over a train, which runs on tracks above a bridge where cars pass over boats on the river!

In 1945, my grandfather, Ambassador Joseph P. Kennedy, purchased the Mart from Marshall Field & Co for $12.5 million.

"My interest stems from my faith in Chicago and the Middle West," he remarked at that time. "Chicago has a great commercial and industrial future, and I am highly pleased by the opportunity of being associated with it."

The Kennedy family were a real presence in Chicago. My uncle R. Sargent Shriver directed the Mart from the late 1940s until 1961 and also served as president of the Chicago Board of Education.

He left here when his brother-in-law, President John F. Kennedy, appointed him as the first Peace Corps director. Another uncle, Stephen E. Smith, also ran the Mart for many years. His son, my cousin William Kennedy Smith, is a doctor here now.

My father, Robert F. Kennedy, was very close to Mayor Richard J. Daley and his family. The Mart created a bond linking the Kennedys and Daleys for 50 years.

Early Mart residents included NBC studios, which debuted the "Bozo" show there; the federal government, which stored Series E war bonds in the building during World War II; and the "hall-of-fame" sculptures of businessmen which remain today on the South Drive facing the Mart, keeping an eye on business.

ROLLING OUT THE MACHINE

Paul Green
Director of Policy Studies at Roosevelt University

Mayor Anton Cermak (hand on microphone) worked to rid the Democratic party of personality politics and replace it with the principles of business, bringing structure, rewards and punishment.

BY PAUL GREEN

1931 was a terrible year for Chicago and the rest of the nation. The economy was in a deep Depression, and many citizens and cities were sagging and unraveling from the continuous pounding of the crisis.

In Chicago, several hundred millions of tax dollars owed the city went unpaid. City Hall was in arrears to its own creditors; the Chicago School Board could not meet its teacher payroll, and each week hundreds of Chicagoans were evicted from their homes, an action that sometimes caused riots and deaths.

Even the sentencing of hoodlum Al Capone to 11 years in a federal penitentiary for income tax evasion meant little to most Chicagoans.

Enter, Anton J. Cermak. In April 1931, Cermak was elected Chicago's 38th mayor, an accomplishment which made him the city's first foreign-born (Bohemian) mayor, as well as its first mayor not of Anglo-Saxon or Celtic origin.

Al Capone

The good life ended for gangster Al Capone in 1931.

Mayor Anton J. Cermak (sitting) and then-New York Governor Franklin D. Roosevelt

Cermak was a hard-nosed street politician who had battled Republicans and fellow Democrats in city wards for decades. In 1931, he became the founding father of the soon-to-be-legendary Chicago Democratic Machine.

Prior to Cermak's election, Chicago's politics were as dismal as its economics. William Hale "Big Bill" Thompson (the city's last Republican mayor and probably the worst mayor ever elected in American urban history) was ending his third term as mayor as a verifiable buffoon and incompetent scoundrel.

Seizing the moment, Cermak parlayed his recently won chairmanship of the local Democratic party organization,

his unflinching support from East European ethnic Chicagoans, his alliance with powerful new-breed (business-oriented) Irish politicians and his carefully reconstructed image of himself as a master executive and professional administrator into a landslide mayoral win over Thompson.

Cermak's victory changed Chicago.

Into the political and economic void, Cermak brought organization, structure, loyalty, rewards and punishment. By intertwining governmental and political processes into the same system, Cermak became the city's chief executive and ward committeeman.

From the moment he took office, Cermak worked to rid the party of factionalism and personality politics. He and his allies wanted all governmental and political issues to be played out within the party. And, like a business, it would reward success and punish failure.

At a time when old-style urban machine politics was declining everywhere else, 1931 Chicago saw its late-arriving, professionally driven Democratic machine take off. Why?

Unlike in other cities, saloonkeepers, brawlers and outright hooligans were not part of Chicago's machine leadership (although, to be sure, many of these types were lower-level players). Instead, many of Cermak's top lieutenants were businessmen and professional people (largely lawyers) who gave respectability, competence and middle-class appeal to machine politics.

Controlling the nominating process and winning as a party and not as individuals were Cermak's political goals. His game plan initiated in 1931 would remain virtually unchanged for over 50 years, as it successfully dominated the structural framework of Chicago governance, politics and lifestyle.

OCTOBER

Charles A. Comiskey

White Sox founder Charles Comiskey dies, leaving the team to his son, Louis.

"Dick Tracy" begins its regular run in the Chicago Tribune after a couple of trial appearances in a Detroit newspaper. Creator Chester Gould prefers the name "Plainclothes Tracy," but is overruled by his bosses.

DECEMBER

Jane Addams, founder of Hull House, shares in the Nobel Peace Prize for her work with the International League for Peace and Freedom.

Jane Addams

ALSO IN 1931

Prisoners riot at the state penitentiary in Joliet, wrecking prison shops, the dining room and kitchen. One prisoner was killed and three wounded. Four days later, prisoners at Stateville rioted, causing $500,000 in damages and injuries to three prisoners.

FDR LANDS NOMINATION

Anna Eleanor Roosevelt

Executive director of the Brain Research Foundation, an affiliate of the University of Chicago

Franklin D. Roosevelt breaks tradition—and starts a new one—by accepting his party's nomination in person in 1932 at the Chicago Stadium.

BY ANNA ROOSEVELT

My grandfather, Franklin D. Roosevelt, won a hard-fought, fourth-ballot nomination for the presidency at the 1932 Democratic National Convention in Chicago Stadium.

He would laugh and shake his head as he listened to the convention on radio from his study at the governor's mansion in Albany, N.Y. Even though Grandfather had a clear majority of the delegates going into the convention, a two-thirds vote was required to win the nomination. Grandfather finally prevailed when John Nance Garner of Texas withdrew in his favor.

Until the 1932 Chicago convention, presidential nominees didn't formally accept their nomination until weeks later in their hometown. But with America slipping deeper into the Depression, my grandfather took a different approach.

"I thank you," he told delegates at Chicago Stadium by radio from Albany. "It is customary to hold formal notification ceremonies some weeks after the convention. This involves great expense. Instead, may I ask the convention to remain in session tomorrow that I may appear before you and be notified at that time?" The Democratic faithful shouted in the affirmative.

JANUARY

William Wrigley Jr. dies, leaving his interest in the Chicago Cubs to his son, Philip K. Wrigley.

William Wrigley Jr.

JUNE

An earthquake that kills or injures 30 and leaves 6,000 homeless in Colima, Mexico, produces tremors felt in Chicago.

Utility tycoon Samuel Insull, 73, resigns as head of his crumbling financial empire at the urging of bankers upset that his investors have been left penniless.

AUGUST

Wife of blues singer and songwriter Thomas A. Dorsey dies, inspiring him to write "Precious Lord, Take My Hand," later a gospel standard. Called the "Father of Gospel Music," Dorsey organized the first gospel choir at Ebenezer Baptist Church on the South Side.

Thomas A. Dorsey

Franklin D. Roosevelt (center), with Mayor Anton J. Cermak (right), throws out the first pitch of the 1932 World Series between the Chicago Cubs and the New York Yankees.

My grandfather boarded a Ford trimotor airplane in Albany for the first flight ever made in American politics. The historian Arthur M. Schlesinger Jr. wrote: "FDR felt that the disheartened nation would welcome a startling gesture that signified a break with the past."

The flight was supposed to have taken seven hours, including stops for refueling in Buffalo and Cleveland. But they met rough headwinds and arrived two and a half hours late. My uncle John, who was then a fifth grader at Groton, got sick from the turbulence.

Chicago's Mayor Anton Cermak, who a few months later would be killed by an assassin's bullet meant for FDR, greeted my grandfather at the airport. So did my father, James Roosevelt.

"I regret that I am late, but I have no control over the winds of heaven and could only be thankful for my Navy training," Grandfather told delegates on his arrival at Chicago Stadium.

His speech was a message of vision and hope. As he closed his remarks, his strong, clear voice rang with a phrase that would come to characterize his entire administration: "I pledge you, I pledge myself, to a New Deal for the American people. Let us all here assembled constitute ourselves prophets of a new order of competence and of courage."

My grandfather never forgot Chicago's importance to his political career. The New Deal started in Chicago. Three of grandfather's four nominations for the presidency were in Chicago Stadium. On the strength of his Chicago vote, FDR carried Illinois four times. Chicago was—and is—his kind of town.

Nearly everyone assumed that Grandfather would take a train to Chicago. "I may go in a submarine," he quipped when reporters asked him about his travel plans. Then he suggested other possibilities.

"Now, I'll tell you what I'm going to do," he said with feigned seriousness. "I'm going to bicycle out to Chicago. I'm going to get one of those quintets—you know, five bicycles in a row. Father will ride in the first seat and manage the handlebars. Jim (my father) will ride second, then Elliott, Franklin Jr., and then John."

In a reference to his friend and adviser Judge Samuel Rosenman, Grandfather added, "Sam will follow on a tricycle."

OCTOBER

Babe Ruth pops a homer over the center-field bleachers at Wrigley Field during the third game of the World Series. Thus begins decades of speculation on whether the Bambino first "called his shot" with a point of the bat. One thing is undisputed: The Cubs went on to lose the series, 4-0.

Henry Horner

NOVEMBER

Democratic Judge Henry Horner is elected governor of Illinois—becoming the state's first Jewish chief executive and the first governor born in Cook County.

ALSO IN 1932

President Herbert Hoover is nominated for a second term at the Republican National Convention at Chicago Stadium. Three weeks later, Franklin D. Roosevelt is nominated at the Democratic National Convention, also at the Stadium.

Chicagoan Frank R. Steel sets a world record for dry fly casting, earning a perfect 100 score at a tournament in Pittsburgh.

AWE-INSPIRING FAIR

Dan Haar
Sun-Times
assistant metro
editor

Even President Franklin Roosevelt visited the 1933 Chicago World's Fair.

BY DAN HAAR

My grandfather, nearly penniless, left Chicago just as the city was about to put on a world's fair in 1933, trumpeting a century of progress. He must have watched and wondered as bright buildings went up along the lakefront from 12th to 39th streets.

There was the art deco tower of the Dairy Building, where an organist striking the keys of the "Clavilux" would activate colored lights in

Large crowds jammed the Palmer House bar awaiting the repeal of the 18th Amendment.

the "cyclorama"; the Great Havoline Thermometer, a 200-foot pylon with ne tubing to show the temperature; the Skyride, where "rocket cars" would ferry people betwe 628-foot towers; a the midway, a collection of carni acts rimmed by sle concrete buildings where young men would wrestle alligators and Sally Rand would rustle ostrich feathers.

Sally Rand stole the show at the World's Fair in 1933.

FEBRUARY

Chicago's $22 million post office at Harrison and Canal is dedicated. Officials say it is the largest—and best equipped to ensure speedy mail delivery—in the world. Its flat roof is designed as an airplane landing field.

The fire in a Goose Island grain elevator causes $1 million in damage.

MAY

The Pulitzer Prize for best foreign correspondence of 1932 goes to Edgar Ansel Mowrer of the Daily News, for his reports from Berlin describing Germany's political upheaval.

JUNE

Chicago radio host Don McNeill, 26, changes the name of the "Pepper Pot" show to "Don McNeill's Breakfast Club." The following month another show originates from Chicago, "Jack Armstrong the All-American Boy."

JULY

Italian aviator Italo Balbo leads a squadron of 24 planes on a round trip from Rome to Chicago, which names a street after him. Later in the year Benito Mussolini gets the popular Aviation Ministry official out of Italy by naming him governor of Libya.

Sally Rand, the "fan dancer" from the World's Fair, leaves her ostrich plumes at home to attend opening night of the Empire Room in the Palmer House with her date, Abraham Lincoln Marovitz, who now is a 94-year-old U.S. District senior judge.

But there was no work for my grandfather, Anton Aarns, who moved here with his wife and toddler son after losing his down-state home and coal mining job to the Depression. He stayed with a sister-in-law in a small house on South Paulina and tried selling vacuum cleaners door-to-door. He sold his watch to put food on the table. My mom was born in a hospital for unwed mothers.

The world must have seemed a charity ward to him. About 200,000 families in Chicago depended on some kind of private or public assistance. The Near West Side was called Floptown because so many people slept on the streets.

No wonder Mayor Anton Cermak, an old coal hauler who got the Democratic machine humming, was a fan of President-elect Franklin Roosevelt's New Deal and traveled to Miami to meet him. Cermak was standing near Roosevelt's car during a rally Feb. 15 when Giuseppe Zangara climbed a wobbly chair and opened fire, hitting the mayor and four others.

Cermak was said to have uttered to Roosevelt, "I'm glad it was me instead of you." He died March 6; Zangara went to the electric chair March 20 in what is considered the swiftest legal execution in this century.

Yet the year gave as good as it got. The first NFL football championship and the first All-Star baseball game were played, and the city hosted both. The Bears beat the New York Giants, 23-21, at a fogbound Wrigley Field; 49,200 fans crammed into Comiskey Park to watch the American League beat the National League, 4-2. Babe

Mayor Anton Cermak is helped immediately after being shot. He died three weeks later.

Anton Aarns

Ruth hit the first home run during the "Game of the Century," driving a fastball just inside the right-field foul pole.

A few months later, the speakeasies along South State toasted the end of Prohibition as Al Capone prepared to become No. 85 at Alcatraz.

But the fair took center stage, so popular, it was extended another year and drew 39 million people to 427 acres of landfill jutting into Lake Michigan.

It was a curious mix of high tech (for the day) and carny magic. "Living Babies In Incubators," a nearly one-story sign proclaimed as men in straw hats and women in summer dresses ($1.49 from the Sears, Roebuck catalog) snaked along the Midway. But it was the undulations of Sally Rand that stole the show.

A movie actress whose stage name was chosen by Cecil B. DeMille, Rand fell from favor when the talkies took over because of her lisp. She found new fame after pulling a Lady Godiva stunt at the gates of the fair, and soon she was dancing with two 7-foot pink ostrich plumes (and little else) at the "Streets of Paris" concession. In a year, she was appearing with 24 dancers and 16 showgirls, reportedly grossing $6,000 a week.

"I cannot say sincerely that I would have chosen just this road to fortune," she mused. "At any rate, I haven't been out of work since the day I took my pants off."

Just as well my grandfather wasn't around.

AUGUST	SEPTEMBER	OCTOBER	DECEMBER	ALSO IN 1933
Financier Errett Lobban Cord bought Michigan's Checker Cab Manufacturing Corp. to become "taxi king of Chicago."	Ring Lardner dies at age 48. A writer of humorous short stories, many about baseball players, he was a Chicago sportswriter before attaining literary fame.	William L. Veeck Sr., president of the Chicago Cubs, dies at age 56.	The stage comedy "Twentieth Century," by ex-Chicago newsmen Ben Hecht and Charles MacArthur, opens on Broadway in the first of 152 performances.	At international air races at Glenview's Curtiss-Wright Field, James R. Wedell flies 296.94 mph. That barely beats the record set in 1932 by Jimmy Doolittle, a future hero of World War II, but isn't official because Wedell failed to follow the course or carry the required recording instruments.

DILLINGER'S GOOD THEATER

Sara Paretsky
Best-selling
mystery writer

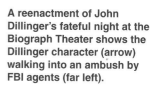

A reenactment of John
Dillinger's fateful night at the
Biograph Theater shows the
Dillinger character (arrow)
walking into an ambush by
FBI agents (far left).

BY SARA PARETSKY

When Nellie and Sydney Garfinkle joined other Chicagoans escaping the 109-degree heat on July 22, 1934, at the air-cooled Biograph, Nellie exclaimed to a woman clinging to a man in front of them, "What an ugly red dress!" Her harassed husband said, "Shh! You don't know who that might be."

Sydney and Nellie Garfinkle

"That" was mobster John Dillinger with the Lady in Red, Anna Sage, in whose boardinghouse-cum-brothel he was staying. The ugly dress tipped federal agents to follow them to the Biograph, where they shot Dillinger after he watched "Manhattan Melodrama."

Dillinger was a hero to many Chicagoans. When the coroner opened the morgue on July 23, hundreds had themselves photographed next to Dillinger's dead body. Entrepreneurs near the Biograph sold bits of paper guaranteed dipped in the gangster's blood for 25 cents, while a local haberdasher sold out of ties identical to the one Dillinger was wearing when shot.

John Dillinger

MAY	JUNE	JULY
A Burlington Railroad diesel-powered train sets the record for the longest and fastest nonstop run, covering the 1,015 miles from Denver to Chicago in 13 hours, 5 minutes to average 77.6 mph.	A Chicago track team wins the National Polish Intercity Meet here, trouncing St. Louis, Cleveland and others.	American Airlines opens sleeper service between Chicago and New York. The U.S. Labor Department lists average retail prices per pound here for sirloin, 32.2 cents; chicken, 24.6 cents; sugar, 5.9 cents; coffee, 27 cents; butter, 30 cents; eggs, 25.6 cents; bread, 7.2 cents.

A death mask of Dillinger's face sold for $10,000 to an anonymous English collector.

Tom Thompson, a retired businessman in his 70s, recalls taking an eight-cent streetcar ride from the far North Side with his mother "so we could see Dillinger's blood and where he died."

Dillinger's death wasn't Chicago's key event in 1934—it's just the one the city preens itself on because we love our reputation as a gangster capital.

After all, Brookfield Zoo opened a few weeks earlier, and that has affected more lives than John Dillinger. The first open habitat zoo in America, its design has been copied many times since.

Brookfield was the brainchild of Edith Rockefeller McCormick, who deeded the land for the project.

Although she believed she was the reincarnation of King Tut's mother and refused to speak to her children unless they scheduled appointments with her secretary, this daughter of John D. Rockefeller loved animals. She hated the close quarters at Lincoln Park Zoo. Unfortunately, she died before her new zoo was finished.

That spring Illinois passed strong equal opportunity legislation for African Americans as a condition of

granting the Century of Progress a charter for its second successful year. And the Chicago Symphony Orchestra under Frederick Stock performed African-American composer Florence Price's First Symphony and her Piano Concerto in One Movement.

Price, who won major national contests in composition, also heard her work featured by the Chicago Women's Symphony Orchestra. Because women were barred from regular symphony orchestras, about thirty cities established women's orchestras. Chicago's was considered the best, with a high level of musicianship and radio broadcasts of its concerts. The Chicago WSO specialized in works by women and African Americans.

It's a pity the WSO no longer exists: it is still hard for women's compositions to gain an audience, and Florence Price, who wrote over three hundred works and pioneered the blending of American rural folk music with classical structures, almost doesn't exist. She isn't mentioned in the Grove Dictionary of Music, the Encyclopedia Britannica, or Compton's Encyclopedia; few people know her music.

In architecture, Chicago's pride, 1934 was a somber year: completion of the La Salle Bank building at 135 South La Salle marked the end of new construction in the Loop for almost two decades, as the Depression and World War II depleted the city's resources.

And in another long-standing tradition, the Chicago Cubs made an important postseason trade. When St. Louis won the World Series in 1934 behind the power pitching of Dizzy Dean, Chicago dealt the Cards Pat Malone, their only pitcher able to beat Dean.

This giraffe arrives in preparation for the opening of the Zoological Park at Brookfield Zoo in the summer of 1934.

DEPRESSION-ERA MEMORIES

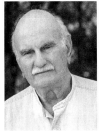

Harry Mark Petrakis

Author of *A Dream of Kings* and *Tales of the Heart*

The Petrakis family poses for a portrait. From left: Tasula, Mark, Dan, Irene, Mike, Harry (author), Barbara and Presbytera.

BY HARRY MARK PETRAKIS

In 1935, when I was a green-boned 12, the Great Depression had reached our neighborhood on the South Side of Chicago.

Beyond our Washington Park community were soup kitchens and bread lines, veterans selling apples, strikes and labor wars. Many of our neighbors were working men, and we sympathized with them. "When they tie a can to a union man, Sit down! Sit down!"

But we were full of youth's vitality, nested within our village in the city. We could lose ourselves in Saturday afternoon heroics at our local movie theater, raptly watching Flash Gordon battle the almond-eyed Ming the Merciless, who was evil incarnate. (We weren't sure what *incarnate* meant.)

We were not conscious of poverty. My mother was adept at cooking large steaming pots of savory pilaf and cutting a single desiccated chicken into it to give the meal some weight.

Our neighborhood was a bazaar of nationalities, Irish, Polish, German, Italian, Greek. We were entwined in one another's lives. When a person was ill, friends would bring in a bowl of chicken soup. Troubles were also shared. My mother went to court with a woman whose son had been arrested for breaking into a car.

Author Harry Mark Petrakis remembers his anguished walk down the aisle of Sts. Constantine and Helen Greek Orthodox Church.

JULY	AUGUST		SEPTEMBER	OCTOBER
Cook County funds for unemployment relief and administration total $5.8 million, up 17 percent from July 1934.	In a Chicago bout, Joe Louis KOs King Levinsky in the first round. The following month the "Brown Bomber" puts away ex-heavyweight champ Max Baer in the fourth round.	 Joe Louis	Santa Fe Ry. diesel-driven train hits 111 mph on Chicago-Los Angeles run.	The Detroit Tigers, featuring Hank Greenberg, Mickey Cochrane and Charlie Gehringer, beat the Cubs, with Gabby Hartnett, Billy Herman and Stan Hack, 4-2, in the World Series. Shortest game: 1 hour 49 minutes. Longest: 2 hours 28 minutes.

Thousands of Greek immigrants entered the food business when they arrived in Chicago.

We went to the church at 61st and Michigan and waited in a rear pew until the moment a hundred parishioners rose and knelt before my father, who slipped the tiny golden spoon with communion into each devout mouth.

My mother and I knelt beside them. Our turn came. My mother received communion. My father bent toward me.

"The boy ate a piece of a banana," my mother whispered. "Can he still take communion?"

The candles reflected across my father's stern, unyielding face.

"No," he said.

She also helped new immigrants, working with Jane Addams, who died in 1935. Because of the many Greeks that Addams helped, all Greek businesses in Chicago closed the day of her funeral.

The word resonated from my ears to my feet. My mother and I rose and began an endless walk through the church. Every parishioner stared at me in shock, wondering what foul crime of murder, pillage, arson I had committed to make my own father turn me away!

In the midst of major events throughout the country, a small personal catastrophe befell me. This took place during the Holy Week leading to Easter in our parish church—Sts. Constantine and Helen, where my father was the Greek Orthodox priest.

Sts. Constantine and Helen Greek Orthodox Church

I looked at them in anguish, my throat aching to shriek, "A banana! It was only one piece of a banana!"

Such is my memory of that year full of significant events in the city. The Cubs won their last 21 games and clinched the pennant, and Big Ed Kelly

For 40 days we abstained from meat and dairy products to make us worthy of Holy Communion. For the final twenty-four hours, we ate nothing. By Sunday morning, my stomach groaning with hunger, a bright yellow banana was more than I could bear. I reached for it as Eve reached for the forbidden apple.

was elected mayor of Chicago.

But now, more than 60 years later, I do not recall these events, but remember only my anguished, humiliating walk down the church aisle, feeling the world's scorn and censure swirl around my sinner's head.

My mother's shriek lodged the first bite in my throat. I tried valiantly to stop its descent. Too late. My mother's stricken face witnessed me swallow.

DECEMBER

Instead of Christmas cards, Chicago printing salesman Duncan Hines sends out pamphlets listing his favorite eating places. He went on to lease "Recommended by Duncan Hines" signs to restaurants and write best-selling guide books.

Sol Polk

ALSO IN 1935

An 18-year-old entrepreneur named Sol Polk opens an appliance store at 334 N. Central and brings his four older brothers and sister to help. Polk Brothers comes to revolutionize retailing with volume buying, sensational promotions and low prices.

Novelist James T. Farrell publishes *The Young Manhood of Studs Lonigan*, second in his trilogy on the tragic life of an Irish-American in Chicago.

Chicago entrepreneur Irvin Schwartzberg, ordered by his doctor to start the day with lemon juice and water, tires of squeezing lemons and introduces ReaLemon juice.

1936

Abner Mikva
Former congress-
man, U.S. Court of
Appeals judge and
White House
counsel

HAPPY DAYS FOR FDR

Unemployed Chicagoans stand
in line at State and Harrison to
apply for jobs. The
unemployment level neared 17
percent in 1936.

BY ABNER MIKVA

In 1936, Franklin Delano Roosevelt had just won reelection in a landslide against a very nice Kansas governor who didn't even get FDR to work up a sweat.

Ralph Metcalfe and Jesse Owens had just knocked a big hole in Adolph Hitler's racial supremacy theory by sweeping their events in the Olympic games in Berlin.

Olympic stars Jesse Owens (left) and
Ralph Metcalfe

But the breadlines were still long, and unemployment in America was almost 17 percent of the workforce. Hitler and Mussolini were just beginning to assert their territorial demands, while America and its future allies in Western Europe ignored the obvious threat to civilization.

The Supreme Court was striking down some of the key New Deal legislation as unconsti-

Sox star Luke Appling with the
Yankee Clipper, Joe DiMaggio

Richard
Loeb

JANUARY

Richard Loeb, imprisoned for the notorious "thrill kill" murder he committed with Nathan Leopold, is slashed to death by another inmate.

Heavyweight fighter Joe Louis KOs Charley Retzlaff in the first round. But in June, Louis loses to Max Schmeling in New York in 12 rounds.

FEBRUARY

"Machine Gun" Jack McGurn, a former lieutenant to Al Capone, is slain in a bowling alley on Milwaukee Avenue.

APRIL

Richard J. Daley wins his first election—as a Republican—for the State House. Daley staged the campaign when the formal candidate died. He switched back to the Democratic Party as soon as he took office.

MAY

The Super Chief, a new luxury train that cuts travel time between Chicago and Los Angeles to 39 hours, heads out of Dearborn Station for the first time.

tutional, and the dust bowl drought was driving tens of thousands of farmers from their land.

And in Chicago, while White Sox shortstop Luke Appling set the team batting record of .388, his team was out of the running. So why were Chicago and the nation in an upbeat mood? Why was "Happy Days Are Here Again" still the anthem of the Democratic Party and FDR?

Franklin Roosevelt had learned the key to a successful presidency was not only in programs or fancy economic theories. It was in the style of the president. FDR made people feel optimistic about the future, even though there was no reason for the optimism.

The campaign promises that Roosevelt had made in the 1932 election—reducing government spending and reducing the number of government employees—had long been abandoned. Instead, he had generated all kinds of new federal programs.

Some of them worked. The Civilian Conservation Corps—the CCC—had taken young males and put them in boot camps, where they worked on some public projects but mostly had a roof over their heads and three square meals a day.

A more important program was the Works Progress Administration—the WPA. Despite ridicule about make-work ideas, there exists even today many courthouses and other public buildings built by the WPA.

Franklin D. Roosevelt

I still remember the excitement when my father got a WPA job and we were able to leave welfare. His job was not very suitable to his talents. He was hired to type plays for the WPA theater, even though he couldn't type, and English was his second language.

But it was a job and a paycheck—and the return of his dignity. The economy really didn't get better until World War II heated up in 1940.

Famed University of Chicago economist Dr. Milton Friedman recently told me he agrees that the employment programs, such as the WPA and the CCC, were helpful and necessary, but he is of the opinion that the economic programs, such as the National Recovery Act (NRA) and the Agricultural Assistance Act (AAA) that Roosevelt had put in, made things worse.

It's a good thing that Dr. Friedman never ran for public office, especially during the New Deal. No matter how many graphs and charts he could have put together, he never could have persuaded my family that FDR wasn't the country's economic savior.

Even if happy days hadn't quite arrived, Americans were convinced they were on the way. What Roosevelt lacked in economic acumen, he made up in knowing how to be a cheerleader.

And, as for Cub fans, they were waiting for next year—again.

WPA workers

A NIGHT TO REMEMBER

Timuel Black
Professor emeritus at City Colleges of Chicago

COMISKEY PARK —CHICAGO—
35th Street and Shields Avenue
JIM BRADDOCK VS. JOE LOUIS
15 ROUNDS
Tues., June 22, 1937
8:15 p.m.
RINGSIDE $27.50

Seated at a table on the stage of the Auditorium Theater in view of 2,000 spectators are challenger Joe Louis and champion Jim Braddock.

Joe Louis celebrates his victory over Jim Braddock.

BY TIMUEL BLACK

I taught history for many years, but one night in 1937, I actually witnessed history. On June 22, I was among thousands packing the 8th Regiment Armory—historic home of an all-black Illinois National Guard unit—to hear Chicago's own Benny Goodman's band, which included two of America's greatest black jazz musicians, pianist Teddy Wilson and vibraphonist Lionel Hampton. (Goodman just a year earlier had been the first white bandleader to include black musicians in his ensemble.)

That same evening, a few blocks away at Comiskey Park, another earthshaking event took place as black boxer Joe Louis, one of the greatest athletes ever, beat Jim Braddock for the heavyweight championship of the world.

What a night!

I was a recent DuSable High School graduate working at a jewelry store on 47th Street. My friends and I went without dinner to make it to the Armory in plenty of time for the jazz event.

When we heard that Louis had TKO'd Braddock in the 8th round, we went crazy. I remember the band was playing a really smooth "Moonglow," and that my heart glowed as well when they announced Louis was the champ.

Benny Goodman

It was even sweeter because his victory came only a year after Louis' defeat by Max Schmeling, a product of Hitler's Germany. That had cast a pall over the entire black community of Chicago.

But now the mostly white crowd at Comiskey Park was crying, shouting, laughing. Horns were tooting. They were singing in the streets for joy.

After the fight, Louis and his entourage walked over to the Armory at 35th and Giles for the fun. It was bedlam outside and inside. Police had to close the doors and stop the band from playing for a bit.

But when they resumed, everyone was dancing and singing along with Hampton and Wilson, doing that swing with Goodman's clarinet and Gene Krupa's drums.

Republic Steel Plant workers striking

This historic evening was less than a month after a bloody tragedy at the Republic Steel Plant. My uncle was employed there, and my dad, by then a stockyard worker, had also been at Republic.

Things had been simmering at the plant in South Chicago for a long time. In May, they reached the boiling point and spilled over. The steelworkers union was set on getting a contract. The operators were just as set on not giving in to the union.

As organizers and workers tried to stop and block scabs and other strike breakers from crossing picket lines, all hell broke loose. Guards and about 150 Chicago policemen opened fire on the union organizers and workers.

When the smoke cleared, 10 organizers and workers were dead. Some of my father's former co-workers were among them. Another 60 were injured, some shot from behind.

My parents and I were born in Alabama, as were many Chicago blacks. So in 1937 we all followed the infamous Scottsboro case in which nine young black men were accused of raping two white women, one of whom denied she had been raped.

Most Chicago blacks were pessimistic that racial justice was possible in Alabama. But when word came on July 24 that the case had been dropped against some of the young men and that four were released, there was jubilance in our house and neighborhood. (Over the coming years, four of the five still imprisoned were released.)

Hope and action had triumphed over cynicism, hopelessness and apathy. Joe Louis, Teddy Wilson, Lionel Hampton, Republic Steel and Scottsboro. This was 1937 for me.

SEPTEMBER

Bill Veeck Jr., a member of the Cubs' promotion staff, suggests planting ivy and vines on Wrigley Field's outfield walls.

OCTOBER

Rail unions win a pay raise of 44 cents a day.

President Roosevelt gives his "Quarantine" speech here, saying peace-loving nations must quarantine those spreading the infection of war.

NOVEMBER

Recovery, Inc., the oldest self-help group for people with mental health problems, is founded by Chicago psychiatrist Abraham Low.

DECEMBER

Demolition of the Armour mansion on Prairie Avenue begins.

ALSO IN 1937

More than 120,000 people jam Soldier Field for the Leo vs. Austin high school championship football game between public and Catholic leagues.

IRISH, GERMANS GAIN POWER

Roger Flaherty
Sun-Times
assistant metro
editor

The German side (above) and the Irish side (right) of the Flaherty family illustrated in its own way that the two largest ethnic groups in the area had learned how to deal with each other.

BY ROGER FLAHERTY

Justice was swift in 1938, as noted January 2 in the Chicago Daily News: "Pretty Woman First Speeder Jailed in 1938." Mrs. Elsie Danick, "an attractive 26-year-old brunette," got five days in jail for going 57 mph on Lake Shore Drive between Ohio and Schiller.

A few days later, on January 5, Cubs manager Charlie Grimm was announcing his decision to make Phil Cavarretta his first baseman come spring. Illinois Attorney General Otto Kerner was expressing reservations about a

Charlie Grimm

Chicago ordinance allowing licensing of bookmakers. Marlene Dietrich was starring in "Angel" at the Gateway Theater, and no one named Flaherty turned up in the death notices.

That made us one up. I was born that day, adding to the area's two largest ethnic groups, fifth of eight in an Irish-German family. Neither the Irish nor the Germans had been popular with Chicago nativists 75 years earlier, both for their drinking habits and, as Roman Catholics, their religion.

JANUARY

Rene Curtis McLaughlin of Lake Forest asks the court to force her estranged husband, Maj. Frederick McLaughlin, to pay for furnace repairs.

Ten South and Southwest Side female teachers give the required official notice to the Board of Education that they had married in the previous year.

FEBRUARY

Giant panda Su-lin was joined at Brookfield Zoo by panda Mei-mei or "little sister." Su-lin died of pneumonia a few weeks later, and Mei-mei was joined by Mei-lan "the little flower" later that year. All three pandas, thought to be females, were actually males. Mei-mei died in 1942, but Mei-lan lived until 1953.

JULY

Utilities magnate Samuel Insull dies. Once worth $150 million, he leaves $1,000 in cash and debts of $14 million.

The city buys the Scientific Crime Detection Laboratory from Northwestern professor Fred Imbau.

AUGUST

James Smith Ferebee plays a record-setting 144 holes of golf in one day at Olympia Fields Country Club.

City welcomes Douglas "Wrong Way" Corrigan with a parade.

SEPTEMBER

Cubs catcher Gabby Hartnett hits his 9th-inning "homer in the gloamin'," the hit that came after the Pittsburgh Pirates complain that it is too dark for the game to go on. The homer knocked the wind out of the Pirates and propelled the Cubs into the World Series.

In August 1938, the Daily News reported that Niles Center (later Skokie), a bastion of Germans and Luxembourgers, had 56 saloons, catering to the blue noses of North Shore towns where liquor was outlawed. The bars paid a quarter of Niles Center's bills.

By 1938, Irish and Germans were formidable in politics, the professions and business. There were about 200 churches of the predominantly German Missouri Synod of the Lutheran Church, and at least some services were conducted in German at about three-quarters of them.

Manager Frank Frisch peers through batting cage as Phil Cavarretta belts a few with Mickey Owen behind the plate.

Cardinal George Mundelein, a grandson of a German immigrant who fought in the Civil War, was in his 20th year at the helm of the Chicago Catholic Archdiocese. German Catholics dominated more than a dozen parishes and ran Angel Guardian Orphanage at Ridge and Devon, thanks to profits from cemeteries.

Charles Gross, my grandfather, husband of Catherine and son of Civil War veteran Nicholas Gross, once ran one of them—St. Boniface Cemetery.

Judge Thomas Courtney (left) and Police Captain Dan Gilbert

A great-grandfather, John Peter Daleiden, a German immigrant from Wallendorf, owned the city's largest supplier of church goods in a building at 1530 N. Sedgwick, now a shelter for battered women.

In August 1938, about 25,000 people attended the 61st harvest fete at Riverview Park, sponsored by the Germans' Schwaben-Verein. Chicago Mayor Edward Kelly was among those attending. The Irish and the Germans had figured out how to deal with each other.

My grandfather Morgan Flaherty, a streetcar motorman, came here from Terrivane, County Kerry, Ireland, shortly before the turn of the century. He and my grandmother Ellen lived above Stalmierski's tavern in Bucktown (Poles such as the Stalmierskis made up the third-largest ethnic group in the city) and raised most of their six children there before moving out to Portage Park.

By 1938, the Irish were long ensconced in streetcar barns, firehouses, police stations and political patronage jobs. In August, about 30,000 people were at Riverview, where 62 colleens vied for Queen of Irish Day.

But a couple of Irishmen were feuding—Mayor Kelly and State's Attorney Tom Courtney. With his eye on the 1939 mayoral race, Courtney spent much of the latter part of 1938 conducting dramatic gambling raids, his troops armed with axes to break up the furniture. By year's end, the Daily News had reduced raid coverage to a little box score. Almost all of the cases were tossed out in court.

The year in Chicago played out in a darkening world, as Adolf Hitler's forces invaded Austria and Czechoslovakia. Still, at year's end, British Prime Minister Neville Chamberlain declared that the year left "no cause for pessimism."

And who could argue? Courtney's investigator Dan Gilbert, later known as the "world's richest cop," promised new gambling raids in 1939. A Cook County grand jury was looking into the sale of Police Department jobs, and society favorites, the Walter Dillinghams, revealed they would stay in the East until summer.

OCTOBER

Ludwig Mies Van der Rohe takes over the architecture department of the Armour Institute (later Illinois Institute of Technology).

NOVEMBER

Richard J. Daley wins his first election as a Democrat. He was elected to the state legislature two years earlier as a write-in candidate on the Republican ballot.

Mayor Kelly (right) shakes hands with Secretary Ickes.

DECEMBER

Mayor Edward Kelly and Interior Secretary Harold Ickes break ground for the city's first subway, on State Street in front of Holy Name Cathedral.

The American Medical Association and top officials are indicted for violating antitrust laws.

Chicago River locks at Lake Michigan begin operating, immediately reducing flow from Lake Michigan from 5,000 cubic feet per second to 1,500.

BATTLES HERE AND THERE

Charles Nicodemus
Sun-Times staff reporter

Soon-to-be-slaughtered cattle are held in the holding pens of the Chicago stockyards, which were going full tilt in 1939.

BY CHARLES NICODEMUS

When 17-year-old Alfred Krakau saw the Sept. 1, 1939, headline announcing Germany "had gone into Poland," he rushed home, put on his brown Jugenschaft uniform and headed to the group's headquarters on Western near Irving Park Rd.

"I wanted to be there for any fighting," Krakau recalled. "I believed in that fascist foolishness in those days," he said.

The German invasion on Sept. 1—the start of the war that would reshape the world—sent shockwaves through two of Chicago's largest ethnic communities.

At the headquarters of the Jugenschaft, the youth group of the militant, controversial German-American Bund, Krakau had to muscle his way through "an angry crowd of protestors. They were shouting and cursing." Police surrounded the office to prevent violence, he said.

In the city's huge Polish community the shock was profound. Helen Kotlarz, then a 15-year-old high school sophomore, remembers, "It was something far away for someone young like me." But for her Polish immigrant parents and others in the community, "It consumed them. Poland was a part of their life, their culture."

Clubs and dances to raise money for Polish cities sprang up all over. Kotlarz'

Alfred Krakau

As summer approached, the stockyards were in ferment. Low wages were being cut again. Labor union organizers fought management charges that they were Communists. And strikes flared periodically. Meanwhile, the "Back-of-the-Yards" area southwest of the stockyards was a teeming, worsening slum.

Meegan, with contacts throughout the community, and Alinsky, with an organizing genius and a sure sense of strategy, melded into one giant organization some 185 local groups—scores of parishes, churches and synagogues; all of the unions, social organizations, businessmen's groups and ethnic clubs, to form the Back-of-the-Yards Neighborhood Council, which revolutionized social organizing in America.

After a July 16 rally drew 13,000 people to the Coliseum, the stockyards' top meat-packing companies agreed to a truce that allowed more labor organizing, improved the workers' lot, and opened the door for neighborhood renewal.

Founded in 1865 at the nation's expanding transportation hub, the growing concentration of slaughterhouses, holding pens and meat-packing firms had drawn millions of cattle and thousands of stockmen from throughout the midwest. It helped give the city its wealth and identity.

Saul Alinsky led a community effort to fight the labor practices of Chicago's meat packers.

father headed one. There were giant rallies at Soldier Field and the Stadium, others recalled.

Although the German-American community was split, Krakau remained a pro-German militant until Pearl Harbor. It cost him.

"In early 1942, my father and I were interned as 'enemy aliens,'" said Krakau, now a naturalized citizen. "I wasn't released until 1948."

Earlier in 1939, a different kind of battle was fought by Saul Alinsky, a gravel-voiced West Sider with a criminology scholarship at the University of Chicago, and Joe Meegan, a streetwise local park director from the Near Southwest Side.

Joe Meegan

But animal volume at the mile-square yards peaked in 1926. Eventually, more modern plants built closer to the hog, cattle and sheep markets rendered Chicago's operation as obsolete as the heavy mallets once used to stun animals before slaughter.

In 1971, the yards finally were closed—leaving nothing but their ornate stone portal, preserved as the entrance to an industrial park. And in its final days, the place that had helped bring Chicago fame and fortune had to be sued by the city to force the cleanup of tons of remaining manure.

NOVEMBER

With his brain addled by syphilis, Chicago's famed former mob boss Al Capone is released from federal prison after serving eight years for tax fraud. He died in 1947, at his Miami Beach, Fla., home.

Montgomery Ward's distributes 2.3 million copies of a brief Christmas tale penned by one of its advertising copywriters. Condensed to rhyme and set to music in 1949, it becomes the enduring holiday ditty, "Rudolph the Red-Nosed Reindeer."

Al Capone

DECEMBER

University of Chicago president Robert Maynard Hutchins stuns the athletic world—and his own students, faculty and alumni—when he announces that the once-powerful U of C Maroons are dropping out of the Big 10 and intercollegiate athletics because the school could not continue to compete and still remain faithful to the concept of unpaid student athletes.

ALSO IN 1939

The 1922 song "Chicago" is performed in the movie "The Story of Vernon and Irene Castle."

Chicagoan Frank W. Schwinn introduces a lifetime guarantee on the cantilever bicycle frame he designed.

ARTISTS BRUSH UP THE CITY

Curtis Lawrence
Sun-Times staff
reporter

After groundwork was laid in 1940 for the South Side Art Center, First Lady Eleanor Roosevelt, joined by board chairman Patrick Prescott (center) and co-founder Daniel Caton Rich, dedicated the center on May 7, 1941.

BY CURTIS LAWRENCE

By 1940, Chicago was staggering back to its feet from the Depression and at the same time building a reputation as a tough, creative city that could wield a paintbrush as well as a tommy gun.

President Franklin D. Roosevelt's Works Progress Administration programs, the New Deal projects created to help bring the country through the Depression years, included the works of architect Alfred Caldwell, who designed the Lincoln Park Rookery and the landscaping of Montrose Point. Also included were works by Archibald Motley, who put the struggles and triumphs of the South Side on canvas,

and Lucile Ward Robinson, one of a legion of muralists who documented the century's lean years in school auditoriums and park district field houses.

"I think it was the most magnificent act for the whole country as far as developing art and culture was concerned," said Margaret Burroughs, one of the founders of the South Side Art Center and also the founder of the DuSable Museum of African-American History.

The WPA had laid the groundwork for the art center at 3831 S. Michigan in a vacant brownstone mansion donated by the Charles Comiskey

Margaret Burroughs

JANUARY	APRIL	MAY	JULY		AUGUST
Samuel S. Stritch, Archbishop of Milwaukee, is named by Pope Pius XII to head the Chicago Catholic Archdiocese.	Moses Annenberg, dubbed the "czar of horse racing information services," pleads guilty to evading $1.2 million in federal income taxes. A dozen men shake his hand in court.	Episcopal Church Bishop George Craig Stewart, 60, dies of a heart attack while on his way to teach a confirmation class. He was a founder of the World Council of Churches.	President Franklin D. Roosevelt is nominated for a third term at Chicago Stadium.	President and Mrs. Roosevelt	Mob associate and laborers' union czar Mike Carrozzo, indicted in June for racketeering, dies of a kidney ailment. Carrozzo led 25 locals and was said to be one of the richest labor leaders in the country. He was buried in a $10,000 bronze casket. Within weeks, the first of his three wives said he was a bigamist.

Archibald Motley

At the time, jobs for black artists were scarce, according to *The Federal Art Project in Illinois,* by George J. Mavigliano and Richard A. Lawson. "Few commercial jobs were available, and black artists found it almost impossible to sell their work or find a gallery willing to promote it," they wrote.

While the WPA had done its part to help trim soup lines, 15 percent of Americans were still unemployed in 1940.

Even though times were tough, Chicago's WPA artists were busy creating a history that preservationists are now trying to conserve into the next century.

In 1940, Robinson was putting the finishing touches on her "History of Chicago" mural in the assembly hall at Sawyer Elementary School, 5248 S. Sawyer.

family. The center was founded in 1939, and much of 1940 was spent establishing an extensive arts education program. On May 7, 1941, First Lady Eleanor Roosevelt came to Chicago for the official dedication.

"I just heard it would be a chance to work on the WPA and thereby earn some money," said Robinson, 92.

Like Burroughs, Ward was a graduate of the Art Institute. She also worked on murals at Harrison High School, the Cook County Children's Hospital and Pasteur Elementary School.

"Minority people got a chance to develop in arts and culture," Burroughs said, reflecting on the WPA years. "It's just unfortunate that after the Roosevelt era, the reactionaries came in and cut it out. They figured poor people didn't need anything like that."

"In general, black artists sought to communicate their message by combining an ethnic viewpoint with technical skill," author Alain Locke wrote in 1941. "These artists improved their artistry and their stature as contributors to American culture."

DuSable Museum of African-American History

The WPA, which experts cite as the largest government-funded arts program of its time, began in 1935 and was disbanded in 1943.

"The arts projects were probably the most ethnically diverse, and it's amazing when you look at the women hired," Mavigliano said.

OCTOBER	NOVEMBER	DECEMBER		ALSO IN 1940
The first peacetime military draft in U.S. history begins.	Winds up to 60 miles an hour whip through the city, killing two and injuring scores more. Trees and power lines are felled, buildings demolished and billboards and electric signs toppled.	A United Airlines plane clips the roof of a house, plunges into a garage, shears a power line and crashes at Municipal Airport, killing 10 and injuring 16.	 **Richard Wright**	*Native Son,* African-American novelist Richard Wright's most noted work, is published. Wright came to Chicago in 1934 from Mississippi. He wrote at night and worked as a postal clerk during the day. Some 300 leaders of the Illinois Ku Klux Klan meet in Chicago with Imperial Wizard James A. Colescott. The "baldish, portly" man "looked more like a chamber of commerce executive than a wizard," the Daily News said.

LIBERAL "SUN" DAWNS

December 4, 1941—Historic first front page of The Chicago Sun

Marshall Field V
A direct descendant of department store founder Marshall Field and publisher of the Chicago Sun-Times from 1969 to 1980.

Marshall Field III, founder of The Sun

BY MARSHALL FIELD V

In 1941, my grandfather, Marshall Field III, owned PM, a no-advertising afternoon newspaper in New York. The year-old publication advanced liberal ideas and supported Franklin Delano Roosevelt's policies.

Marshall Field innovation—a "Speedy" delivery wagon

From its inception, conservatives attacked PM as a communist rag. In 1941, the attacks intensified when the New York Post labeled it a "New Deal" organ. Americans on the whole held conservative views. We had not entered World War II, and most people did not want to do so. But my grandfather felt Adolf Hitler was a great threat to the United States and was convinced we must enter the war.

The PM venture only whetted his appetite for buying or starting a newspaper in Chicago to counter the "un-American monopoly" of Col. Robert R. McCormick's arch-conservative Tribune.

JANUARY

Fearing higher milk prices, housewives join farmers and union men to protest the city's plan to make the dairy industry pay the $400,000-a-year cost of milk inspection.

APRIL

Laundry-truck driver Anton Gorczak is clubbed to death with a baseball bat, the latest in a string of apparent mob murders. Businessmen plead with authorities to "do everything humanly possible" to stop the crime wave.

JULY

Detective Daniel Moriarity is convicted of killing a young woman he mistook for her mother in a case that led to the firing of two prosecutors for taking bribes to protect an abortion ring. The mother had threatened to expose the protection scheme.

University of Chicago campus

SEPTEMBER

The University of Chicago celebrates its 50th anniversary.

Daniel Goldblatt confesses to killing Anton Gorczak in April, saying a rival cleaning company owner paid him and two associates $100 each to "take care of" Gorczak.

The Sun newsroom

Although Grandfather lived in New York, the Field family still retained business interests in Chicago. The store on State Street still carried his and his grandfather's name. He felt an obligation to challenge McCormick, another heir to a Chicago fortune.

One day he hosted a luncheon in New York to try to sell his new publication, Parade magazine, to Silliman Evans, operator of a Nashville newspaper. But the conversation at the lunch turned instead to starting a pro-Roosevelt newspaper in Chicago. Shortly after, Evans was asked to head up the project.

Evans felt they must move fast and get the new paper on the street by December to take advantage of the peak advertising season. Initially, no commercial printer would take the job, but Evans persuaded Frank Knox, publisher of the Daily News, to print the new publication and he held a contest to name it.

There were 20,000 entries. Winner of the $5,000 prize was Russell Trenholme, who suggested "the Sun." His

Three days after the Sun's debut, President Roosevelt assured a concerned nation that "all we have to fear is fear itself."

explanation: "When morning comes you look for two things to make your world right: you look for the sun and sunlight, and you look for your morning paper for the truth of what's going on in the world."

Despite many snafus, at 3:30 a.m. Nov. 15, my grandfather pulled the switch for the first dummy run of the Sun. A specially bound volume was sent to Roosevelt.

When the actual first edition was launched Dec. 4, the governor, the mayor and many other VIPs were in the pressroom to witness the big event. The first edition sold 896,000 copies. Its inaugural editorial page warned that "war was very near in the Pacific."

Events three days later showed how true those words were.

The paper, which was shut out of membership in the Associated Press thanks to the Tribune, finally was let in, courtesy of the U.S. Supreme Court. Later, the Sun merged with the Chicago Times and moved into a new building.

I was born the same year as the Sun. I lived in Lake Forest for a few years as a young boy, but after my parents divorced, moved to the East Coast with my mother. I visited Chicago for a month each summer to see my father, Marshall Field IV, who later took over the paper.

One highlight was going downtown to watch him at work. I was fascinated by the pressroom because it made all that noise. Little did I think that one day I would run the newspaper started the year of my birth.

ATOMIC HISTORY AT U OF C

John Simpson
The Arthur H. Compton professor emeritus of physics at the University of Chicago

Members of the Manhattan Project are honored with a memorial plaque (left). Team members celebrate their success with a bottle of Chianti wine (above).

BY JOHN SIMPSON

The mysterious, secret project at the University of Chicago had an ordinary-sounding name: "Metallurgical Laboratory."

But there was nothing ordinary about its mission. The U. of C. was headquarters for much of the early work in the Manhattan Project, the crash program to build the atom bomb. I was among more than 2,000 scientists and workers from across the country who came to Chicago to work in the "Met Lab."

Scientists made rapid progress designing and acquiring materials for an experimental nuclear reactor. In August 1942, the first pure sample of plutonium was isolated. By December, the first nuclear reactor was assembled in the squash court under the stands of Stagg athletic field.

Crude by today's standards, the reactor was a pile of black bricks that contained 22,000 pieces of uranium oxide and 800,000 pounds of graphite. Under the direction of Italian-born physicist Enrico Fermi, scientists produced the first nuclear chain reaction on Dec. 2.

In a chain reaction, the nucleus of a uranium atom splits apart, releasing

Enrico Fermi

JANUARY

Heavyweight boxer Joe Louis volunteers for the Army, a day after knocking out challenger Buddy Baer and two days before he was to report for the draft in Chicago.

MARCH

An interracial-student group of University of Chicago founds the Congress of Racial Equality and holds sit-ins at restaurants that refuse to serve blacks. CORE became a key player in the civil rights movement.

Former Chicagoan Herbert Hans Haupt, 22, is the youngest of eight Nazi saboteurs sentenced to death by a military commission. The eight snuck ashore at night from German U-boats in the Atlantic, carrying explosives to bomb factories and bridges.

JUNE

The American Meat Institute announces in Chicago that researchers have developed a process to dehydrate meat, saving shipping space in the war effort.

JULY

Police Capt. Martin E. McCormick and three officers of the "morals squad" are acquitted by the Civil Service Commission of failing to shut down Loop gambling. A report later says the four are guilty and should have been fired.

AUGUST

The biggest blackout test in the country begins at 10 p.m. The half-hour blackout affects 12 million people in the Chicago area and along the shores of Lake Michigan.

Squash court under the stands of Stagg Field

"The Italian navigator has just landed in the New World," Compton said.

"Is that so?" replied Conant. "Were the natives friendly?"

"Everyone landed safe and happy," Compton replied.

I joined the Met Lab in 1943, staying in a room in Compton's Hyde Park home. I invented an instrument that detected plutonium amid other radioactive products. I was amazed by the atmosphere of two cultures on campus. On one hand, students and faculty freely went to classes, with military cadets training as meteorologists. On the other hand, the Met Lab occupied the physics and mathematics buildings with its secret purpose. The dichotomy was a challenge, but it was successful.

subatomic neutrons. These neutrons smash into other uranium atoms and split them apart, releasing more neutrons, which split more atoms, and so on. Each time an atom splits, it releases energy. Nuclear power plants control the reaction and harness the energy to generate electricity. An atom bomb is a runaway chain reaction.

Fermi initiated the chain reaction by withdrawing a control rod. Excitement gripped the small group of scientists and engineers as the intensity of the chain reaction built up. Enrico, using his slide rule, calculated that the recordings agreed with what was expected. The Hungarian physicist, Eugene Wigner, brought paper cups and a bottle of Chianti wine to celebrate the beginning of the Nuclear Age.

Met Lab director Arthur Compton telephoned the news, in code, to Harvard University President James Conant, the head of the National Defense Research Council.

After Germany was defeated and two atom bombs were dropped on Japan in 1945, I was concerned about the future of the new weapon. I became chairman of the Atomic Scientists of Chicago. I remain as president of the Bulletin of the Atomic Scientists, the magazine with the symbolic doomsday clock on the cover, now set at nine minutes to midnight.

Dr. Albert Einstein (left) and President James B. Conant of Harvard University

After the war, our scientists, engineers and fellow citizens succeeded in achieving civilian control of the development of nuclear energy in the United States. However, we failed to prevent the international buildup of nuclear weapons and their proliferation by many nations.

The good news is that 54 years after Hiroshima and Nagasaki, there has been no further use of the weapon in anger by any nation.

The bad news is that we have not been able to reduce or eliminate existing nuclear weapons.

SEPTEMBER

Carl Sandburg leads the pack in a Story magazine poll to decide "the greatest living American writer." Sandburg wins over John Steinbeck, Eugene O'Neill, Willa Cather and Ernest Hemingway, among others.

OCTOBER

Frederick A. Stock, 69, director of the Chicago Symphony since 1905, dies.

NOVEMBER

With the backing of "New Deal" Mayor Ed Kelly, Republican-turned-Democrat William L. Dawson defeats GOP nominee William E. King in the race for the 1st Congressional District seat, the only black-occupied seat in the House.

University of Chicago student and office worker John Johnson uses a $500 loan on his mother's furniture to start Negro Digest, the first publication of Johnson Publishing Company. This was followed three years later by Ebony, the world's most successful black-oriented and -owned magazine.

DECEMBER

The Bears lose in an upset to the Washington Redskins, 14-6, in football's championship game. The Bears had won 24 straight games.

FBI agents capture the last three of seven "Touhy gang" mobsters who escaped from Stateville prison Oct. 9. The seven were serving life sentences.

SUBWAY OPENS

The offical opening of the Chicago subway in October 1943

Adrienne Drell
Sun-Times reporter and editor of 100 Years • 100 Voices

Legendary performer Cab Calloway

BY ADRIENNE DRELL

It was 56 years ago, but James Kelly still remembers playing hooky from 8th grade to ride Chicago's first subway train.

"It was a little scary because you were down deep in a tunnel for over four miles, but the fluorescent lights and all the bright colors of the different stations were dazzling," recalled Kelly, 69, who attended the Oct. 16, 1943,

James Kelly holds a picture of that historic day when he rode Chicago's new subway.

opening-day ceremony 48 feet below State Street.

"I remember Mayor Edward J. Kelly and other dignitaries cutting the ribbon," said Kelly, whose nose was plastered to the front window of the first car as the train glided past 16 stops to Howard Street. To this day he recalls sitting on the soft green velvet seats which Chicagoans dubbed "plushies."

The opening of the $34 million subway, the first in the city's system, was just one of the events of 1943 in Chicago.

Skater Sonja Henie

JANUARY

"Kup's Column" by the legendary Irv Kupcinet appears for the first time in the Chicago Times.

Irv Kupcinet

FEBRUARY

McKinley Morganfield arrives in Chicago from Mississippi. He changes his name to Muddy Waters and becomes one of the most famous blues musicians of all time.

MARCH

Madame Chiang Kai-Shek, wife of China's leader, speaks to 23,000 at Chicago Stadium and is interrupted frequently by loud cheers and applause. She calls on the United Nations to make an "organized effort" for peace and quotes Confucius and the Bible.

APRIL

Pizzeria Uno opens at the corner of Ohio and Wabash, offering thick-crusted, cheese-packed pizza that becomes known as Chicago-style pizza.

Edward Kelly is elected mayor for the third time.

The crowds stood in line at State and Madison to buy tickets for the opening day of Chicago's new subway.

"These were guys in the Army who were being trained in meteorology at UC and would march down the quad singing, 'Wait til the Sun Shines Nellie.' They were a lot of fun," recalled Oostenbrug, now a Hinsdale grandmother.

In 1943, UC was also the scene of the first bone marrow transplant (on a lab mouse) and the first successful cancer chemotherapy (on a patient with advanced untreatable Hodgkin's disease who lived another 10 years).

Despite preoccupation with the war, Chicagoans managed to have a good time. Sonja Henie charmed thousands with her skating at the Chicago Stadium, and Duke Ellington, Cab Calloway and Lawrence Welk performed at the Boulevard Room of the Stevens Hotel, the Aragon Ballroom and the Hotel Sherman's College Inn.

Dominating the year, of course, was World War II, with attention focused on Allied forces' efforts in Europe and in the Pacific. The war's impact on Chicago was key, too. When Democratic party leader Benjamin Adamowski was inducted into the Army in late 1943, it made front-page news.

Many people still associate the year with memories of victory garden vegetables. "It filled our whole backyard," marveled Raymond DeGroote, 68, who as an 8th grader at Stone School was assigned to write about that first subway train ride.

"My father was away in the Navy, but my mom let me take the L downtown to watch the parade. Everyone who bought a war bond got a free ride," he said.

Betty Oostenbrug, a junior at the University of Chicago, and her dorm roommate set up a dating service for coeds in 1943 because there were few men around campus "except for the meteorologists."

Musician Fred Rundquist worked clubs such as the Review Lounge on Randolph Street, the Capitol Lounge on State and The Brass Rail on Dearborn.

"Things were just starting to evolve from swing into be bop. Everyone was out in the jazz clubs," he said.

Jean Tempkins Goodman, a young bride at the time, remembers, "one wonderful night when we saw the new hit "Oklahoma!" at the Shubert Theater and then went to Fritzel's for a late-night dinner."

Goodman recalls riding downtown with a fur-coat-clad friend to buy three dozen eggs on sale for $1 (a bargin in war-rationing days) at Stop & Shop, the gourmet food emporium.

"I suggested we take a cab home, but she insisted on the subway. Would you believe all the eggs were crushed and started leaking all over her coat? I teased her that the cleaning bill would cost more than she saved at the sale," said Goodman.

OCTOBER

The city's first commercial TV station, WBKB, begins broadcasting. The first commercial, for Elgin watches, is shown. WBKB is sold to ABC in 1953 and becomes WLS.

Judy

ALSO IN 1943

After refusing to enter the truck intended for her transfer, Judy the elephant walks the 18 miles from Brookfield Zoo to Lincoln Park Zoo. Accompanied by her keepers, Judy excites onlookers and police as she ambles down Congress Avenue to her new home. Judy only made one stop during the eight-hour trip at a gas station to down 66 gallons of water.

During WWII, rationing is a vital part of the war effort on Chicago's homefront. Merchants such as this Clark St. store owner (right) accepted precious stamps for goods.

TRUMANS TAKE ON CITY

Clifton Truman Daniel

Public relations director for Harry S Truman College

Bess, Harry S and Margaret Truman at the 1944 Democratic National Convention in Chicago. Only Bess seems to foresee what's in store.

BY CLIFTON TRUMAN DANIEL

For my grandfather, Harry S Truman, the summer of 1944 might have been called the Great Summer of Avoidance. It was in Chicago that year, at the Democratic National Convention, that he did his best to duck his destiny.

"I have no intention of running for Vice President," he wrote to my grandmother, Bess Wallace Truman. "I don't want the job, have never solicited it and don't expect to."

In another letter he wrote that "the Vice President simply presides over the Senate and sits around hoping for a funeral."

Grandpa, by then a U.S. senator representing Missouri for nine years, felt he could make a greater contribution to the war effort where he was, presiding over a committee exposing waste and fraud in the defense industry.

While Grandpa wrestled with history at the convention, my mother, Margaret Truman, then a 20-year-old history major at George Washington University, was enjoying Chicago. One of her favorite landmarks was Buckingham Fountain.

"I could stand for hours at night and watch that fountain change colors," she said.

My mother had been to Chicago on several previous occasions, when my grandfather had business in the city. She

Buckingham Fountain

JANUARY

A national network of "MacArthur for President" clubs is formed in Chicago to recruit Gen. Douglas MacArthur for the Republican nomination.

FEBRUARY

Mayor Kelly leads a massive torchlight parade down State Street to recruit war workers.

APRIL

The Chicago Blackhawks lose to the Montreal Canadiens in the Stanley Cup hockey playoffs.

Soldiers carry Montgomery Ward board chairman Sewell Avery out of his office when he rejects a presidential order to recognize a new union.

Sewell Avery

MAY

The University of Chicago announces it is dropping all intercollegiate athletic competition. Football had been dropped in 1939.

Margaret Truman

remembers the Christmas tree at Marshall Field's, but her fondest memories are of shopping and getting into mischief at Field's and Carson Pirie Scott.

"I liked to ride the escalators," she said. "In those days, they had little tin steps, sloping downward, and covered with wooden boards. If you weren't very, very careful, you could fall all the way down."

My grandmother was acutely aware of the peril and clung sensibly to the railing, while my mother cavorted up and down the mechanical stairs.

"Carson Pirie Scott had the worst escalators, and I loved those the best," she said. "They were dangerous."

Carson's has no doubt upgraded its escalators several times since then. And my mother has gone on to much more dangerous pursuits, killing people in Washington, D.C., one at a time in a series of murder mysteries.

At the 1944 convention, the major danger was that Grandpa was going to be drafted for the Democratic ticket. Party leaders were trying to decide among six men for the vice presidency, including incumbent Henry Wallace, who was trying mightily to hang onto his job.

In the end, my grandfather won out, courtesy of, among other things, a sterling Senate record, coming from a border state and having a good record on civil rights. Still, he fought it.

Finally, it took a call from President Franklin D. Roosevelt himself, who assured my grandfather that if he wanted to wreck the Democratic Party, he could go ahead and not run.

"That," my mother said, "is what got to Dad."

Resigned to his fate, he put his heart and soul into the campaign.

He, my mother and my grandmother found themselves in a special box up away from the convention floor at the Chicago Stadium, surrounded by delegates and well-wishers. In photos taken of the scene, only my grandmother seems to know what's in store for them.

"I'm laughing to beat the band," my mother said. "And Mother's just sitting there with a grim look on her face."

Helen Bleicher (left), a government worker, and a friend sell war bonds at a downtown department store.

AUGUST	SEPTEMBER	OCTOBER	NOVEMBER	DECEMBER
The Rialto Burlesque is shut down and turned into a movie house. It started as a vaudeville venue in 1907.	John Thompson, founder of the Chicago Temple in the Loop and known as the "Shepherd of the Loop," dies at 82. Thompson was an outspoken advocate for public welfare and often attacked corruption.	The Daily News is sold to Knight Newspapers for $2.15 million. President John S. Knight promises the paper will remain politically independent.	A week-old railman's strike prompts layoffs of 1,600 nonoperating workers for the Chicago, North Shore & Milwaukee and the Chicago, Aurora & Elgin lines. The railmen struck for a 9-cents-an-hour pay hike. Baseball commissioner Kenesaw Mountain Landis, 78, dies. Landis took the job after the "Black Sox" scandal of 1919.	"The Glass Menagerie," Tennessee Williams' first major play, opens at the Civic Theater. Author Saul Bellow publishes *Dangling Man*.

ON THE CUSP OF THE BOOM

Rev. Andrew M. Greeley

Chicago Catholic priest, sociologist and novelist

Marshall Field's, V-J Day

BY REV. ANDREW M. GREELEY

It was the last year the Cubs made the World Series. They lost, of course, to the Tigers.

The same year, a bunch of my grammar school classmates, with Roger Brown, son of the legendary sportswriter Warren Brown, at quarterback, won the city football championship for Fenwick High School.

People my age hung out at Hayes at Harlem and North or Peterson's ice cream (the best on the West Side, and the other two sides didn't matter) or, if they wanted something more than a malted milk, at the Sky Club farther north on Harlem. For

really big dates, they went to the College Inn at the Sherman House and evenings to the Chez Paree.

Young men wore crew cuts, young women short skirts, oversized sweaters, bobby socks and either saddle shoes or penny loafers. They also tended to wear two-piece bathing suits, either piece composed of at least twice the fabric of contemporary two-piece suits.

A ride on the L cost 10 cents (3 cents for children under 12) and on the streetcars 8 cents. Transfers were free. You could still get anywhere that counted on public transpor-

---

JANUARY

A federal court fight begins over the government's seizure of Montgomery Ward's property because of the company's position against unionism.

FEBRUARY

Wrigley stops making chewing gum because of a wartime raw materials shortage.

MAY

Germany surrenders to the Allies, setting off V-E Day celebrations in Chicago.

A referendum approves public ownership of a unified transportation system for Chicago.

Street sweeper swamped in ticker tape

JUNE

President Truman orders the Office of Defense to seize Chicago's strike-bound trucking industry. Workers trickle back, and seized truck lines are returned to owners in August.

Andrew Greeley is in the second row from the left, fifth from the front.

Clifton Utley updated us on the news every morning after 55 minutes of light classical music presided over by Norman Ross Sr.

Women assembled Douglas C-54 bombers up at the Orchard airport, which became the Orchard-Douglas Airport (whence the airport's abbreviation, ORD), then O'Hare. Catholics among them went to the Sorrowful Mother novena every Friday to pray for the return of their fathers and husbands and sons and boyfriends. Chicago boasted five newspapers—the Herald-American, the Times, the Sun, the Tribune and the Daily News. Moreover, they each published several editions each day. You could monitor progress in the war by glancing at the newsstands every hour or two.

There were a few special things that would never happen again. World War II ended—V-E (Victory in Europe) day in May, V-J (Victory in Japan) in August. Two atomic bombs were dropped on Japan.

Something of the evil of the Holocaust was revealed in the news photos of the concentration camps. Young men swarmed home from the service, with the promise of $20 a week. Some married almost immediately. The younger ones hung around drugstore corners. They talked about going to college, but the wave of enrollments would begin next year. My peers rejoiced that they had avoided the war—only to find themselves in the snow-covered mountains of Korea five years later.

tation. There weren't many cars because the automobile industry was making tanks and bombers. There was no disgrace in taking your date on a streetcar or bus.

The motormen were all white males.

A first-class stamp was 3 cents, air mail 8 cents, a gallon of gasoline a quarter.

The Kelly-Nash Democratic machine ran city government, though there were 16 Republican aldermen. Beyond the old suburbs—Evanston, Oak Park, Cicero— there were hardly any suburbs that mattered, only what the machine called "country towns." You could reach some of these tiny places on the Aurora and Elgin trolley line. Ed "Sewer Pipes" Kelly was mayor, and you could hear him deliver a pious message every weekday morning on the radio.

A sailor meets a girl at State and Madison streets during V-J Day celebrations.

We hunkered down, awaiting the return of the Depression. But the world of ever-expanding prosperity was just beginning. The Great Depression would never return. We didn't know that then. Nor did we know that 1945 was the year that represents the most important turning point of the century.

AUGUST

Gen. Charles de Gaulle, feted in Chicago, says Europe will dissolve in chaos without U.S. aid.

SEPTEMBER

Roosevelt College of Chicago, founded in protest against racial discrimination, opens.

University of Chicago faculty and researchers petition President Truman to share the secret of the atom bomb with other nations for world security.

OCTOBER

Chicago and most of the northeast quadrant of the nation are hit by a Greyhound Bus strike that runs until January.

DECEMBER

Mayor Kelly pushes airlines to start Chicago-Europe service.

Movie star Mary Astor, born Lucile Langhanke of Quincy, marries Chicago broker Thomas Wheelock.

HEAVEN'S UGLY SIDE

Vernon Jarrett
Former Sun-Times columnist, now a senior fellow at the Great Cities Institute of the University of Illinois at Chicago.

Fear of trouble as a result of "Negroes moving in" brought police to this South Side neighborhood.

BY VERNON JARRETT

I served in World War II, and after my discharge from the Navy in 1946 returned to my home town of Paris, Tenn. Here my contempt for racism was refueled by one incident.

On a fateful March day I decided to tolerate a Jim Crow theater balcony just so my mother could see a Marx Brothers movie. The two of us were walking home when a car of drunken whites drove by and shouted that my mother was a "nigger bitch."

Too much. I already had visions of becoming a journalist in Chicago. That incident speeded up the process. I was on my way north within days.

Chicago's new citizens from the South contributed to the great post-World War II migration. We would help Chicago's black population leap from 277,731 in 1940 to 492,265 by 1950, when the Census Bureau would for the first time in history describe America's black people as "largely urban."

When a little girl on the train north asked me, "Where do you live and how big is your home?" I paused. My answer was "3639 Giles Avenue, Shaw-

Many blacks migrated northward after WWII to take advantage of the business opportunities available in Chicago's black community.

JANUARY

At the Blackstone Hotel, the upstart All-American Football Conference says it will have teams in Chicago and seven more cities. The short-lived league shuts down in 1949.

The brutal murder of 6-year-old Suzanne Degnan stuns the city. Parts of the child's butchered body were found less than a block from her Edgewater home. In August, police report University of Chicago student William Heirens, 17, had confessed to the murder. In September, looking "cool and bored," Heirens escapes the electric chair, but gets three life terms in prison.

APRIL

Forty-five people are killed and at least 100 hurt in a Burlington-Northern train crash near Naperville. Two sections of a train headed west from Chicago collide as the train rounds a curve.

JUNE

City Hall becomes a temporary morgue when fire sweeps through the 23-floor LaSalle Hotel, killing 61 and injuring 200. The blaze apparently started in an elevator shaft next to a cocktail lounge.

Jewels and historical items stolen in a $1.5 million heist from a German castle are discovered in the Roosevelt Road station of the Illinois Central railroad. An Army colonel and his wife are suspects. They were arrested at the LaSalle Hotel, two days before the fatal fire in June.

JULY

Pope Pius XII canonizes Mother Frances Xavier Cabrini, the first American to become a saint. Cabrini founded Columbus Hospital.

104

Tuskegee Airmen Lt. Craig Williams (left) and Lt. Felix Kirkpatrick are both graduates of Chicago's Englewood High School.

kaw-ga, population 3,500,000." That was the address of my cousin, retired packinghouse worker Bill Griggs, and his daughter Beatrice. That was my new home in Heaven.

It was an emotional experience just saying "Shaw-kaw-ga" with my feigned Northern accent.

Well, it turned out Shah-kaw-ga was not Heaven. But overall the city represented a big powerful plus for black people. It was certainly Heaven compared to the Deep South. Chicago blacks publicly defied the system.

But I discovered that Chicago's Loop restaurants and hotels were committed to discrimination. One downtown nightclub featured a short run of Duke Ellington, but management advised him to limit the attendance of his black friends. Jobs appeared rather plentiful, but discrimination was rife.

Many white cops talked down to blacks, and they openly shook you down for minor traffic violations. Just

Homer Jack

as bad were outright denials of mortgages and fire insurance to black buyers regardless of their financial capabilities.

And mob violence was the usual white response to "negroes moving in" to their neighborhoods regardless of the blacks' wealth and acclaim.

That first winter I barely escaped death when, as a new Chicago Defender reporter, I covered racial violence on the Southwest Side.

I was called "nigger" more times in one two-hour period at Airport Homes than during an entire lifetime in Tennessee. Never in Tennessee had a mob covered my back with spit. The same mob damaged civilian and police cars and attempted arson on the federally owned homes. No arrests.

In 1946, most older Chicago neighborhoods were loaded with racially restrictive covenants outlawing black residency in white-organized blocks. On May 2, 1948, the U.S. Supreme Court ruled the covenants illegal.

That's when the mobs really began to mobilize and when Chicago's Joseph Beauharnais organized the White Circle League, a Northern Ku Klux Klan.

I was introduced to examples of great courage—on the parts of whites as well as blacks. I recall Elizabeth Wood, executive secretary of the Chicago Housing Authority, a white woman fired for trying to end racial discrimination.

And I recall white ministers and activists such as the Rev. Homer Jack, who defied mobs and physically helped blacks move into their new homes, and Hall Branch librarian Vivian Harsh, who constantly encouraged me to "keep writing."

Despite everything that I discovered wrong or right about Chicago in 1946, hope abounded here in the black community. And blacks enjoyed their sense of potential political power in their numbers and spirit.

OCTOBER

The Navy Pier campus of the University of Illinois opens. The campus moved to its current location on Chicago's West Side in 1965.

Laszlo Moholy-Nagy

NOVEMBER

Laszlo Moholy-Nagy, Hungarian born Chicago artist and founder of the Institute of Design, dies. In 1938, he came to Chicago to direct the New Bauhus, an American school of design founded by the Association of Arts & Industries located in the old Marshall Field residence on Prairie Avenue.

ALSO IN 1946

Boxer Jack Johnson's body is shipped to Chicago to be buried in Graceland Cemetery. Johnson, the first black heavyweight champion, died in a car wreck.

Argonne National Laboratory is established in Palos Park. Originally part of the Manhattan Project at the University of Chicago, Argonne was one of the national laboratories devoted to development of nuclear physics.

ADAPTING IN POSTWAR WORLD

Hedy Weiss
Sun-Times theater
and dance critic

Harold Washington speaks at a
Roosevelt student assembly.

Roosevelt student council
officer Harold Washington
(standing left) poses with his
fellow class officers.

BY HEDY WEISS

In 1947, a young African American by the name of Harold Washington was making his mark at what is now called Roosevelt University as student council officer.

After serving in the U.S. Army, Washington had returned home and retrieved his former job in the bond department of the U.S. Treasury, whose offices were in the Merchandise Mart. He also joined the great wave of former soldiers who took advantage of the G.I. Bill's generous education benefits to pursue a university degree. These were heady days on campuses nationwide. By 1947—a peak year—more than 2.5 million veterans had become college students.

Washington, a political science major, thrived at Roosevelt, which had created a unique openness to black students—a policy in stark contrast to the still largely segregated world of downtown Chicago restaurants and hotels. But he also learned an important lesson in 1947 as he watched a local political boss undermine his father, attorney Roy L. Washington, in a race for 3rd Ward alderman. It was his first taste of some very nasty campaign tactics.

Politics, however, was not the only game in town.

JANUARY

Al Capone, the gangster who permanently scarred the image of Chicago, dies Jan. 25 at the age of 48. Already racked by syphilis, he was felled by a stroke in his Miami mansion.

FEBRUARY

Chicago writer Nelson Algren meets visiting French intellectual Simone de Beauvoir, and a long-distance romance gets under way.

Steve Reeves

JUNE

Steve Reeves, who went on to make the Hercules movie, wins the Mr. America title at Lane Technical High School over 29 other contestants. His broad-shouldered, narrow-physique look launched bodybuilding into a new era.

OCTOBER

The Chicago Transit Authority (CTA) is created by state legislation and begins operating on Oct. 1.

Nelson Algren

the movie industry with communist propaganda. The witch-hunt era had begun.

On stage, Tennessee Williams' "A Streetcar Named Desire" was the smash hit of the Broadway season, but Chicago audiences flocked to the Harris Theatre to see Noel Coward's "Private Lives," starring Tallulah Bankhead. Claudia Cassidy, grand empress of critics, called Bankhead "the season's volcano."

In writing about the season, Cassidy also noted that in mid-November, the linotype workers went on strike against Chicago's major daily newspapers, so her reviews came out a day late.

The strike was called despite passage of the Taft-Hartley Labor-Management Relations Act, which gave employers wider protections against union actions. Labor attorney Leon Despres, now 91, remembers it all.

"It went on for 28 months, and the newspapers looked awful," he said. "In a way, it presaged the change of technology."

On the literary front, there was the publication of *The Neon Wilderness,* a collection of 24 short stories by Nelson Algren, poet laureate of Chicago's Northwest Side. Among its now classic tales was "The Captain Has Bad Dreams"—part Dostoyevski, part Damon Runyon— which captured the desperate parade of lowlifes, losers and thugs passing through the nightly lineup at a police precinct. In February, Algren's personal life underwent a radical change as French feminist writer Simone de Beauvoir arrived in Chicago. Algren took her drinking in Polish bars, and the unlikely couple began a romance that lasted many years.

Simon de Beauvoir

Meanwhile, another Chicago-born literary light, screenwriter Ring Lardner Jr. ("A Star Is Born," "Woman of the Year" and the 1947 "Forever Amber," a racy historical romance that made censors' eyebrows curl), was sentenced to jail for refusing to cooperate with the House Un-American Activities Committee. One of the "Hollywood Ten," Lardner was suspected of infiltrating

And then there was television—still in its infancy, but already well aware of the power it could wield over an audience of children.

It was in 1947 that RCA Victor invited the brilliant puppeteer Burr Tillstrom and his Kuklapolitans to do an hour-long show for WBKB Chicago. Radio star Fran Allison joined Tillstrom, the doll-like Kukla, the sad-sack dragon, Ollie, and all the others for "Kukla, Fran & Ollie." The first show aired locally on Oct. 13. It was so successful that by 1951, it was seen nationwide.

A writer for Television magazine at the time noted, "The mid-show commercial is smoothly worked in, with Kukla handing Fran an RCA Victor children's album [which she] puts on a RCA Victor record player. Thus a five-minute commercial becomes an entertainment feature." Sound familiar?

NOVEMBER

David Mamet, who has come to be Chicago's best-known contemporary playwright, is born Nov. 30. The Pulitzer Prize-winning author of "American Buffalo" and "Glengarry Glen Ross" drew on Chicago street types for his characters and invented a cryptic form of dialogue thickly laced with obscenities.

ALSO IN 1947

RCA Victor sponsors the local television debut of "Kukla, Fran & Ollie." The show is so popular that within a few years it is broadcast nationwide, setting a high standard for children's programming.

Southwest suburban Park Forest, the first packaged community in America, is founded.

Real estate mogul Arthur Rubloff formally dubs North Michigan Avenue "The Magificent Mile," claiming credit for a phrase that had been in play since 1910.

Kukla, Fran and Ollie

BEST OF MANY GOOD YEARS

Irv Kupcinet
Sun-Times
columnist

Fun Ahoy! Anchors aweigh! Kup's fourth annual Purple Heart Cruise sets sail with a crew of 500 convalescing war veterans off on a day of fun.

Irv Kupcinet

BY IRV KUPCINET

Everybody has a favorite year. I'm lucky enough to have had many: 1939, when I married my lovely Essee; 1943, when I began "Kup's Column"; 1945, when I held the first of 50 years of Purple Heart cruises; 1953, when I began my 23 years of broadcasting Bears football with my dear friend Jack Brickhouse; 1959, when I began Kup's Show.

But 1948 holds a special place in my heart. My old friend Harry Truman won an election that the pundits and know-it-alls were certain he would lose (this reporter's column, I'm proud to say, was among the first to support Truman).

He called me whenever his daughter, Margaret, was coming to town. You never forget those times when the phone rings and it's the president. You sit up straighter, taking that call.

Irv Kupcinet with President Harry Truman

JANUARY

Chicago grants 14-25% pay raises to its 14,000 public school teachers, averting a strike.

MAJCZEK TELLS $5,000 'GIFT' TO ILL. LEGISLATOR

The first-ever front page of the Sun-Times

FEBRUARY

The merger of Marshall Field's Sun newspaper and the Chicago Daily Times is announced, creating the Chicago Sun-Times.

Chicago meat and grain markets suffer their worst-ever fall in a 10-day period, with corn down 21 percent, triggering a drop in retail food prices.

APRIL

Bluesman Muddy Waters records "I Can't Be Satisfied," his first hit for the Aristocrat label, later Chess Records, the label that made Chicago blues famous.

Muddy Waters

"My baby is coming to Chicago," Truman would say. "Take good care of her."

And I would. I'd meet her at Union Station and escort her to the Pump Room. I'll never forget her stopping by on her way to a West Coast singing engagement on a television show. On the way there, we sat in Booth Two, and I didn't think much about it.

But on her way back, we were ushered to Booth One, which was (and is!) center stage at the Pump Room. Afterward, I asked the manager, Phil Boddy, why. "On the way to Los Angeles she was just the president's daughter," he said. "But coming back, she was a television star."

That was the year Israel became a nation. I had been there the year before, when it was still called Palestine. I sent back touching stories of refugees from concentration camps struggling to carve a nation out of the desert. I was proud of those stories, prouder still when Israel became a nation, and very proud when Truman made the United States the first to recognize the country (with key encouragement, it should be noted, from Jacob Arvey, the famed Chicago Democratic power broker).

Irv and Essee Kupcinet in Israel

Irv Kupcinet, daughter Karyn and son Jerry with Elvis Presley

I had two regular radio shows in 1948, and had already dabbled in the infant medium, television.

It was a good time to be alive. Chicago, for me, was a place of exciting nightclubs—the Chez Paree, the Shangri-La, the Hi-Hat, the Trade Winds, among oth-

ers—each with its own personality, its own gimmicks and flair. My wife would go with me, sometimes wearing a blouse with my column stenciled on it. That might sound silly now, but in 1948 women wore that kind of thing, along with elaborate hats and white gloves. And a man wasn't dressed without a hat, a necktie and a shine on his shoes. It was a stylish time.

I think back on that year, and in some ways it is a whirr of late, late night cups of coffee, people leaning in close to whisper the latest news above the sound of a full orchestra launching into "Red Roses for a Blue Lady." You could chat informally with a star— Clark Gable was "Clarkie." Everybody else was "buddy-boy." My column was carried all over the world—in Rio de Janeiro, in Germany. The Sun-Times—created that February, in yet another highlight of the year—gave me a 50 percent raise in 1948, to a princely $22,500 a year.

But the nightclub life wasn't my entire world. My daughter, Karyn "Cookie," was 7 years old in 1948. When kids that year asked her what her father did for a living, Karyn said, "He writes the best damn column in town, and if I don't say so, they twist my arm." Her murder years later cut short a promising life and career. Essee and I, as well as our son Jerry, miss her terribly every day.

I was 36 years old in 1948, and if you think I wouldn't happily go back tomorrow, you're wrong.

JUNE

Adolph Herseth becomes principal trumpet for the Chicago Symphony, a post he still held in 1999.

SEPTEMBER

At 6:15 p.m. on Wednesday, Sept. 1, WNBQ makes its first television broadcast, a soundless test pattern.

NOVEMBER

The Chicago Tribune guesses wrong with a front-page headline the morning after the presidential election: "Dewey Defeats Truman." President Harry S Truman had surprised the pundits and GOP candidate Thomas Dewey. The Tribune subhead was also wrong: GOP Sweep Indicated in State— Paul Douglas was elected senator and Adlai Stevenson was elected governor in a Democratic landslide.

DECEMBER

Meigs Field officially opens at 15th Street and the lakefront.

Chicago's police censor bans John-Paul Sartre's play "The Respectful Prostitute," saying it would disturb race relations.

1949

JAPANESE FIND DIGNITY

Sandra Otaka
Attorney with the
U.S. Environmental
Protection Agency

Sam Ozaki (right) visits his parents at their internment camp in Jerome, Ark. Inset: Osaki today.

Chiye Tomihiro's mother, Satoru (right), and a friend stand near the barracks of the Minidoka Relocation Center near Twin Falls, Idaho. Inset: Chiye Tomihiro today.

BY SANDRA OTAKA

In 1949, Chiye Tomihiro lived on the North Side with her parents in a run-down, one-room apartment with an icebox but no sink in the kitchen and a bathroom shared with four other Japanese families.

It was a far cry from the lovely flat the Tomihiros once owned in Portland, Ore., but still better than the animal pen where the family lived after Japanese-Americans were ordered interned as a security measure during World War II.

In one of the most shameful periods in U.S. history, more than 110,000 persons of Japanese ancestry (two-thirds of them American citizens) were relocated to internment camps to live behind barbed wire and under armed guard.

My family, originally from Seattle, was interned in the same camp as the Tomihiros in Minidoka, Idaho. There was no sewage system. You had to walk more than a block in the cold winter to an outhouse, and there were long meal lines.

Internees kitchen crew at Minidoka

"To this day I won't eat apple butter or Spam," said Tomihiro, who was finally allowed to leave the camp for college.

Orchard Place military airport is renamed O'Hare, after fighter pilot and war hero Navy Lt. Edward "Butch" O'Hare.

When the war ended, Tomihiro's parents moved to Chicago to be closer to her at the University of Wisconsin in Madison. She joined them after receiving a degree in mathematics. Her father, a law school graduate, could only get a job in a factory doing piecework.

My grandparents got jobs in South Bend, Ind., but moved to Chicago in the early '50s. My grandfather had been an accountant, and my grandmother owned a flower shop in Seattle. Here they were both factory workers.

The Tomihiros and my family were among more than 20,000 Japanese internees who moved to Chicago during and after World War II. Prior to 1940, there were fewer than 400 persons of Japanese origin here.

The new arrivals chose Chicago for various reasons. They were barred at first from returning to the West Coast. There were jobs available here. And most important, they hoped to escape the prejudice encountered on the West Coast.

"We had nothing to go back to in Portland anyway," said Tomihiro, now a retired accountant.

Sam Ozaki moved to Chicago after the war to join his sister. Born in Los Angeles, Ozaki and his parents were interned in an Arkansas relocation camp.

Ozaki, however, volunteered for the all-Japanese 442nd Infantry Regimental Combat team, which served in Italy and France. It was one of the war's most decorated combat units.

"We besieged the U.S. government to let us serve and prove our loyalty," said Ozaki, who won a Purple Heart in France. In Chicago after the war, he attended Roosevelt and Loyola universities on the G.I. Bill and became the first Japanese and Asian-American school principal in the Chicago public schools.

Fifty years later, Tomihiro resides in Lincoln Park, not far from where she lived in 1949. The Japanese community, once confined to Oakenwald on the South Side and Uptown and Near North areas, now is dispersed.

The Japanese have been joined by newcomers from Asia. Many of these Koreans, Pakistanis, Indians, Vietnamese and Cambodians—to name a few—arrived here via O'Hare Airport, which was officially named in 1949.

Overt housing and job discrimination are now addressed by federal law and local human rights ordinances. But organizations such as the Japanese American Citizens League and the Japanese American Service Committee continue to fight discrimination and hate crimes against Asians, such as the 1999 murder of Naoki Kamijima in Crystal Lake and Benjamin Smith's shooting at two Asians in Northbrook.

Despite the hate crimes, the Japanese have been happy here.

"I am glad I came to Chicago. People were very fair to us here," said Tomihiro.

JUNE

South Chicago Savings Bank is robbed by five bandits who take $920 in cash and $377,000 in nonnegotiable checks. Two Brinks guards are killed. Four of the five bandits are caught within a month.

OCTOBER

More than 4,000 CIO Farm Equipment Union members end a monthlong strike at Harvester's Chicago tractor plant.

DECEMBER

The Midwest Stock Exchange opens for trading.

Work begins on the Congress Expressway. The highway was later renamed for President Dwight D. Eisenhower.

Wholesale egg prices drop to 33 cents a dozen, 29 cents below where they stood in September.

ALSO IN 1949

Charles Lubin establishes the Kitchens of Sara Lee, named for his 8-year-old daughter Sara Lee Lubin, and produces its first bakery product, Sara Lee Cream Cheesecake.

Municipal City Airport is renamed Midway to honor the WWII Battle of Midway.

PULITZER LIGHTS UP HER LIFE

**Gwendolyn
Brooks**
Poet Laureate of
Illinois

Gwendolyn
Brooks

*Illinois Poet Laureate Gwendolyn Brooks
contributed to this account of the momentous
night in 1950 when she won the Pulitzer Prize
for* Annie Allen.

*She also offered readers a segment of the final
chapter of her poem because she feels it reflects a
mood prevalent in 1950.*

The power was out but not the phone
when the call came late in the afternoon of
May 1, 1950, informing Gwendolyn Brooks
she had won the Pulitzer Prize for her poem
Annie Allen.

But the electricity mysteriously came on
by the next day as reporters and photogra-
phers swarmed into Brooks' home at 9134
S. Wentworth to interview the first black
person to win the award.

The sudden illumination of the scene by
electricity and the Pulitzer transformed her
life in many ways.

"More invitations, more awards," said
Brooks.

In 1950, Brooks was a published poet of
renown. Yet she, her husband, Henry
Blakely, and their 9-year-old son were poor.
They, like so many blacks, confronted the
reality of limited job choices and discrimi-
natory housing.

**Gwendolyn Brooks and poet and
playwright Langston Hughes speak at
the Chicago Public Library.**

FEBRUARY

Scientists on the
University of Chicago
round table say the
hydrogen bomb
could exterminate
the world's entire
population.

MARCH

Edgar Lee Masters, a
Chicago
Renaissance writer
and author of *Spoon
River Anthology,*
dies.

Edgar Lee Masters

MAY

Lincoln Park Zoo
director Marlin Perkins
starts Zoo Parade radio
broadcasts on NBC.

The Chicago Daily
News wins a Pulitzer
Prize for articles
exposing Illinois
newspapermen on
state payrolls.

JUNE

The Chicago Railroad
Fair opens on the
lakefront for a 73-day
run that draws
1,709,004 visitors but
finishes in the red.

Nelson Algren wins the first-
ever National Book Award for
The Man with the Golden Arm.

"There were places you couldn't go to, such as certain restaurants. You couldn't stay in certain hotels."

The prize-winning *Annie Allen,* a series of poems about black life, captured the rejection blacks encountered, as well as the usual human sorrows and joys.

When the phone call came from Sun-Times reporter Jack Star, breaking the news that she had won the prize, Brooks could "not believe it at first. I remember grabbing my son and dancing around the room. Then we went to a movie, and to celebrate, but to this day I can't remember what we saw."

The next morning, when the official Pulitzer telegram came from then-Columbia University President Dwight D. Eisenhower, Brooks was suddenly besieged by calls, flowers, requests for interviews, and letters from friends.

Brooks, now 82, warms at memories of May 2, 1950. But she remembers, also, the time's veneer of "niceness" by patronizing whites and the veiled racism that exists to this day. She remembers—and observes today—the Graceful Gliders.

She says, "in 1950, the word 'moderation' was a popular word-toy. I did not consider it a niceness. I did not consider it pretty. When those who loved it used it, they meant 'Let's be not completely evil. Let's be moderately evil. Let's practice evil this far— and perhaps not farther.'"

Brooks goes on to say, "Any major changes in Graceful Gliders? No. I responded to the essence of that non-prettiness at the end of *Annie Allen*. Here is some of it— representing much of a certain mood of 1950."

Selection from *Annie Allen*

Men of careful turns, haters of forks in the road,
The strain at the eye, that puzzlement, that awe—
Grant me that I am human, that I hurt,
That I can cry.

Not that I now ask alms, in shame gone hollow,
Nor cringe outside the loud and sumptuous gate.
Admit me to our mutual estate.

Open my rooms, let in the light and air.
Reserve my service at the human feast.
And let the joy continue. Do not hoard silence
For the moment when I enter, tardily,
To enjoy my height among you. And to love you
No more as a woman loves a drunken mate,
Restraining full caress and good My Dear,
Even pity for the heaviness and the need—
Fearing sudden fire out of the uncaring mouth,
Boiling in the slack eyes, and the traditional blow.
Next, the indifference formal, deep and slow.

Comes in your graceful glider and benign,
To smile upon me bigly; now desires
Me easy, easy; claims the days are softer
Than they were; murmurs reflectively "Remember
When cruelty, metal, public, uncomplex,
Trampled you obviously and every hour...."
(Now cruelty flaunts diplomas, is elite,

Delicate, has polish, knows how to be discreet):
Requests my patience, wills me to be calm,
Brings me a chair, but the one with broken straw,
Whispers "My friend, no thing is without flaw.
If prejudice is native—and it is—you
Will find it ineradicable—not to
Be juggled, not to be altered at all,
But left unvexed at its place in the properness
Of things, even to be given (with grudging) honor.
    What
We are to hope is that intelligence
Can sugar up our prejudice with politeness.
Politeness will take care of what needs caring.
For the line is there.
And has a meaning. So our fathers said—
And they were wise—we think—At any rate,
They were older than ourselves. And the report is
What's old is wise. At any rate, the line is
Long and electric. Lean beyond and nod.
Be sprightly. Wave. Extend your hand and teeth.
But never forget it stretches there beneath."
The toys are all grotesque
And not for lovely hands; are dangerous,
Serrate in open and artful places. Rise.
Let us combine. There are no magics, or elves,
Or timely godmothers to guide us. We are lost, must
Wizard a track through our own screaming weed.

AUGUST

President Truman orders the Army to seize and operate railroads to avert a scheduled nationwide strike. Unions immediately order members to work, and private management continues the actual operation of trains.

Chicago bans the movie "No Way Out," a violent study of racial prejudice, on grounds it could "cause trouble." The ban is lifted after a one-minute scene is deleted.

OCTOBER

Kefauver Senate crime committee holds hearings in Chicago, and says it finds ties between Chicago and other big city syndicate operations. Dan Gilbert, chief investigator for the state's attorney's office for three decades, says he made his $360,000 fortune on stock and grain markets, not graft.

NOVEMBER

Timothy O'Connor is named police commissioner after John Prendergast resigns following criticism for failure to wipe out crime.

DECEMBER

A wildcat "sick-out" strike idles trains in Chicago, St. Louis and Washington. President Truman orders men back to work on the grounds that rail tie-ups are interfering with the Korean War effort.

COMEDY, MUSIC AND ROMANCE

Dave Hoekstra
Sun-Times staff
reporter

Dean Martin and Jerry
Lewis ham it up on their
visit to Chicago.

BY DAVE HOEKSTRA

Jerry Lewis and Dean Martin headlined the Chicago Theater in July 1951. The comedy team was at the peak of its popularity, which underscored America's playful postwar atmosphere.

After finishing their first stage show in a week-long engagement to promote their film "That's My Boy," Martin and Lewis invited the audience to come to the backstage door to receive a picture. More than 1,500 fans stormed the door.

Martin and Lewis climbed to a fire escape for safety. They began dropping the pictures to the ground like ticker tape.

The crowd kept knocking on the door.

And the city was open to a world of possibilities.

A Chicago Theater fire escape provides refuge for
Dean Martin and Jerry Lewis from screaming fans.

"Chicago was integral to my career," Lewis told me in a 1996 interview. "I played the Oriental Theater as a single act. After the Chicago Theater, in 1951, Dean and I played the State-Lake. We went in for two weeks at the Chez Paree (a nightclub at 610 N. Fairbanks) and stayed for 12. I don't even

JANUARY

Bushman the gorilla, 23, dies at the Lincoln Park Zoo. In two decades on display, Bushman attracted 100 million visitors—120,000 on one day—and the nation's zoo directors voted him "the most outstanding single animal of any zoo in the world."

FEBRUARY

Dorothy Mae Stevens Anderson attracts national attention as "The Deep Freeze Woman" when she is found frozen—but alive—in a South Side alley, having passed out after a night of drinking. Her body temperature was 64 degrees. Until then, no person was known to have lived with a body temperature below 75 degrees.

APRIL

An estimated 4 million people, more than the city's population, line the parade route to greet Gen. Douglas MacArthur, 15 days after his dismissal from Far East command by President Truman.

Gen. Douglas MacArthur

The Edgewater Beach Hotel

know if a lot of the people I knew at that time are still alive."

In 1951 Martin and Lewis appeared on the NBC-TV "Colgate Comedy Hour," filmed live at the Studebaker Theater, 418 S. Michigan (now the Fine Arts movie theaters). The late choreographer-theater director-filmmaker Bob Fosse worked on the show with Martin and Lewis.

Further north and earlier in the year, my parents honeymooned at the Edgewater Beach Hotel at Sheridan and Balmoral. The hotel was billed as the "Site of America's Most Successful Meetings."

When my mother opened the door to her hotel room, she found a surprise from my father—a bouquet of a dozen red roses.

The Edgewater could do that to you. The romantic hotel had 1,000 feet of private beach, including a Cabana Club. A promenade led guests

Al and Irene Hoekstra

to the lakefront. It was a perfect setting for 1951's soundtrack, which featured hits like Les Paul and Mary Ford's "How High the Moon" and Johnnie Ray's "Cry."

Bandleaders Xavier Cugat, Guy Lombardo and Woody Herman played to a nationwide radio audience from the sunken 1,200-seat Marine Room. "There was a big dance floor," my mother recalled. "And from all the windows you could see out on the lake." It was a stately view for a young woman from downstate Illinois who had fallen in love with a shy purchasing agent from Logan Square.

Celebrities like President Franklin D. Roosevelt, Babe Ruth and Mahatma Gandhi stayed at the Edgewater. Most National League baseball teams stayed there because it was close to Wrigley Field. My father's bill for the hotel room, drinks and dinner for a wedding party of four was $49.89.

My father remembered the hotel's "Yacht Club." He said, "You went down an imitation gangplank, and it moved back and forth as if you were actually getting on a ship. Portholes had little waves moving back and forth." The Yacht Club had a piped-in ambiance of booming surf, ship's bells and foghorns.

In the mid-1960s a northern expansion of Lake Shore Drive cut off the beach from the hotel. The hotel's elegance dimmed, and by 1967, the Edgewater filed for bankruptcy. It was razed in 1969. My parents aren't so sad about the hotel's demise. Some of life's most memorable doors are hinged from the heart.

Only a short distance from Wrigley Field, the Edgewater Hotel served as the Chicago home for many visiting baseball greats such as Babe Ruth.

JUNE	JULY	AUGUST	NOVEMBER	ALSO IN 1951
Robert Maynard Hutchins resigns as University of Chicago president, ending a 21-year reign marked by intellectual ferment and the university's withdrawal, in 1939, from intercollegiate football.	The electric blues movement takes shape when Muddy Waters (McKinley Morganfield) hands off his guitar to Little Walter before recording "Still a Fool" (with Leonard Chess on bass drum). Waters goes on to become one of the most dynamic vocalists in modern blues.	Jake "Greasy Thumb" Guzik and Rocco Fischetti, alleged leaders of a revived Capone gang, are indicted by a federal grand jury.	Chicago publishing magnate John Johnson starts Jet magazine, which immediately becomes the number one weekly news periodical featuring black Americans.	The Weber Grill is invented in Palatine by George Stephen, an employee of Weber Brother Metal Works who didn't like barbecue grills that were then available.

PARTY FOUND A WINNER IN IKE

Steve Neal
Sun-Times political
columnist

President Harry Truman (left) encouraged a reluctant Adlai Stevenson II to seek the presidential nomination at the 1952 Democratic National Convention in Chicago.

BY STEVE NEAL

It was the summer of Ike and Adlai.

In July 1952, the Southwest Side's International Amphitheatre was where the man who beat Hitler faced his toughest political battle and where the Democratic governor of Illinois sought to avoid one.

President Truman had decided that spring not to seek reelection. With both major political parties holding their conventions in Chicago that July, there was fierce competition for the Democratic and Republican nominations. On the eve of both party gatherings, the outcomes were far from certain.

The GOP met first. Sen. Robert A. Taft of Ohio, who was known as "Mr. Republican," had 530 committed delegates to Gen. Dwight D. Eisenhower's 427. Taft, who controlled the GOP national committee and whose allies were in charge of the convention, needed just 74 votes for the nomination.

Taft became the first casualty of the little screen. As Theodore H. White noted, television discovered its political power at the '52 GOP convention. This was the first time that television networks provided gavel-to-gavel coverage of the national conventions. When Taft's forces refused to allow television coverage of a credentials

Adlai Stevenson II was the Democratic presidential nominee in 1952 and 1956.

Vice presidential candidate Richard Nixon (left) and GOP presidential nominee Dwight D. Eisenhower celebrate with their wives, Pat Nixon and Mamie Eisenhower, at the Republican National Convention in Chicago in July 1952.

fight over disputed delegates, the networks portrayed Taft as the villain.

Even though Taft was awarded most of the disputed delegates by the credentials committee, Ike's forces challenged this decision on the convention floor. With that vote, the momentum suddenly shifted. After 20 years of losing presidential elections, Republicans were desperately seeking a winner. Taft was first in the hearts of GOP delegates, but many of them doubted he could win the presidency in the fall. Eisenhower was nominated because he was a sure winner.

In his surprise choice for vice president, Ike selected California Sen. Richard M. Nixon, then only 39 years old. The cheering GOP throngs greeted their new ticket with a sea of "Ike & Dick" posters.

William G. Stratton (left), at the 1952 convention, became Illinois' governor that year.

When the Democratic convention opened later in the month, Sen. Estes Kefauver and 74-year-old Vice President Alben Barkley were the leading contenders. Barkley withdrew when labor bosses told him he was too old. Kefauver was bitterly opposed by Truman, who viewed him as a loose cannon.

Stevenson had declined Truman's invitation to seek the nomination. "I have been in politics only three years," he wrote a friend in March, "and while I have learned a great deal, I have a great deal more to learn. My ambitious program in Illinois is well under way, but there is still much to be done."

In short, Stevenson wanted to run for reelection as governor. Stevenson also thought that a change in administrations might not be a bad thing in '52. His plan was to seek the presidency in '56.

But the '52 delegates had other ideas. Stevenson charmed and captivated them in his opening remarks to the convention: "Where we have erred, let there be no denial; and where we have wronged the public trust, let there be no excuses. Self-criticism is the secret weapon of democracy, and candor and confession are good for the political soul," he declared.

The "Draft Stevenson" movement led by Chicago boss Jake Arvey gained steam. Later that week, on the third ballot, Stevenson won the prize he didn't want. Eisenhower later confided to his son John that he wouldn't have run if he had known that Stevenson, whom he admired, would be the Democratic nominee.

Eisenhower won the election handily that fall. Republican William G. Stratton succeeded Stevenson in the '52 election as Illinois governor.

AUGUST	**SEPTEMBER**	**OCTOBER**	**ALSO IN 1952**
The city endures a one-day invasion by hordes of crickets. CTA pays $16.5 million for Chicago Motor Coach Co.	*Great Books of the Western World*, a $2 million, nine-year project of the University of Chicago and Encyclopedia Britannica, is published. The 54-volume, 32,000-page collection sells for $500.	A strike by 1,500 elevator operators in high-rises is settled with a 2-cent hourly raise, to $78 a week, and the cutting of the 48-hour week to 40 without a pay cut.	In his book *Chicago: The Second City* (based on a series of New Yorker articles) A.J. Liebling blasts the city's provincialism and lack of humor. Later, the internationally known comedy troupe picked this title for its own name.

Vicki Quade
Editor, writer and
playwright

POLIO STRIKES CHICAGO

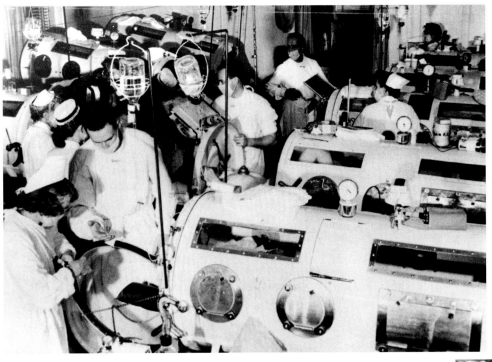

The polio outbreak of
1953 required drastic
medical attention (left)
for many of Chicago's
children. The more
fortunate victims, such
as Sugar Rautbord
(below), escaped the
disease relatively
unscathed.

BY VICKI QUADE

Children heard it all the time: "Don't go near the water, don't go on the beach, don't go into crowds." The year was 1953, and a silent disease stalked Chicago. Polio.

"It was the fear on every parent's mind," recalled Sugar Rautbord, Chicago-born author and socialite. "I remember that my parents went off to their golf club for the day, and the nanny took my two sisters and me to the Museum of Science and Industry. It was

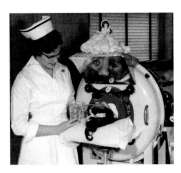

Columbus Hospital in the polio ward

late August. We crossed the street right there and went to the beach. I, being the gutsy one, jumped into the water."

Two and a half weeks later, Rautbord should have been getting ready for kindergarten. "My mother called me to come and I couldn't. I was paralyzed from my waist down."

Rautbord was rushed to Michael Reese Hospital,

Sugar Rautbord

MARCH

In its 45th year, the Chicago Auto Show is recognized as the largest of its kind, as it remains today. The 1953 show runs nine days and draws 481,000 visitors.

APRIL

Thirty-four people die when a flash fire hits the plant of Haber Corp., an electrical appliance firm.

Baha'i
Temple

MAY

Baha'i Temple in Wilmette is dedicated. Chicago area residents petitioned the faith to build the edifice in 1904, but it took decades to raise the $2.6 million construction cost from the worldwide Bahai community. Ground had been broken in 1921.

University of Chicago's Stanley Miller announces production of amino acids under conditions thought to have existed early in Earth's history.

Frank, Francois and Robert Pope

"I still have a few little things with my muscles, but I knew I was going to be OK that summer when I could move a little bit," she said.

The fear of playing outdoors was so palpable, children looked for alternatives. Child psychologist Frances Horwich started the "Ding Dong School" on WMAQ-TV that February in 1953, becoming one of television's best known preschool teachers. "Kukla, Fran and Ollie" kept kids laughing.

And Frank Pope became an unlikely celebrity when he was cast with his brother, Robert, on their father's "Creative Cookery Television Show." Long before there was Julia Child or Emeril Legasse, there was Francois Pope, who taught gourmet cooking classes every morning until 1963.

where her grandparents had donated money to build a new wing and a pavilion. But polio was the great economic equalizer. Children of wealth like Rautbord were just as subject to the disease as youngsters from public housing.

"We were opposite 'Howdy Doody,' but a lot of kids watched us. I know that sounds strange, but it's true," Frank Pope said.

"They were stacked in the aisles, lobbies, halls, doorways—everywhere, there were paralyzed children," she recalled. "They would wheel two or three in, and if they hadn't moved, they would go into the iron lung room. There was another room for children who had lighter cases. All I knew is there was door one and door two. Everyone behind door two was weeping. Door one was where parents looked relieved. I was determined with every ounce of strength I had to get myself into door number one."

Rautbord was one of the luckier polio victims.

With Marilyn Monroe on its cover, Playboy magazine was an instant success in 1953.

The show was a spin-off from the Antoinette Pope School of Fancy Cookery on Michigan Avenue, where Frank's mother created recipes made famous in her Antoinette Pope School Cookbook. Sales topped 1 million, and the book was a best-seller at Marshall Field's for years.

By the end of 1953, another entrepreneur was busy making his own history. Hugh Hefner's Playboy magazine had become a success. The first issue featured Marilyn Monroe.

Gale Morin, who modeled under the name Diane Hunter, appeared on the inside back cover of that issue.

"I didn't keep any of the old magazines," she said. "Boy, am I sorry now!"

OCTOBER

Waukegan native Ray Bradbury publishes *Fahrenheit 451*. It involves a book-burning society of the future. The title refers to the temperature at which paper burns.

Former Oak Parker Ernest Hemingway, now living near Havana, wins a Pulitzer Prize for *The Old Man and the Sea*. Its protagonist is a Cuban fisherman.

Driven indoors by the polio scare, children turned to TV shows like "Kukla, Fran and Ollie."

DECEMBER

Carter H. Harrison II, Chicago mayor from 1897 to 1905 and 1911 to 1915, dies on Christmas Day at age 93.

ALSO IN 1953

U.S. meat packers begin moving out of Chicago to plants closer to the western feedlots.

Chicago-based Sara Lee Kitchens proves that properly frozen baked goods can be marketed successfully.

LYRIC TAKES CENTER STAGE

Danny Newman
Press agent for the
Lyric Opera

The globally publicized photo of
Maria Callas' reaction to getting
a subpoena helped spread her
and the Lyric Opera's fame.

Maria Callas sang
Violetta opposite
Canadian tenor
Leopold
Simoneau's
Alfredo in the
Lyric's 1954
production
of "La
Traviata."

BY DANNY NEWMAN

Two stars were born in Chicago on Nov. 1, 1954.

Maria Callas skyrocketed to fame in the title role of Bellini's "Norma."

And the Lyric Opera Company, by giving Callas her American debut, was launched on the international stage.

Time, Life, Newsweek and the New York Times cheered the Chicago debut of the American-born soprano who later that season also scored mightily in Lyric's "Lucia di Lammermoor" and "La Traviata."

The first eight-opera season and the one that followed were artistically glorious but financially disastrous for a company with no start-up capital. However, the public and critics were inspired by such "Big Name, Big Voice" singers as Callas, Renata Tebaldi, Giulietta Simionato, Nicola Rossi-Lemeni, Tito Gobbi, Eleanor Steber, Jussi Bjoerling and Dorothy Kirsten.

Somehow bankruptcy was avoided, and two years later, co-founders Larry Kelly and Nicola Rescigno departed, leaving onetime opera student Carol Fox in sole control of a new corporate entity—The Lyric Opera of Chicago.

JANUARY

The Chicago area passes Pittsburgh as the world's leading maker of steel. Pittsburgh protests that the Chicago figures include the U.S. Steel plant in Gary, Ind., and says it's still No. 1 if a nearby plant in West Virginia is counted.

"The Breakfast Club"

FEBRUARY

The Board of Health, after ordering anti-rabies shots for all dogs and cats, rejects an offer from former dancer Irene Castle, an inoculation foe, to let herself be bitten by a rabid dog to prove the disease will not kill humans.

"The Breakfast Club" debuts here on ABC television, with standbys from the 21-year-old radio show including host Don McNeill and guests Fran Allison—of "Kukla, Fran and Ollie"—comic Sam Cowling and singer Johnny Desmond. The TV show runs only one season but the radio broadcast continues until 1968.

JUNE

Four people drown and seven are missing after a 10-foot wave, or seiche, hits the Chicago beaches. The seiche was caused by high winds and a sudden drop in air pressure along the lakefront. One couple who drowned left behind 11 children.

Maria Callas (center) poses backstage with the Lyric Opera chorus after a performance of "Lucia di Lammermoor" in 1954.

Our first production was Mozart's "Don Giovanni" in February. Then Carol was off to Milan, where she outbid the Met's Rudolf Bing by $250 per performance for Callas. As a result, history was made that November with arias like "Casta Diva" in Callas' incandescent voice.

Chicago opera fans flocked to hear her that year and the next season when, after a final performance as Cio-Cio-San in "Madame Butterfly," Maria was served with a subpoena over a contract dispute. Photos of her apoplectic reaction went around the world, adding to her fame and that of the Lyric.

Callas left Lyric after two years. But the company survived. Conductor Bruno Bartoletti, who joined us in 1956, remained for 42 years. New productions and a training school for young singers were added.

Fox was the driving force behind the company. Her optimism that Chicago could sustain an opera troupe was undaunted by the earlier failures of half a dozen major predecessor companies that had strutted their brief hours across the stages of the Auditorium Theatre and the Opera House.

When the last pre-Lyric entity, the Chicago Opera Company, bit the dust in 1946, I went down with that ship. But I learned an important lesson: that without a subscribed, committed audience, no opera company can survive, much less thrive.

From 1947 through 1953, I promoted visits here by the New York City and Metropolitan Opera Companies. But in 1954, I became press agent of the fledgling Lyric. Early on, I began, in mounting crescendo, to build what has become an army of subscribers.

Carol Fox

Lyric has produced 2,382 performances of 145 different operas, has a $35 million budget, recently completed a $100 million renovation of the Opera House, and boasts 39,000 series ticket subscribers and 13,000 regular contributors. Its original three-week season has grown to five and a half months.

In 1954, the shepherd boy in Puccini's "Tosca" was sung by Children's Chorus soloist William Mason. He is currently our general director, following the 1997 death of Ardis Krainik, the successor to Carol Fox, who died in 1981.

I am now 80 years old, and the last survivor of Lyric's founding staff. In 2004, Lyric will celebrate its 50th anniversary. Few people in 1954—especially board members of all those bankrupt old companies—would have bet on such longevity.

SEPTEMBER

The Union Stock Yard and Transit Co. slaughters its one billionth animal, a Hereford steer.

OCTOBER

The Chicago River floods the Loop. High water from the river and other streams kills 19 people and causes $50 million in damages in the city and north suburbs.

Agostino "Gus" Amedeo, sought in the slaying of police detective Charles Annerino, is killed by police after his girlfriend's sister-in-law helps set a trap for him.

NOVEMBER

Swift & Co. introduces the Butterball Turkey, a new breed of bird that promises the end of pined feathers and a deeper breast with more tender meat. It is now the leading brand of turkey in the U.S.

ALSO IN 1954

Harlem-Irving Plaza in Norridge opens as a shopping plaza with a Walgreens drugstore and Wieboldt's as the main department store.

DALEY ASSUMES COMMAND

Frank Sullivan
Former press
secretary to Mayor
Richard J. Daley

Richard J. Daley is sworn in for his first term as mayor of Chicago. By the time he died in 1976, Daley had been sworn in an unprecedented six times.

BY FRANK SULLIVAN

When Richard J. Daley was elected mayor on April 5, 1955, some observers assumed he would allow old-time bosses Jake Arvey and Joe Gill to run things.

But 43rd Ward Alderman Paddy Bauler had it right:

"They're gonna run nothin'. They ain't found it out yet, but Daley's the dog with the big nuts, now that we got him elected. You wait and see. That's how it's going to be."

Mayor Daley with Muhammad Ali

Daley was, in fact, a shrewd and farsighted politician who became the first of the modern big-city managers and builders. He served 21 years.

Within days of besting Republican Robert Merriam, the mayor—who was also chairman of the Democratic Party—used his political know-how to take the city's budget-making authority out of the hands of aldermen and transfer it to himself.

Mayor Daley and his wife, Eleanor

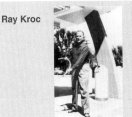

JANUARY

Ray Kroc

The London House restaurant, 360 N. Michigan, becomes a hot spot for live talent when it begins presenting live jazz. Artists such as Oscar Peterson, George Shearing, Ahmad Jamal and Ramsey Lewis play the room before it closes in 1975.

APRIL

The first McDonald's franchise opens in Des Plaines. Ray Kroc, a 55-year-old Chicagoan, was selling milk-shake mixers when he noted the success of a California restaurant owned by Dick and Mac McDonald. Kroc bought the brothers out in 1961.

Col. Robert R. McCormick, 74, publisher of the Chicago Tribune, dies.

JULY

Chuck Berry records "Maybelline" for Chess Records in Chicago, and the song begins its climb to No. 1 on the Billboard charts.

Chuck Berry

The Daley mayors have controlled the political scene in Chicago for most of the second half of the century.

The new man at City Hall was showing he would become a very special mayor.

Like Harry Truman, whom he admired, Daley based his actions on firmly held beliefs, not the polling data or focus groups used so widely today.

A politician for 40 years, Daley kept his private thoughts to himself. His wife, Eleanor, was his only confidante. However, during the years I was allowed inside his inner circle as press secretary, I derived some measure of the man. He was honest, forthright and smart.

Daley's brand of politics was formed in a pre-television era. But through television, in his sometimes ungrammatical way, he spoke to real people.

Mayor Daley greets his constituents.

He truly was the essence of all the folks who lived on the side streets of the city, and he spoke to them directly. Daley's remarks were sometimes impolitic—but usually effective. He bonded with most ethnic groups.

Near the end of his life, Daley told a Sons of Italy gathering at the Sheraton Hotel that "World War II was won by the sons of the Irish, Polish and Italian families of America."

The crowd erupted with applause and cheers. The mayor had just eliminated most of the American people from having anything to do with the war victory, but this particular ethnic audience liked what he said.

The mayor's major political confrontation came in 1966, when Dr. Martin Luther King Jr. selected Chicago for the northern phase of his civil rights campaign, maintaining the city—and its schools—were the most segregated in the nation.

But Daley believed that King was being unfair to expect northern cities like Chicago to rectify, in a short period of time, injustices of a century.

"These problems were created thousands of miles from here in Georgia, Mississippi and Alabama. This deprivation of education can't be laid to the people of Chicago. They had nothing to do with it," Daley said.

The very next year Daley carried all the black wards of Chicago. He had done so in every election—even those following his intemperate "shoot to kill order" in the wake of the rioting after King's assassination.

In 1974, before undergoing what he was convinced was life-threatening surgery to clear a blocked carotid artery, he chatted with me about lucrative moneymaking offers he had received, even in his first weeks as mayor. One could have brought him more than $1 million. Of course, he declined.

"Some people thought that because I was an Irish Catholic, that I was going to seek a profit from being in office," he said. "That made me all the more determined to show them that the office wasn't for sale."

AUGUST
African-American Emmett Till, 15, of Chicago, is murdered in Money, Miss., while visiting relatives. One of the two white men arrested for the kidnapping, beating and shooting says the youth spoke obscenely to his wife, grabbed her waist and whistled at her. A September trial ends in acquittal.

SEPTEMBER
Ex-marine Jack Johnson is appointed warden of Cook County Jail. To shield his three daughters, he invented the widely accepted story that three jail officials—not just he—pulled levers to execute killers in the electric chair.

OCTOBER
The first advice column by a 37-year-old housewife named Eppie Lederer, who won a contest to write under the name "Ann Landers," begins running in the Sun-Times. Lederer's twin sister Abigail Van Buren begins writing her own "Dear Abby" column just nine months later.

NOVEMBER
Chicago's tallest building is dedicated. The 40-story Prudential Building is crowned by the Top of the Rock restaurant, named for the insurance company's symbol, the Rock of Gibraltar.

A DREAM TICKET THAT WASN'T

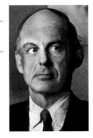

Adlai E. Stevenson III

Former Democratic U.S. senator from Illinois and state treasurer and now president of SC&M International Ltd.

Democratic nominee Adlai Stevenson II privately lobbied for Massachusetts Sen. John F. Kennedy to be his running mate, only to see the convention nominate Tennessee Sen. Estes Kefauver instead.

BY ADLAI STEVENSON III

It was a tough year for the Democrats.

Divisions which had surfaced within the Republican Party four years earlier had subsided. President Eisenhower was renominated by acclamation at the Republican National Convention in San Francisco. William G. Stratton, a popular Republican governor, was seeking reelection. The Republicans fielded a strong ticket in Illinois, and the public was not in a mood for change anywhere.

As usual, the Democrats were less orderly. My father, former Gov. Adlai Stevenson, or the "Guv," as he was known to family and friends, contested with Sen.

Estes Kefauver of Tennessee for the presidential nomination in the nation's first significant primary contests, winning in California.

Harry Truman announced his support for New York Gov. Averell Harriman. But there was never much of a contest for the dubious privilege of facing off against Eisenhower. With a roar that reverberated through the Chicago Stockyards International Amphitheatre, reflecting more

On vacation from Harvard Law School, Adlai Stevenson III joins his father on the campaign trail.

FEBRUARY

In its 51st year, the Chicago Defender newspaper goes daily and expands coverage to include stories of general interest in addition to news affecting the African-American community.

MARCH

Chicago Daily News fashion editor Peg Zwecker begins writing about a talented young milliner named Roy Halston Frowick. Several years later she introduced him to designer Lilly Dache, who launched the multimillion-dollar fashion career of Halston.

Roy Halston Frowick

APRIL

Foreshadowing the VCR, the Chicago firm AMPEX displays a device that records TV shows on magnetic tape.

enthusiasm for the Guv than optimism for his prospects, the Democratic Convention nominated him on the first ballot.

He secretly had chosen a young freshman senator from Massachusetts to be his running mate, which is why he asked John F. Kennedy to nominate him. The speech was eloquent and drew national attention to Kennedy. Then, to infuse the convention with excitement, the Guv threw open the contest for the vice presidential nomination, expecting Kennedy to win.

State Auditor Orville Hodge ran afoul of the law by forging vouchers for state funds.

The first part of the plan succeeded. At one point during the seesaw balloting, Kennedy's nomination seemed assured. I raced down the stairs at the Stock Yards Inn to Kennedy's room, where Sargent Shriver, his brother-in-law and manager of the Merchandise Mart, was manning the barricades.

Kennedy was pulling up his trousers, getting ready to accept the nomination. I congratulated him enthusiastically and hurried back to the Guv's suite just in time to see Kefauver win on the second ballot.

The Eisenhower-Nixon ticket, paradoxically aided by the Soviet Union's suppression of the uprising in Hungary and the British-French-Israeli invasion of Egypt, swept the country. In Illinois, the Republicans won every

Not all the fighting in 1956 took place in the political arena. Floyd Patterson knocked out rival Archie Moore in the fifth round of their heavyweight bout in Chicago in late 1956.

statewide office and even elected the state's attorney of Cook County, Ben Adamowski.

Four years later, Kennedy won the presidency. He later acknowledged that if he had won the 1956 vice-presidential nomination and gone down to certain defeat, he might not have gotten a second chance in 1960. As it was, Kennedy's nominating speech and the dramatic contest for the vice-presidential nomination catapulted him into the front ranks of the party and the consciousness of the American people.

The Guv spelled out his program—his New America—in his acceptance speech and in the fall campaign. He failed to win against an American folk hero running on a platform of peace and prosperity. But the New America became the genesis of the New Frontier and Great Society. Many of the programs carried out by Presidents Kennedy and Johnson were first proposed by my father.

While the Guv was on the national hustings, a political scandal dominated Illinois' political scene. State Auditor Orville Hodge got caught forging vouchers for state funds, which he would then authorize and collect. Hodge was forced off the Republican ticket, indicted, convicted and served time.

A PIÑATA OF OPPORTUNITIES

Carlos Tortolero
Founder and executive director of the Mexican Fine Arts Center Museum

Chicago's Mexican-American community celebrates Mexican Independence Day with a State Street parade.

BY CARLOS TORTOLERO

I was only a toddler in 1957, but I can remember watching "Romper Room" on TV. There was a daily segment in which the star of the show would look in a magic mirror and call out different names of children that she would see.

She never called my name. She never called out any Mexican kids' names.

There were no Mexicans on TV then. And in 1957, it was hard to say how many Mexicans lived in Chicago.

That's because the U.S. Census Bureau

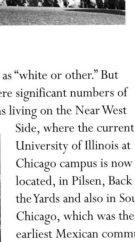

Mexican pride

listed us as "white or other." But there were significant numbers of Mexicans living on the Near West Side, where the current University of Illinois at Chicago campus is now located, in Pilsen, Back of the Yards and also in South Chicago, which was the earliest Mexican community here.

In January of that year, though, the Mexican population increased by five, as my mother, two brothers, a sister and I accompanied my father to Chicago. He had

Mayor Daley joins in the celebration of Mexican Independence Day.

JANUARY

The bodies of the Grimes sisters—Barbara, 15, and Patricia, 13—are found on German Church Road near DuPage County, lying in a ditch next to a bridge. They had been missing 26 days and were last seen leaving a Southwest Side theater. No one has ever been charged.

FEBRUARY

Communist Party convention delegates vote to move their headquarters to Chicago. Mayor Daley says they're not welcome, and the party stays in New York.

New Trier High School grad Bruce Dern, later to become a movie actor, quits the University of Pennsylvania track team rather than shave his Elvis Presley-style sideburns.

MARCH

Robert Taylor, chairman of the Chicago Housing Authority from 1939 to 1950, dies of a heart attack at 56. Decades later, the complex named for him becomes one of the most crime-ridden CHA developments.

MAY

The Daily News wins a Pulitzer Prize for exposing fraud in the office of former state auditor Orville Hodge, who was slapped with a 10-year sentence for stealing state funds.

first come here in December 1955, found a job and housing and then returned to Guadalajara, Mexico, to bring his whole family back with him.

I was two months shy of my third birthday when we went from living in a city with one of the world's best climates to Chicago in the middle of winter. A cultural shock, to say the least.

We had left behind my parents' families, including our grandmother, whom I affectionately called "Chula," or pretty one. Two years later, we picked her up at Midway Airport to join the family. All of my parents' families—with the exception of an aunt—came to Chicago in the succeeding years. They came for the same reason all Mexicans did in the '50s—jobs.

I didn't know it at the time, but 1957 was also a memorable year for me, because in a little town in Mexico called San Miguel, Nayarit, my beautiful wife, Maria, was born.

We lived in a second-floor apartment at 1437 W. Taylor Street on the Near West Side. (The new National Italian Sports Hall of Fame is being built right next door to where I grew up.) There were Mexicans, Puerto Ricans and Italians living on my block. Near my house was a Chicago Housing Authority project consisting mainly of African Americans. Yet, there wasn't a lot of interaction.

One could get a few Mexican products in a couple of neighborhood stores, but when we wanted to load down

Parade festivities

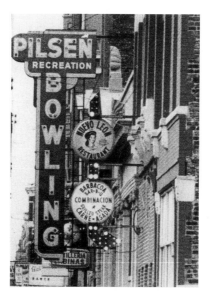

The Pilsen neighborhood is home to many of Chicago's Mexican Americans.

on Mexican staples like tortillas, cheese and pan dulce, we would go to 18th Street or *la dieciocho* in Pilsen.

Some of my earliest memories are of going to Mexican movies at a local theater called the Tampico, located on Roosevelt and Paulina. I remember seeing triple features that usually included a film starring Cantinflas (still the funniest person ever in movies), a "Santo" movie about a masked wrestler who did good deeds and then a soaper in which a disaster-stricken woman would finally live happily ever after.

My father, Rodolfo, a repairman for Hot Point Electrical Company, loved driving. On weekends we traveled all over the Chicago area, picnicking and visiting museums, the zoos and different Catholic churches. The two most popular churches frequented by Mexicans were St. Francis of Assisi on Roosevelt and Our Lady of Guadalupe in South Chicago. Both churches, although very small, still hold a special place in the hearts of most Chicago Mexicans.

As a kid sitting in front of the TV, I never imagined the day would come when 75 percent of the 1.1 million Latinos in the metropolitan area would be Mexicans, and that 25 percent of all children in the Chicago Public Schools would be Mexican. And some things never change. There are still hardly any Mexicans on TV today.

AUGUST

The dismembered body of Judith Mae Andersen, 15, is found between two oil drums in Montrose harbor. The Northwest Side teen disappeared on her way home from a friend's house. No one was ever charged.

NOVEMBER

The Illinois NAACP calls Chicago's public schools the most segregated of any major Northern city. The NAACP charges that new schools are being built in white areas with empty classrooms while South Side black schools are so overcrowded that children must attend school in shifts.

DECEMBER

The Old Town School of Folk Music opens at 909 W. Armitage, becoming the nation's first such school. With new headquarters at 4544 N. Lincoln, the Old Town School today has 3,000 students a week.

The Detroit Lions humiliate the Chicago Bears 59-14 to take the National Football League title.

ALSO IN 1957

Sam Cooke, reared on the South Side, cuts "You Send Me," the first of 29 Top 40 singles he wrote and recorded before he was shot to death seven years later, at age 33, in a seedy Los Angeles motel.

AND THE ANGELS WEPT

Phillip J. O'Connor

Retired reporter and rewriteman for the Chicago Daily News and later the Sun-Times

Spectators mingle with panic-stricken parents outside fire-wrecked Our Lady of the Angels Catholic School, a death trap for scores of children.

BY PHILLIP J. O'CONNOR

In 1958, a fire stunned the city and the nation.

Three nuns and 92 children were killed in the Dec. 1 blaze at Our Lady of the Angels Catholic School at 3810 W. Iowa, sending the city into mourning.

It was Chicago's deadliest fire since the 1903 Iroquois Theater blaze claimed 602 lives.

An injured student is comforted by a nun and a fireman.

Rosalie Lutzka, who was an eighth-grader in second-floor classroom No. 209, has vivid memories of the heat, dense smoke and children's screams.

"A day doesn't go by that I don't think of it," she said. "You wonder why you were spared. You wonder what could have been, if friends killed in the fire had grown up, married and had children.

Rosalie Lutzka survived the Our Lady of the Angels fire. She holds a photo of her 1959 class.

MARCH

At Chicago Stadium, Sugar Ray Robinson wins the middleweight boxing title for a record fifth time, defeating Carmen Basilio in a 15-round decision.

MAY

The U.S. Labor Department adds Chicago, along with New York and Cleveland, to the list of major labor centers with 6 percent or more unemployment.

JULY

In U.S. Senate hearings on labor racketeering, the attorney for the Chicago Restaurant Association takes the 1st, 5th, 6th and 16th amendments in refusing to talk about his activities.

Ernie Banks

SEPTEMBER

The Cubs' star shortstop, Ernie Banks, completes one of his greatest seasons, hitting 47 home runs, knocking in 129 runs and earning league MVP honors.

An Argonne National Laboratories report financed by the Atomic Energy Commission says experiments with mice show that current fallout levels from nuclear weapons tests could not produce leukemia or bone cancer.

"Some who survived had no physical scars, but they were scarred mentally. You don't forget. But you go on with your life," said Lutzka, of Streamwood, now married and the mother of two grown children.

Chicago's final streetcar—a Green Hornet

Lutzka, who escaped unhurt, said students in her class were among the first to discover the fire when the classroom suddenly became hot, and black smoke billowed under the door. "We were scared to death," she said.

Their teacher, Sister Davidas Devine, who suffered burns in the fire and was praised for her quick thinking, helped save all but two of her 62 eighth graders. The nun had students pile books against classroom doors to try to keep out smoke.

Then, most boys and some girls in 209 leaped to the top of a wood first-floor canopy, Lutzka said. A parish priest, the Rev. Joseph Ognibene, who suffered burns, and a neighbor, Sam Tortorice, teamed up to swing trapped students, including Lutzka, from a window in Room 209 to an adjoining classroom, where they exited safely, Lutzka said.

Dan Rostenkowski begins his long career in Congressional politics.

The cause of the fire was listed officially as unknown, but a number of investigators said it appeared to be arson. They theorized it was set in a trash can in a basement stairwell. The fire led to changes in building codes in Chicago and elsewhere.

Less somber was the passing in 1958 of the last streetcars. They were the so-called Green Hornets, sleekly styled and in green—a pronounced change from the old, red streetcars. Green Hornets were quiet, accelerated quickly and caused no pollution on the streets, since they ran on electric motors powered by overhead power lines.

The Green Hornets were later refashioned into L cars and spent years more in service before hitting retirement.

In politics that year, a young Dan Rostenkowski, the son of a Chicago politician, was first elected to Congress. He went on to become chairman of the House Ways and Means Committee, one of the most powerful in Congress. But in 1994, he was defeated for reelection by an unknown Republican while under indictment and was later convicted and imprisoned.

1958 was also the year Nathan F. Leopold Jr. was paroled in the 1924 thrill murder of 14-year-old Bobby Franks, which was committed by Leopold and another Chicago boy genius, Richard A. Loeb.

Chicago attorney Elmer Gertz, who won Leopold's parole, said the murderers "wanted to commit the perfect crime and thought they would get away with it."

Leopold was a law student at the University of Chicago, while Loeb, who had an IQ of 160, had graduated from the University of Michigan at the age of 17.

Gertz, who had Carl Sandburg testify as a character witness, convinced the parole board to allow Leopold to move to central Puerto Rico, where he worked in a religious hospital. He died there 12 years later. Loeb was fatally stabbed by another inmate several years after entering prison.

OCTOBER

Editors of the University of Chicago's literary quarterly, Chicago Review, are ordered not to print excerpts of William S. Burroughs' book *Naked Lunch*, with its raw sex, violence and drug talk. They create a new magazine, Big Table, which is banned from the U.S. mails when it runs the excerpts the following March.

NOVEMBER

Milwaukee Archbishop Albert G. Meyer becomes Roman Catholic archbishop of Chicago, succeeding the late Cardinal Samuel Stritch.

Chicago's oldest school

ALSO IN 1958

The play "A Raisin in the Sun" moves to Broadway after opening at Chicago's Blackstone Theater. Written by Chicago writer Lorraine Hansberry, it stars Sidney Poitier, Ruby Dee and Louis Gossett Jr.

Chicago's oldest school, Olea Thorpe, built in 1871 to serve the farm community at Addison and Narragansett, is torn down.

SECOND CITY SCORES A FIRST

The Second City
ESTABLISHED 1959

Bernard Sahlins
Co-founder of Second City, now an independent producer, director and writer

Early members of The Second City cast included (left to right) Eugene Troobnik, Barbara Harris, Alan Arkin, Paul Sand, Bill Mathieu, Mina Kolb, Severn Darden and Andrew Duncan.

BY BERNARD SAHLINS

It was Beethoven's 189th birthday on Dec. 16, 1959, when we opened Second City in a converted Chinese laundry on North Wells Street.

I figured no one would show up for the opening, but there were 200 people in the crowd that night. The audience couldn't stop laughing and applauding. And they kept on coming—although for a few months I thought some of the people just wanted to pick up their shirts.

Who would have thought that a group of out-of-work actors would become one of the great bastions of American comedy? When we opened, the Chicago theater

scene was almost at a standstill, except for touring shows that played big downtown houses like the Selwyn, Blackstone and the Shubert.

Of course there was the Gate of Horn, a counter-culture nightclub featuring folk singers and offbeat comedians.

But our unique feature was that we came from the theater and applied theatrical forms to popular entertainment. That is why a lot of the people who started the new theater movement here in the 1970s came to us for advice on survival.

Several of Second City's most famous alums: John Candy, Dan Aykroyd, Eugene Levy, Rosemary Radcliffe and Gilda Radner

---

FEBRUARY

The FCC orders that equal time on Chicago TV stations must be granted to mayoral candidate Lar "America First" Daly because Mayor Richard J. Daley had appeared in broadcasts greeting the Argentine president and opening the March of Dimes campaign. The ruling is set aside before Daley buries Daly in the Democratic primary by a record landslide, tallying 84.4 percent of the vote.

A U.S. Senate committee is told that Chicago juke-box owners pay mob-connected interests $100,000 a year "for peace." The testimony is that many owners switched distributors under the threat of picketing by a local electrical workers' union headed by Fred Thomas "Juke-Box Smitty" Smith.

Chicago's Soldier Field was the setting for the 1959 Pan-American Games.

APRIL

The head of the Bureau on Jewish Employment Problems charges that at least 1,484 Chicago firms bar Catholics, Jews and Protestants from office jobs.

We have been around 40 years, and our 300 alums have gone on to great careers. It is amazing how many have stayed in the business.

I'm talking about writer, director and actor Harold Ramis, actor and writer Tim Kazurinsky, director and actor Bonnie Hunt, Hollywood stars Peter Boyle, Alan Arkin and Robert Klein and actor-comedians Joan Rivers, Paul Sand and Barbara Harris. Then there is the "Saturday Night Live" crew: the late John Belushi and Gilda Radner, Bill Murray, Mike Myers, the late Chris Farley and Dan Aykroyd.

Avery Schreiber, Joan Rivers, Bill Alton and Del Close star in an early production at Second City.

It all began in Hyde Park in 1953, when a bunch of University of Chicago students such as Mike Nichols, Elaine May and Paul Sills began doing improvisational theater under the guidance of Sills' mother Viola Spolin.

Later, we regrouped as the Playwrights Theater Club at North Avenue and LaSalle and then as the Compass Players at various North Side holes in the wall. I was always the producer, Sills the director.

In 1959 someone suggested we start a coffee shop where we could just sit around. (After all, this was the beat era.) But Paul proposed having a little cabaret-like revue. So we kept trying to find a unifying theme for it.

It wasn't connecting. Finally, Mike Nichols, by then starting to be a success with Elaine on Broadway, came and said, "Get rid of the theme. Just do the scenes." So we did.

During that first show, we did a takeoff on Superman that was called Businessman. The cast that night was pianist Bill Mathieu and actors Howard Alk, Andrew Duncan, Eugene Troobnick, Barbara Harris, Mina Kolb and Severn Darden.

Director Sheldon Patinkin remembers we did a funny song about modern education and a spoof about WFMT radio with a guitarist who strummed poet William Blake's "Tyger, Tyger Burning Bright" like a mournful folk song.

We didn't acknowledge Beethoven's birthday, and—even though it would have been good material—didn't do anything on Fire Commissioner Robert J. Quinn frightening thousands with air raid sirens when the White Sox won the pennant.

Within four or five months, we were selling out every performance. Time magazine called us the "Temple of Satire." Still, we couldn't believe we were a success. One night there was an empty table in the house. Sills said, "That's the beginning of the end."

But it wasn't. We expanded to Canada and Detroit and started the syndicated "SCTV." Sheldon says we were the first comedy club at a time when standup comedians—such as Mort Sahl, Lenny Bruce, Bob Newhart and Woody Allen—were the kings. We did scenes rather than routines. Nobody wrote. We worked it out in rehearsal through improvisation. It was fun and always different.

1959 White Sox

JULY

In the first visit to Chicago by a reigning British sovereign, Queen Elizabeth tells a luncheon crowd the newly opened St. Lawrence Seaway will be a new bond between Britain, Canada and the Midwest.

Mayor Daley and Queen Elizabeth

OCTOBER

"The Untouchables" debuts on TV, starring Robert Stack as a treasury agent fighting Chicago mobsters. It gets great ratings over its four seasons, but is widely criticized for its violence.

ALSO IN 1959

Bill Veeck Jr. buys the White Sox and steers them to their first pennant in 40 years. To celebrate, Fire Commissioner Robert J. Quinn orders a five-minute sounding of the air raid sirens, and many frightened Chicagoans run to shelters. The Sox lose the World Series to the Los Angeles Dodgers.

THE ORIGINAL PLAYBOY

Hugh Hefner
Playboy magazine
founder

Even in the midst of the media storms that often surrounded his controversial Playboy magazine, publisher and editor-in-chief Hugh Hefner maintained an island of calm by working in solitude on the famous round bed in his private quarters at the Chicago Playboy Mansion.

BY HUGH HEFNER

The year 1960 was the start of a decade that would change America and the world.

It was a year of tremendous promise and optimism. It was a year of transition from postwar conservatism to new beginnings. The birth control pill arrived, and a handsome young president was about to move into the White House with his equally young and beautiful wife.

Television had become America's favorite form of entertainment in the 1950s. In the 1960s, it changed our world—electing a president and changing American attitudes on civil rights, segregation and a stupid little war in Southeast Asia.

I believed in the power of television and started using it to promote Playboy, hosting a syndicated show titled "Playboy's Penthouse" that first aired in January 1960 on Channel 7 at 11:30 p.m. on Saturday. Our local competition was Kup's "At Random" on Channel 2.

Our first show featured Playmates Joyce Nizzari and Eleanor Bradley, Lenny Bruce, composer Cy Coleman, author Rona Jaffe, the incomparable Ella Fitzgerald and Nat "King" Cole (another Chicago boy and a graduate of Wendell Phillips High School on the South Side).

Americans ushered in the most dynamic decade of the century by sending the youngest president ever, John F. Kennedy, and his glamorous first lady to the White House.

JANUARY

Dina Halpern

Chicago actress Dina Halpern founds the Chicago Yiddish Theater Association with a production of poet-dramatist I. Manger's "The Witch."

Chicagoans enjoy the world premiere of the movie "Scent of Mystery" featuring "Smell O Vision" which wafted different odors at the audience.

MARCH

Three Chicago women exploring the woods in the Starved Rock State Park are robbed and murdered by resort dishwasher Chester Weger, who is convicted and receives life in prison.

Chester Weger assists police in reenacting his crime at Starved Rock.

SEPTEMBER

At the WBBM-TV studios, presidential candidates Richard Nixon and John F. Kennedy engage in the first nationally televised presidential debate.

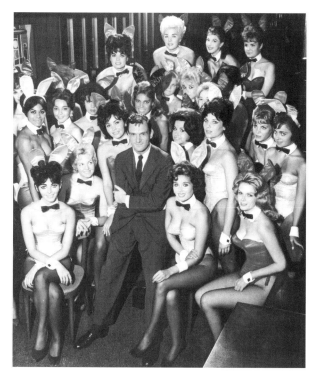

Hugh Hefner is surrounded by two dozen of the original Bunnies at the first Playboy Club in Chicago.

The appearance of black performers on "Playboy's Penthouse" in a social setting in what appeared to be my apartment assured no syndication in the still-segregated South, but it made me a hero on the South Side.

Playboy already was the most successful men's magazine in America, but it was also the most controversial. The show added to the controversy with its interracial entertainment and performers like Lenny Bruce.

Bruce got his first national exposure in the February 1959 issue of Playboy, but in 1960 he began having problems with authorities across the country.

Lenny Bruce

He was arrested for a performance at the Gate of Horn on the Near North Side in December 1962, and when I

came to his defense in an editorial series I'd started writing titled the "Playboy Philosophy," they arrested me as well. The supposed reason was a Jayne Mansfield pictorial in the June 1963 issue, but we had published similar pictorials in the past without incident.

My trial ended in a hung jury, and Jayne Mansfield's movie "Promises, Promises" opened in the Loop soon after. It was the beginning of the end of this sort of censorship in Chicago, although Lenny Bruce never lived to see it. He was convicted of obscenity in Chicago and New York and died before the convictions were over-turned on appeal. I always felt he died for our sins.

We opened the first Playboy Club in Chicago on Feb. 29, 1960, and even that was controversial. Authorities objected to the Bunny costume, and we had to go to court to get our liquor license.

It was the year I came out from behind my desk and started living the life espoused in the magazine—smoking the pipe, wearing the smoking jacket, driving a Mercedes Benz 300SL.

I moved into the original Playboy Mansion at 1340 N. State on the legendary Gold Coast that spring. It was my own Aladdin's Castle, a childhood memory from Riverview Park, with secret panels, an indoor swimming pool, an underwater bar, game room, bowling alley, a rotating, vibrating bed and gadgets galore—the sort that would have made James Bond proud.

We introduced Bond in the March 1960 issue, and the association between the magazine and Agent 007 would continue through the end of the century. The comparisons between Bond's life and mine seemed obvious, but his was fictional and mine very real—an adolescent's dream come true.

OCTOBER

The final segment of the $183.5 million Congress Expressway opens. Four years later, it is renamed for former president Dwight D. Eisenhower.

NOVEMBER

The McCormick Place Exposition Center opens. The $35 million lakefront building will be destroyed in a January 1967 fire, and a new black-steel design hall will open on the site in 1971.

Gov. William Stratton opens the $237 million Northwest Expressway, saying that the new expressway will save 50 lives a year by offering safer driving.

Presidential candidate JFK ends his whirlwind campaign with a giant street parade leading to a rally at Chicago Stadium. Kennedy narrowly beats Nixon, as Republicans charge that Mayor Daley used vote fraud to elect the first Irish-Catholic president.

John F. Kennedy

ALSO IN 1960

Expansion of the northwest-to-southwest runway at O'Hare Airport—from 8,838 to 11,600 feet—makes it one of the world's longest runways for commercial jet aircraft.

CUBA COMES TO CHICAGO

Maria de los Angeles Torres

Associate professor of political science at DePaul University and author of *In the Land of Mirrors: Cuban Exile Politics in the U.S.*

The Chicago area bids a warm welcome to a planeload of Cuban refugees arrriving at O'Hare Airport from Miami.

BY MARIA DE LOS ANGELES TORRES

On the night of April 16, 1961, Chicagoans celebrated the Blackhawks' first Stanley Cup victory in 23 years. In Havana, Cuba, that same night, my mother put my sister and me to sleep in the bathtub in case our house was bombed.

The next day, a U.S.-backed force of Cuban exiles tried to invade the island through the Bay of Pigs. Their defeat spurred a massive exodus of 14,000 children without their parents, myself included.

Our journey was part of a classified

Maria Bechily

government program known as Operation Pedro Pan. Spearheaded by the State Department, it gave a Catholic priest in Miami the extraordinary power to waive visas for children under 16.

As time passed, many of us who were living with foster families and relatives started to reclaim our parents. But for 8,000 of the children, the United States shut the doors on immigrants after the October Missile Crisis.

The federal government's massive relocation program reunited many Cuban families in Chicago.

MAY	JUNE	JULY	AUGUST
Chicago attorney Newton Minow, chairman of the Federal Communications Commission, in a speech to the National Association of Broadcasters, calls television "a vast wasteland."	Bill Veeck sells his White Sox holdings to a former business associate, Arthur Allyn Jr. In 1975, Veeck buys the team back, but later (1981) sells the team to a group headed by the current owners, Jerry Reinsdorf and Eddie Einhorn.	The month is marked by racial disturbances in which 65 blacks are arrested and accused of beating whites in retaliation for the unsolved fatal shooting of a 17-year-old African-American boy. Later in the month, 12 whites are arrested for refusing to disperse when close to 200 blacks attempt a wade-in at Rainbow beach. More than 200 police are on hand to keep the peace.	James Benton Parsons is appointed U.S. District Court judge by President John F. Kennedy, becoming the first African American to hold the post.

Maria Bechily, then 12, and her younger brother arrived in Chicago in the dead of winter and were placed in different foster homes. Bechily's first foster family did not speak Spanish. Eventually, she was placed with a Spanish-speaking family in Evanston, but she still wanted her parents.

The 1960-61 Blackhawks brought home Chicago's first Stanley Cup in 23 years.

important Cuban neighborhood, with the restaurant La Lechonera as its anchor.

But police corruption here paled in comparison to what the Cubans had left behind. Eventually, 45,000 Cubanos moved here. They settled first in the Lakeview area, where a local priest had pressured banks to give loans to Puerto Rican homebuyers, making it a friendly neighborhood for Cubans as well.

The first Cuban-American lobby was born, as Bechily and other kids began a letter-writing campaign to Sen. Paul Douglas and President John F. Kennedy. They succeeded. The United States agreed to let their parents emigrate on cargo ships used to deliver food and medicine in exchange for Bay of Pigs prisoners.

These mothers and fathers first arrived in Miami and then were shipped to their kids around the country. Many families wanted to remain in Miami, but locals there had grown leery of the large influx of refugees.

The federal government initiated a massive relocation program, with Chicago a key destination. Recruiters armed with photographs of the lakefront in summer tried to entice immigrants by suggesting similarities to Havana's Malecon. No one mentioned the marrow-chilling "hawk." So Cubans came.

But the ghosts of government abuse and corruption they knew on the island were to haunt them here. Headlines in 1961 blared the news that eight police officers of the Summerdale district had been convicted of helping Richard Morrison, the "babbling burglar," in a string of robberies.

The mayor brought in a new police superintendent, O.W. Wilson, to clean things up. And the city renamed Summerdale the Foster district, which became an

They also moved into Edgewater, where a special bus route was set up to take them to work at Motorola in Melrose Park, and later to the Logan Square area. Here, we developed Milwaukee Avenue's business strip with Arencibia's Jewelry Store and Elias Sanchez's Tania's restaurant, perhaps the first Cuban restaurant in the world to have a menu including both Cuban and Mexican food.

Later, Cubans moved westward to Albany Park. My Chicago-born husband was amazed when I took him to a New Year's Eve party at the Jose Marti Club de Leon on Lawrence and more than 70 of my relatives were there.

Many of the Pedro Pans made important contributions to the city's education, communications and social services. Maria Bechily would become a leading advocate for women and a champion of the arts.

Some of our parents, though, opted to return to much warmer and more Cuban Miami. Today there are an estimated 16,000 Cubans in Chicago, a small percentage of the burgeoning Latino community.

SEPTEMBER

WGN-Channel 9's "Bozo's Circus" begins its reign as the longest-running children's show on local television, with Bob Bell wearing the big shoes and the red nose. He was later replaced by Joey D'Auria, who still runs the popular show.

A TWA Constellation crashes into a field minutes after takeoff from Midway Airport, killing 78 persons aboard. The same month, 37 die when a Northwest Orient Airlines Electra II crashes and burns seconds after takeoff from O'Hare.

Henrici's restaurant at 67 West Randolph for 71 years is razed to make room for the Civic Center. It started as a German pastry shop with donuts as big as a plate made by baker Philip Henrici.

DECEMBER

Tow truck driver by day and blues man by night, Buddy Guy cuts his hit record "Stone Crazy" for Chicago's legendary Chess Records, which also recorded works by Muddy Waters, Chuck Berry and Koko Taylor.

Buddy Guy

ALSO IN 1961

A University of Chicago study leads to fluoridation of drinking water.

CAMPUS BORN OF CONFLICT

Ken Towers
Northwestern University Medill School of Journalism adjunct lecturer; former Sun-Times editor.

The ruins of famed Hull House were visible through a broken window pane in the Holy Guardian Angel School, which was also torn down to make way for the new UIC campus.

BY KEN TOWERS

Chicago in 1962 burnished its worldwide reputation for powerful—and controversial—architecture.

The federal government and the University of Illinois took the crucial steps to buy and clear land for a Chicago campus on the Near West Side, despite fierce opposition from residents of the heavily Italian neighborhood.

The victor was Mayor Richard J. Daley; the vanquished foe was Florence Scala, a longtime community activist, who led protests and sit-ins at City Hall until two black-powder bombs went off at her home.

The bombs did minor property damage, and no one was ever arrested. But Scala decided to call off the public protests and focus on court challenges, which ultimately proved unsuccessful.

"I'd do it again," Scala says today, explaining that she felt there were other suitable locations for the campus and that the mayor reneged on a promise to let the area around Harrison and Halsted prosper as a residential community.

"Daley wanted to build a monument to himself at any cost," she reflects.

Florence Scala

MARCH

Eli Schulman opens Eli's Stage Delicatessen, a popular Oak Street destination frequented by the likes of Barbra Streisand, Woody Allen, Joe E. Lewis, Henny Youngman and Bobby Short. The deli closed after a 1968 fire, but Schulman's Eli's Place for Steak lives on at 215 E. Chicago.

APRIL

Voters defeat Mayor Richard J. Daley's $66 million bond issue to finance urban renewal projects, new sewers, streetlights and other projects.

MAY

The Billy Graham crusade draws 55,000 to Soldier Field.

Soldier Field

JULY

Sixteen state policemen are suspended for allegedly taking bribes to allow overweight trucks to stay on the highways.

Mayor Daley won his fight against the Halsted-Harrison Community to build the new UIC campus.

Not many bother to take photos of the Robert Taylor Homes, the massive public housing development that came to life in a four-mile area around 47th and State in 1962. It bears the dubious distinction of being the nation's largest and most densely populated continuous segment of high-rise public housing.

This "warehousing" of low-income families is now viewed as misguided, and high-rises are being torn down at Robert Taylor and elsewhere in the CHA system.

That monument also revives troubling memories for Walter Netsch, its world-renowned chief architect.

Netsch says he and the university started out on the same page in creating structures to represent several disciplines—centering on a plaza inspired by classical Greek models. But later, the university went its own way and tore down the centerpiece plaza and its surrounding 200 columns.

"I don't go to that campus anymore," Netsch declares, although he admits that friends tell him he achieved his goal for a place of learning in an urban setting.

Convicted murderer Paul Crump and mob boss Tony Accardo both got lucky in 1962. Crump, photographed reading his Bible on Death Row, said he was rehabilitated and won the support of a vocal coalition seeking clemency. Gov. Otto Kerner, a foe of capital punishment, commuted Crump's sentence to 199 years.

Paul Crump

And Accardo, who boasted he never spent a night in jail, was acquitted on a charge of income tax evasion.

Also in 1962, tenants moved into Marina City, the first circular apartment towers in history, built on the Chicago River at State and Dearborn.

Marina City

The "city within a city" houses 896 apartments, a 16-story commercial and office building, a marina for 150 boats and restaurants and shops. It has become one of the most photographed structures of our time.

Meanwhile, times were good, as men checked out ads at the Fair Store for an $89 cashmere topcoat, and women could buy a Goddess bra for $3.95 at Field's. Downtown, such hit movies as "The Music Man," starring Robert Preston, and "Lolita," with James Mason and Shelley Winters, played.

For those who liked their entertainment live, Vic Damone and Keely Smith headlined at the Sahara on Mannheim Road, while Erroll Garner held forth at the London House, and Eartha Kitt was at Mister Kelly's.

AUGUST

City health commissioner Samuel Andelman assures worried Chicagoans that, while 29,000 tablets of the drug thalidomide—the cause of severe birth defects—have been distributed to physicians, none have been passed on to women of childbearing age.

SEPTEMBER

Averting a strike with the Chicago Symphony Orchestra, the Musician's Union signs a new three-year contract after bitter negotiations.

NOVEMBER

Republican Richard B. Ogilvie is elected sheriff of Cook County.

Chicago Patrolmen's Association demands the firing of Police Supt. O.W. Wilson, the California academic who took over the city's police force in the wake of the Summerdale police scandal.

Orville Hodge

DECEMBER

Gov. Otto Kerner commutes the 12- to 15-year prison sentence that former state auditor Orville Hodge received for stealing official funds, making him eligible for parole.

Welfare recipients are made eligible for birth-control information and prescriptions when the Illinois Public Aid Commission votes 6-4 to make such services available.

CIVIL RIGHTS MOVE CHICAGO

Don Rose
Political consultant

South Side protesters march around the portable classrooms known as "Willis Wagons."

BY DON ROSE

"End plantation politics!" declared Timuel D. Black, a teacher and civil rights leader, introducing the slogan that stayed a battle cry for two decades.

Black was leader of a coalition of seven independent Negro (as we said then) aldermanic candidates who, during the February 1963 election, shook the political establishment. They assailed both Mayor Richard J. Daley and the "Silent Six"—the incumbent black aldermen beholden to him—in announcing a joint platform to fight segregation and discrimination.

One independent actually won: Charlie Chew made history by trouncing the white

incumbent in a runoff in the majority black 17th Ward. His slogan: "A vote for Chew is a vote for you."

The election campaign was the first salvo fired against the Daley administration in the year the civil rights movement became a central force in the life of the city.

He felt its sting shortly after his reelection. The NAACP held its national meeting in the city. The night before Daley was scheduled to address the organization at a Grant Park rally, he

Timuel D. Black

JANUARY	FEBRUARY	MARCH	APRIL
Former state auditor Orville Hodge, convicted of stealing a million and a half dollars from the state treasury, is released from Menard prison after serving more than six years.	Ald. Benjamin F. Lewis (24th ward) is shot and killed in his office. The murder of an elected city official triggers one of the city's most intensive police investigations, but no one is ever charged.	Gov. Otto Kerner establishes a hold-the-line policy on tax increases and signs into law bills that plug many loopholes in the collection of state sales tax. President John F. Kennedy pays what proves to be his last visit to Chicago when he attends the dedication of O'Hare International Airport.	Dick Portillo begins selling classic Chicago hot dogs (Vienna all-beef natural-cased on steamed bun with mustard, onions, pickles, tomatoes, peppers and celery salt) out of a trailer in a Villa Park shopping center. By 1999, he had sold more Vienna hot dogs than anyone else in the area. Richard J. Daley wins a third term for mayor, even though he loses the white vote to Republican Benjamin Adamowski, former Cook County state's attorney.

Al Raby

A coalition of civil rights organizations, called the Coordinating Council of Community Organizations, was formed in 1962; in 1963 it grew from a dozen to nearly 40 groups. The CCCO, under Timuel Black's leadership, organized nearly 3,000 people who rode two "Freedom Trains" to Washington, D.C., to hear the Rev. Martin Luther King Jr. deliver his famous "I Have a Dream" speech Aug. 28.

When the school year began, Willis and Daley continued to deny there was segregation, let alone unequal education. The CCCO, now led by Al Raby, called a one-day school boycott. On "Freedom Day," Oct. 22, virtually every black student in the system stayed home. Thousands of protesters marched on City Hall. The administration acknowledged that a majority of students were black.

Within two years, the federal government shut off funds to Chicago schools. Daley's clout brought the money back, but he could not stop the federal courts from finding segregation and discrimination in the system.

delivered one of his most notorious gaffes: "There are no ghettos in Chicago!"

He never got to deliver his speech. He was booed off the platform.

That spring, as Sandburg Village housing complex was unveiled on North Side urban renewal land, a brushfire of sit-in demonstrations erupted at South Side schools in protest of portable classrooms. They were called "Willis Wagons," after School Superintendent Benjamin Willis, widely accused of perpetuating school segregation.

Parents of schoolchildren protest segregation and discrimination in Chicago's public schools.

John F. Kennedy was murdered that November, and the city went into mourning. But the year ended on a happy note for Chicago when the Bears won the NFL championship.

The civil rights movement brought King to Chicago in 1965; in 1983, with Raby as Harold Washington's campaign manager, it elected a mayor.

SEPTEMBER

Jacqueline Mayer becomes Northwestern University's first Miss America.

OCTOBER

Abraham Lincoln Marovitz is appointed to the U.S. District Court, where at the age of 94 in 1999, he was still serving as a senior judge.

NOVEMBER

Mayor Richard J. Daley bursts into tears and leaves for home after issuing an expression of his deep grief and sorrow over the tragic death of President John F. Kennedy. City Hall was draped in black, and on the Monday following the Nov. 22 assassination, all public offices and most businesses are closed in memory of the slain president.

Mob loan collector Leo Foreman is tortured to death and mutilated in the basement of Mario DeStefano's suburban Westchester home for reneging on a juice loan debt to Sam DeStefano. Ten years later, Mario DeStefano is convicted and receives 20 to 40 years in prison. Co-defendant Anthony Spilotro was acquitted.

ALSO IN 1963

Ground is broken for the Civic Center just east of the County Building.

LAST HURRAH FOR ARCHITECTURE

Lee Bey
Sun-Times
architecture critic

Chicago's architectural style
comes in all shapes and sizes,
reflecting both old and new,
oftentimes standing side by side.

BY LEE BEY

Chicago had two downtowns in 1964. One was an aged and fading urban core lined with ornate, 19th-century buildings. The other was an emerging new city outfitted in modernist steel-and-glass office towers and bold forms.

Most of Chicago's best postwar buildings were either built or in some stage of construction in 1964. Bertrand Goldberg's marvelous Marina City and Ludwig Mies van der Rohe's stellar Chicago Federal Center were taking shape then.

The new buildings represented a second Chicago School of architecture, with architects using the latest technology to

build a better building—just as Frank Lloyd Wright, Adler & Sullivan and Holabird & Root did 70 years earlier.

But 1964 is important because it represents both the apex and the last hurrah of Chicago's architectural dominance. The economic good times that are so important in the creation of topflight architecture ended abruptly when the economy worsened by the late 1960s and early 1970s.

"It was a very exciting time," retired Skidmore Owings & Merrill architect Hal

Gov. Otto Kerner presents Ludwig
Mies van der Rohe with an Order
of Lincoln ribbon and medal to
salute the architect's great
achievements.

JANUARY	MARCH	MAY	JUNE	JULY	SEPTEMBER
Chicago police find the mob's main weapons cache stored in a warehouse at 2101 S. Wabash	Police Supt. Orlando Wilson confirms a federal probe of allegations that cops took protection money from downtown "B-girl" clubs.	The Chicago Daily News offers a $10,000 reward for the return of a kidnapped baby.	Harold and Lillian Calhoun become the first African Americans to move to Kenilworth.	A Chicago jury convicts Teamsters president Jimmy Hoffa in a scheme to defraud $25 million from the Teamsters Pension Fund.	The Beatles debut in Chicago, receiving $30,000 for a 34-minute concert before 13,000 mostly screaming female fans. Paul, John, George and Ringo play 11 songs.

U.S. Gypsum Building

Iyengar said. "There has been no class of architecture built here since that approached it."

The late great U.S. Gypsum Building, 101 S. Wacker, was only a few months old in 1964. The Equitable Building, 401 N. Michigan, a riverside slice of Mies—although Mies didn't do it—was under construction. The Daley Center, built as the Chicago Civic Center, was nearing completion in 1964. The 31-story building was daring in 1964 because it was a municipal building—a courthouse, essentially—that looked and functioned like a modern office building. The Picasso statue only added to its cache.

At the same time the glass-and-steel courthouse was being erected, the Brunswick Building was going up

across the street at 69 W. Washington. Structurally, the building was a triumph. Instead of carrying weight on a steel skeleton—as the typical skyscraper did—the 38-story building's heft is carried by its concrete exterior and a massive concrete central core.

The effort was designed to make the building flexible and functional. There are no support columns to interrupt floor space. The Brunswick's exterior is simple and clean; an upward, screenlike sweep of windows above a glass lobby.

Amid the new architecture, there was growing concern for old buildings.

"People were still smarting over the demolition of [Sullivan-designed] Garrick Theater in 1964," said Timothy Samuelson, curator of architecture for the Chicago Historical Society. "Discussions were taking place on how to prevent something like that from happening again."

Sullivan's great Chicago Stock Exchange Building was still standing in 1964. So was the First Leiter Building at Wells and Monroe.

"In 1879 it was a building that had more glass than wall," Samuelson said of the building's design. "Then you'd go inside [in 1964] and there would be two old guys with a wind-up novelty toy business."

John Hancock Center was completed in 1969. By 1974, when the Sears Tower was completed, 1964 would be just a memory. With a worsened economy and fears over the city's future, Chicago began turning out more architectural clunkers than masterpieces. The good stuff often wound up in Asia and Europe—often put there by Chicago architects.

There was a bright spot. The newly formed Commission on Chicago Landmarks had full powers to designate landmarks and protect them from demolition. If Chicago could not turn out any more distinctive architecture, it at least had the good sense to keep what it had.

OCTOBER

The Dirksen Federal Building, designed by architect Ludwig Mies van der Rohe, opens on Dearborn between Adams and Jackson.

NOVEMBER

Gov. Otto Kerner holds off Charles Percy and retains the governorship.

DECEMBER

Chicago actress Mary Hartline, bandleader of WENR-TV's Super Circus Sunday afternoon variety show, marries millionaire Woolworth Donahue.

Mary Hartline

ALSO IN 1964

"My Kind of Town (Chicago Is)" is introduced by Frank Sinatra in the Oscar-nominated film "Robin and the Seven Hoods."

MARCHING FORWARD AND BACK

Rev. Martin E. Marty

Author, Lutheran minister and the Fairfax M. Cone Distinguished Service Professor Emeritus at the University of Chicago

Dr. Martin Luther King, Jr. (center) joins members of the Chicago clergy to protest racial segregation in Chicago's public schools.

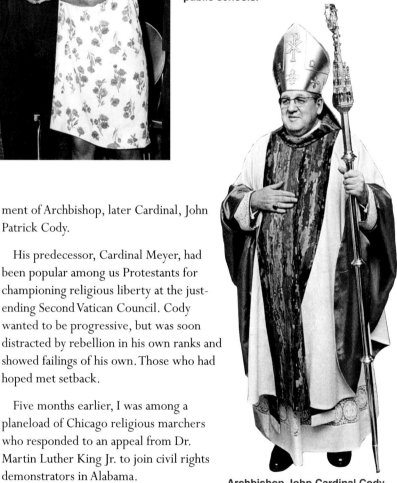

Archbishop John Cardinal Cody

BY REV. MARTIN E. MARTY

Many things, including the '60s and the nation, broke in two in 1965. Chicagoans and others who entered the year with hope ended it in disarray. Through it all, we marched....We marched forward. We were set back.

"Another Catholic march. I'm getting tired of those damn cathedral bells ringing your Lutheran tune, 'A Mighty Fortress Is Our God.'" The Episcopal church official who muttered that was kidding.

At the time, I was joining clergymen of all faiths for the ecumenical march into Holy Name Cathedral for the Aug. 24 enthrone-

ment of Archbishop, later Cardinal, John Patrick Cody.

His predecessor, Cardinal Meyer, had been popular among us Protestants for championing religious liberty at the just-ending Second Vatican Council. Cody wanted to be progressive, but was soon distracted by rebellion in his own ranks and showed failings of his own. Those who had hoped met setback.

Five months earlier, I was among a planeload of Chicago religious marchers who responded to an appeal from Dr. Martin Luther King Jr. to join civil rights demonstrators in Alabama.

Alabama state troopers stand on the steps of the state capitol in Montgomery as the protesters end their 54-mile march from Selma.

The call came in late afternoon, and within a couple of hours, we flew to Atlanta and rented cars for the journey to Selma. My colleague Dean Peerman and I, both staff members of the Chicago-based The Christian Century magazine, wrote about the March 9 event for the Sun-Times.

"A Great Day in Selma" was the headline for our account of the mile-long procession into the Dallas County seat in support of voter registration for African Americans.

School Superintendent Benjamin Willis was the target of Martin Luther King Jr.'s protests.

We cowards lined up at the end when participants assembled in Browns Chapel A.M.E. Church. But when the march began, the tail became the front, and so there I was in the front ranks.

Many of the bishops, seminary deans, eggheads, ministers and senators' wives, such as Emily Taft Douglas, wife of Paul Douglas, who marched found the first step difficult—not because of the prospect of 50 miles, but because of the implications.

Our ungainly group of freedom fighters quaked our way across the Edmund Pettus bridge over the Alabama River and stared Gov. George Wallace's battle-ready state troopers in the eye.

Both sides blinked. A federal judge barred us from going further, and our column was ordered to turn around and head back to the church.

That spring, Americans saw the most progressive legislation yet for civil rights, education, welfare and racial integration. But soon setback followed.

In July, King returned to Chicago to back demonstrators protesting the reappointment of public schools superintendent Benjamin C. Willis. The Christian Century covered speeches by religious leaders attacking Willis and Mayor Richard J. Daley for their "arrogant and stubborn refusal to deal adequately with racial segregation in Chicago schools."

Thousands showed up for King's "largest civil rights protest (yet) in Chicago history," but The Century observed that Chicago "dissipated King's coming as though it were a temporary entertainment … or a passing irritant."

The day after King left, the demonstrators could only rally about 100 people. A month later, in a dress rehearsal for long, hot summers to come and as a smaller encore to the very recent Watts upheavals in Los Angeles, many blacks turned from marching to rioting for two nights in West Garfield Park.

As President Johnson committed troops in Vietnam, America's youth also started rebelling. The forward lurches in church and state turned into stumbles, and hope waned. Neither Chicago nor America at large fully regained the spirit that had existed early in 1965—the year that broke in two.

JUNE	JULY	SEPTEMBER	NOVEMBER	ALSO IN 1965
Astronaut James McDivitt Jr., a West Side native and graduate of St. Mel's grammar school, is cheered during his walk in space with fellow astronaut Edward White.	**Adlai Stevenson II** Adlai Stevenson II, U.S. ambassador to the United Nations, former Illinois governor and two-time Democratic presidential candidate, dies in England.	Manny Skar, a front man for syndicate gambling operations in Chicago, is murdered on the Gold Coast as he is about to turn police informant. Ground is broken in Glencoe for Chicago Horticultural Society's Botanic Gardens—now 385 acres with 8,500 different kinds of plants.	Comedian Dick Gregory is fined $400 after his conviction by an all-white jury on disorderly conduct charges. Gregory had participated in a march near the home of Mayor Daley in which 40 persons were arrested. Marshall Field Jr., 49, editor and publisher of the Sun-Times, dies of acute congestive heart failure.	The Chicago Symphony Orchestra, for its 75th anniversary, commissions works from Gunther Schuller and Jean Martinon and performs world premieres of Stravinsky's Variations and T.S. Eliot in Memoriam.

Samuel Betances
Professor emeritus of sociology at Northeastern Illinois University

THE LONG, HOT SUMMER

Humboldt Park riots

BY SAMUEL BETANCES

Before the long, hot summer of 1966 ended, not only would Chicago's Puerto Rican community blow up, but jeering mobs would stone Martin Luther King Jr. It was also the summer that Richard Speck slaughtered eight student nurses.

There was other news that year: Richard B. Ogilvie became president of the Cook County Board. Republican business executive Charles H. Percy trounced Democratic U.S. Sen. Paul H. Douglas. And Benjamin C. Willis stepped

Valerie Percy

down after 13 tumultuous years as superintendent of Chicago's public schools.

But crime and violence dominated the times. An example: Percy's victory followed the murder of his daughter Valerie in the family's Kenilworth mansion.

At the beginning of the summer, the city was braced for confrontation between Dr. King and residents of the seething South Side and West Side ghettos who were seeking employment, housing and educational equality, but the first explosion came from an unexpected sector—the Puerto

Martin Luther King Jr. gets hit with a rock in Marquette Park.

Tootsie Roll
"Making the World Sweeter"

JANUARY

The Chicago Bulls are formed, and Johnny "Red" Kerr takes over as the team's first coach.

FEBRUARY

The Sweets Company of America changes its name to Tootsie Roll Industries, Inc., and moves from Hoboken, N.J., to Ford City Industrial Park on Chicago's Southwest Side.

MAY

A group of University of Chicago students takes over the administration building in a four-day sit-in to protest the school's cooperation with the Selective Service System's policy of basing draft deferment on class ranking. At Roosevelt University, 39 students are arrested for refusing to leave administration offices at closing time.

Chicago School Supt. Benjamin C. Willis announces his resignation, effective Aug. 31. He is replaced by James F. Redmond.

JULY

Dr. LeRoy A. Smith, a Cook County Hospital emergency room physician, calls the police after treating an unemployed seaman, Richard Benjamin Speck, for self-inflicted arm and wrist wounds. Dr. Smith also reported seeing a distinctive "born to raise hell" tattoo on the wanted man's upper left arm.

Rican community in the Humboldt Park area.

"Riots on Division Street," headlines screamed after successive nights of disturbance when angry crowds overturned police cars and set them afire.

The match that lit the fuse was the shooting of 20-year-old Puerto Rican Arcelis Cruz by a police officer. By the time order was restored two days later, 50 buildings had been destroyed, 16 persons injured, 49 arrested and millions of dollars in damages inflicted.

It was a time to remember, and I, then one of only four Puerto Rican college graduates on the city payroll, had been dispatched to the community in turmoil by Chicago's anti-poverty chief Dr. Deton J. Brooks. I joined religious and business leaders who gathered at the Latin American Boys Club on North Washtenaw to help solve the crisis.

The Puerto Rican community—the second-largest Hispanic group after Mexicans—was splintered through gerrymandering and had been denied a voice in the forums of official city leadership. No Puerto Rican held political office. None was an administrator with the Board of Education, and none held any prestigious position in the Police Department.

The riot changed that. In its aftermath, social service centers were established, such as Mirta Ramirez' Chicago branch of ASPIRA, Northeastern Illinois University's storefront El Centro and a city Urban Progress Center, which I headed.

Richard Speck

National Guardsmen patrol the streets of Chicago's West Side.

The next month, religious leaders including Archbishop John P. Cody attended Dr. King's peaceful equal rights rally in Soldier Field. But two days later, the West Side ignited after two youths were arrested for turning on a fire hydrant.

Over the next four days, two persons were killed, many injured and 300 arrested as pillaging crowds looted shops despite King's pleas to stop. In the end, National Guardsmen quelled the riot.

But as civil rights activists marched in white neighborhoods, tension increased. In Marquette Park, King was struck by a rock when 2,000 whites attacked the peaceful paraders.

The city obtained an injunction stopping the marches at the same time officials met with King in a summit meeting. The conclave spawned goals to end segregated housing patterns and the establishment of the Leadership Council for Metropolitan Open Communities.

Barely a month after the Puerto Rican riots, headlines reported the brutal eight murders by Speck, a slow-witted drifter with a "born to raise hell" tattoo on his arm. It could easily have been nine, but nurse Corazon Amurao managed to hide under a bed and live to identify the murderer.

It occurred to me then, as now, how no group of people can claim a monopoly on suffering. That season of anguish and consternation in 1966 can best be described as the summer of our city's discontent.

BREADBASKET AND BEYOND

Rev. Jesse Jackson

Founder and president of the Rainbow/PUSH Coalition

In the 1960s, the Rev. Jesse Jackson was a top deputy of Dr. Martin Luther King Jr., who assigned him to start Operation Breadbasket in Chicago.

BY REV. JESSE JACKSON

In 1967 there was a thirst for social and political change in Chicago. At the time, I was 26 years old and national economic director of the Southern Christian Leadership Conference. My mentor, Dr. Martin Luther King Jr., wanted me in Chicago to launch Operation Breadbasket, SCLC's economic social justice project.

I grew up in South Carolina, and knew Dr. King as a legendary figure who directed the successful Montgomery, Ala. bus boycott in 1955. Ten years later, when I was a student at the Chicago Theological Seminary, I joined my hero in Selma to march for the right to vote.

Because of Dr. King, an urge for liberation, dignity and a defiance toward oppression became part of my personality all through high school and into college. Because of him, I made the civil rights movement my career—my life.

As a CTS student, I lived in campus housing. Later, with my wife, Jacqueline, and then three children, Santita, Jesse Jr., and Jonathan, I lived in a rented apartment in a racially tolerant area of South Shore, which fortunately allowed me to avoid the ugly bigotry many blacks encountered in seeking suitable housing. But in my new position, I saw how racial segregation

---

JANUARY

McCormick Place, the city's new lakefront convention center, collapses under the intense heat of a spectacular blaze.

Alternating balmy and below-zero days are suddenly replaced by a massive snowstorm that smothers the city with 23 inches of snow in 26 hours and takes weeks to uncover.

APRIL

Sharon Percy, daughter of Illinois Sen. Charles H. Percy, marries John D. Rockefeller IV, great-grandson of the billionaire oil magnate. Her twin, Valerie, was murdered the previous year.

A jury took only 49 minutes to convict Richard Speck of stabbing and strangling eight student nurses. He received the death penalty, later changed to life imprisonment.

Mayor Richard J. Daley is reelected to a fourth term, winning 73 percent of the votes.

JUNE

When the Six Day War breaks out, Chicago-area Jews raise more than $7 million for Israel—$2.5 million of it in just one hour.

housing ordinance. Their criticism, along with the support of Dr. King, may have forced Daley to enforce a 1963 ordinance and to suspend the licenses of three real estate brokers for refusing to show homes in white neighborhoods to blacks.

Jesse Jackson (far right) joins Al Raby, Dr. King and Edwin C. Berry at the Civil Rights Summit meeting in Chicago.

At our weekly Saturday Breadbasket rallies at Friendship Baptist Church, the Parkway Ballroom and the Capital Theater, celebrities including Robert Culp, Bill Cosby and Nancy Wilson joined parents, children, teachers and supportive whites to discuss our pattern for a black economic revolution.

Through boycotts and negotiations, we brought jobs and additional income to many blacks and reached agreements with major food store chains and companies to stock and merchandise food products manufactured by black-owned companies.

confined African Americans to geographic "islands" on the West and South sides.

In late summer 1966, as a result of our open housing marches, a summit conference between Mayor Richard J. Daley and community and religious leaders led to the formation of the Leadership Council for Metropolitan Open Communities.

In 1967 the Council organized a public education program and campaign among whites for pledges to help African Americans find better housing.

Ironically, the effort was helped by the January 1967 snowstorm, as

A. A. "Sammy" Rayner and William Cousins

many whites, who would not allow blacks to live in their neighborhoods, found themselves stranded and having to seek help in black communities.

Open housing also enjoyed support that year from two newly elected black independent aldermen William Cousins (8th) and A. A. "Sammy" Rayner Jr. (6th), who tried to force the City Council to consider a stronger fair

Chicago, torn by racial violence in 1966 and 1968, had only a spate of upheaval in the summer of 1967, while Newark, Detroit and Cleveland were besieged by rioting in black ghettos.

Dr. King, in a 1967 speech at Friendship Baptist Church, blamed Congress for failing to enact legislation to eliminate the roots of this violence.

The battle was not to be won that year. The same divisive issues encouraged me to organize People United to Save Humanity (PUSH) in 1971, now the Rainbow/PUSH coalition.

African Americans have won practically everything we fought for—emancipation from slavery, laws to end segregation and the right to vote. But we still don't have all that we need. The legacy of 1967 is to strive for the final frontier—full economic inclusion.

AUGUST		SEPTEMBER	OCTOBER	DECEMBER	ALSO IN 1967
A 162-ton, 50-foot high abstract Cor-Ten steel sculpture by artist Pablo Picasso is unveiled on the plaza of the new Civic Center, "with the belief that what is strange to us today will be familiar tomorrow."		The Lyric Opera's season is canceled after the Company failed to reach a contract with its orchestra.	Riverview Amusement Park closes its doors after 63 years of allowing visitors to "laugh your troubles away."	Edward H. Levi is appointed president of the University of Chicago to replace George Beadle, who retired.	After being unused for 26 years, the Auditorium Theater has a red carpet reopening with the New York City Ballet company presenting "A Midsummer Night's Dream." Bob Crawford begins a 32-year run covering city hall and politics for WBBM-Radio.

CITY UNDER SIEGE

John Callaway
Retired host of
Channel 11's
Chicago Tonight

In one of the most dramatic convention-week pictures, photographer Paul Sequeira catches a police officer spraying mace into a crowd. Moments later, Sequeira also was maced.

BY JOHN CALLAWAY

As a human being, I wish 1968 had never happened.

As a journalist who directed the start-up of Chicago's first all-news radio operation at WBBM-CBS, and as a reporter who had a front seat to so many of that year's unforgettable, shocking and tragic events, it stands out as the most memorable year of my life.

So forgive me a first-person account of a year that deeply scarred Chicago, forever changed American politics and race relations and that played out before the backdrop of the continuing U.S. misadventure known as the Vietnam War.

The first bombshell hit on the evening of March 31 when President Lyndon B. Johnson announced that he would not run for re-election!

We hadn't totally absorbed that story when less than a week later, on April 4, the bulletin bells in the wire room summoned us to the sickening news that Martin Luther King Jr. had been shot in Memphis.

A view west into the Madison Street inferno

JANUARY	FEBRUARY	MARCH	JULY	OCTOBER
The Chicago Public Library declares an amnesty and 104,813 books are returned. The first kidney transplant in Illinois is performed at the University of Illinois Medical Center.	The Executives Club of Chicago gives Alabama Gov. George Wallace a standing ovation.	Four downtown Chicago department stores are hit by 12 different fires. Arson is suspected. Peace groups and flower children force the closing of a realistic Vietnam War exhibit at the Museum of Science and Industry.	The Chicago City Council passes a new open housing ordinance.	35,000 black students boycott classes every Monday because they feel the Chicago high schools are not responsive to black student concerns. Silent screen idol Ramon Novarro is murdered in Los Angeles by Chicago brothers Tom and Paul Ferguson, who wanted to find where he had hidden his fortune. The brothers were nabbed after calling Chicago to talk to a girlfriend. They were sentenced to life in prison.

Despite the harsh criticism Mayor Daley received for his handling of the events outside the convention hall, he enjoyed nearly unanimous support inside the hall.

For the next several days, I found myself crouched behind cars trying to capture the sounds of rioting, burning and looting on Chicago's West Side. Nine persons were killed, more than a thousand persons were left homeless and 2,500 were arrested.

Mayor Daley, unhappy with reports that his police had demonstrated restraint in handling the riots, then issued his infamous police order to shoot to kill arsonists and shoot to maim looters. It would not be a good year for hizzoner or for his city.

Robert F. Kennedy was assassinated on June 5 in Los Angeles.

Chicago felt so much under siege that by the time WBBM officially went all-news on May 6, our slogan was "Radio Free Chicago." Our hastily assembled new staff was quickly tested.

On the evening of June 5, shortly after he had declared victory in the California Democratic presidential primary, Robert F. Kennedy was shot in the head in Los Angeles. He died a day later.

Two Kennedy brothers were assassinated within five years of each other. Chicago and the nation wept as they watched that weekend's national television coverage of the funeral train making its way to Washington.

Then, in late August, came the Democratic National Convention in Chicago. The Yippies, led by Jerry Rubin and Abbie Hoffman, had threatened to hit town with more than 100,000 demonstrators. In fact, fewer than 10,000 mostly white, middle-class demonstrators took to the streets, where they encountered a like number of armed police and investigators.

Jerry Rubin (left) and Abbie Hoffman

I covered it all, from the ugly police beating of demonstrators and news reporters in Lincoln Park to the bloody, tear-gas encounter in front of the Conrad Hilton in Grant Park, where many policemen were hurt as they manhandled demonstrators into paddy wagons.

Much of it was televised to a "Whole world watching" and Chicago's Mayor Daley, who felt the demonstrations were an affront to his city and his political organization, was held in contempt by the national media.

Three facts that most people don't remember:

In the midst of all the violence and chaos, no one was killed.

It all happened in simply glorious, beautiful late-summer weather.

Most Americans approved of how Daley and his police handled the demonstrations, not to mention Chicagoans, who returned him to office by a landslide in the next election.

NOVEMBER

Democratic presidential candidate Hubert H. Humphrey comes to town for a torchlight parade on the Friday night before the election. Police brace for clashes that never occurred.

Republican Richard Ogilvie defeats Democrat Sam Shapiro for governor. Democrat Paul Simon is elected lieutenant governor.

DECEMBER

Two days after Christmas, a twin-engine plane from Minneapolis crashes into an O'Hare hangar, killing 27 and injuring 26.

John Hancock Building

ALSO IN 1968

John Hancock and First National Bank buildings are topped out.

Chicago has its first successful heart transplant.

Mitch Lee, creator of the Broadway musical "Man of La Mancha," writes the jingle, "Nobody Doesn't Like Sara Lee," which becomes the core of all ads for the Chicago-based company.

Gary Wisby
Sun-Times staff
reporter

TURMOIL IN THE STREETS AND COURTROOM

The trial of the Chicago Seven defendants (six of the seven are shown at left) set a new low for legal decorum and triggered the infamous "Days of Rage" street demonstrations. Former U.S. attorney Tom Foran described the trial as "vulgarity, threats, noise and foolishness."

BY GARY WISBY

Historians see the Chicago Seven trial as the biggest political trial of the tumultuous '60s.

But Tom Foran remembers it as "a little like getting a root canal every morning."

Foran, who was U.S. attorney when the trial began late in 1969, personally prosecuted a group of protesters charged with inciting riots at the Democratic National Convention a year earlier.

There were eight defendants at first, but boisterous Bobby Seale was first bound and

Judge Julius Hoffman

gagged and then removed from the courtroom to face a separate trial (which never occurred). And then there were seven: Abbie Hoffman, Jerry Rubin, Tom Hayden, David Dellinger, Rennie Davis, Lee Weiner and John Froines.

"They were a bunch of, in my opinion, bad people," Foran says. Disruption replaced decorum as the defendants moved their antics from street to courtroom, to the delight of the media and the distress of the judge and prosecution.

Former U.S. attorney Tom Foran

Hoffman, the clown prince of the proceedings, addressed federal Judge Julius Hoffman as "Julie" and one day strolled into court wearing judicial robes, which he stripped off, threw on the floor and stepped on.

"It was more than theater," Foran says. "It was vulgarity, threats, noise and foolishness."

The trial took four months, as defense attorney William Kunstler called to the stand a parade of witnesses that included Judy Collins, Allen Ginsberg, Arlo Guthrie, Timothy Leary, Norman Mailer, Pete Seeger, William Styron and Mayor Richard J. Daley.

The jury convicted all but Weiner and Froines, but ultimately all the riot charges and contempt-of-court jail sentences were dropped by higher courts or the government.

Though they escaped punishment, the Chicago Seven "didn't accomplish a thing," says Foran, 75, now a successful defense attorney.

John Schultz, a Columbia College professor and author of *The Chicago Conspiracy Trial,* couldn't disagree more. Juries in this and other political trials performed their classic function of "insulating citizens from the dangers of governmental oppression," Schultz says.

Case after case against antiwar and civil rights protesters ended in not-guilty verdicts or hung juries. Schultz says his investigation showed the Chicago Seven jury would have been hung, too, if the judge hadn't told jurors through his marshals, "The judge can keep you here as long as he wants."

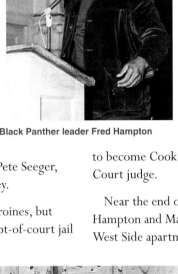
Black Panther leader Fred Hampton

During the trial's first week, a group known as the Weathermen engaged in violent street demonstrations in what they called "The Days of Rage." One day an assistant corporation counsel named Richard J. Elrod was on Madison near Clark when he saw police chasing a protester and yelling, "Stop him!"

"Unfortunately, I did," says Elrod, now 65. He tackled the man, suffered a broken neck and has walked with the aid of canes ever since. Elrod went on to become Cook County sheriff and is now a Circuit Court judge.

Near the end of 1969, Black Panther leaders Fred Hampton and Mark Clark were gunned down at their West Side apartment in a predawn police raid. The Chicago Tribune printed police photos purporting to show holes from bullets fired at the cops.

A tipster told Chicago Sun-Times editor Jim Hoge he should check it out, says Joe Reilly, 60, who was then a general assignment reporter. "Hoge went to the city editor and said, 'Who's free?', and I wasn't doing anything."

With photographer Bob Kotalik, Hoge and Reilly went to the scene and discovered the "bullet holes" were unplastered nail heads.

Hampton and Clark had died in their beds. The Sun-Times' front-page headline next morning blared, "Those 'bullet holes' aren't." And Reilly—later metropolitan editor of the paper and editor of the City News Bureau—had one of his best bylines.

Sun-Times reporter Joseph Reilly examines the so-called "bullet holes."

CARVING A NEW CONSTITUTION

Dawn Clark Netsch

Professor emeritus at Northwestern University Law School

Illinois' top news stories of 1970 involved the state's Constitutional Convention, the emergence on the national political scene of another Stevenson and a shoe box full of money.

BY DAWN CLARK NETSCH

The most dramatic stories of 1970 were not exclusively ours in Chicago.

The near-catastrophic flight of Apollo 13 grabbed headlines, as did the continuing fallout from our engagement in Vietnam and Cambodia.

The protests culminated in the tragic deaths of students at Kent State and Jackson State. And Illinois was not immune from disorders.

Part of the fallout from the anti-war demonstrations at the 1968 Democratic Convention in Chicago—the long and contentious trial of the so-called Chicago

Seven before U.S. District Judge Julius Hoffman—ended in February in a patchwork of guilty verdicts. Not one of the defendants actually served time.

Not nearly as dramatic, but actually quite important to Chicago and the entire state, was the 1970 Constitutional Convention, for which I was one of the delegates. I was vice chair of the committee that redrew the state's revenue and finance responsibilities.

The convention was preceded and prompted by decades of frustration among civic groups at the inability to amend the 1870 constitution to provide more flexibility to meet changed conditions. It was the

Adlai Stevenson III

Daley greets Pompidou

Richard M. Daley   **Michael Madigan**

year the state finally freed itself from the straitjacket of a state constitution which reflected 19th-century Illinois.

This meant that after nine months of intensive deliberations by 116 nonpartisan delegates, voters approved a new constitution on December 15, 1970, with Chicago and suburban Cook County providing the major part of the support. Without Mayor Richard J. Daley's blessing—which was in doubt until shortly before the referendum—the constitution would have failed, the fate suffered by constitutional reform elsewhere.

Of particular importance to Chicago (and likely the deciding factor in the mayor's support) was a broad grant of home-rule power that released Chicago from dependence on downstate legislators to address its big-city issues.

Secretary of State Paul Powell

For example, Police Supt. O.W. Wilson, who was brought in to clean up the latest in recurring police scandals (the Summerdale police burglaries), wanted to use revolving blue—instead of red lights—on police cars. Before the new constitution, however, he couldn't do that until legislation was passed in Springfield.

The new constitution also legalized the long-standing practice in Cook County of classifying the property tax to favor homeowners—another critical ingredient in Daley's support.

It also modernized the operation of state government in many ways and included the strongest bill of rights of any state in the country, including a mini-Equal Rights Amendment.

Con-Con served another unscheduled function: it was a testing ground for two young delegates who later became the major Democratic political powers in Illinois— Richard M. Daley and Michael Madigan.

Chicagoans feast on politics, and there was ample nourishment in 1970. The elder Daley began his 16th year in office, announced he was running for a fifth term and put down a rebellion in African-American Democratic ranks by electing his candidate, Ald. Ralph Metcalfe, over Ald. Sammy Rayner to succeed Rep. William Dawson in the U.S. House.

Adlai Stevenson was elected to the U.S. Senate, defeating Ralph Smith, despite combined charges of Smith and Vice President Spiro Agnew that Stevenson was a "radical liberal." And, oh yes, following the death of one of Illinois' most colorful politicians, Secretary of State Paul Powell, shoe boxes were found in his Springfield apartment stuffed with some $800,000 in cash.

JULY

Kumba is the first gorilla born at Lincoln Park Zoo, and in 1978 she became the first female gorilla born in captivity to give birth.

SEPTEMBER

Ziggy the Elephant, who was confined to an indoor stall at Brookfield Zoo since a 1941 attack on keeper Slim Lewis, is freed after a public crusade. On September 23, Lewis led a reluctant Ziggy into the yard to enjoy the sun. After 40 minutes, the pachyderm turned around and went back inside.

OCTOBER

Former Illinois Secretary of State Paul Powell dies leaving shoe boxes full of more than $750,000 in cash in his Springfield hotel room.

NOVEMBER

Mourners attend the funeral of U.S. Rep. William Dawson. Gospel singer Mahalia Jackson sang and Mayor Richard J. Daley gave the eulogy for the prominent South Side African American.

Adlai E. Stevenson III is easily elected to serve out the remaining four years of the Senate seat of the late Everett McKinley Dirksen.

ALSO IN 1970

Folk singer Steve Goodman, a regular performer at the Earl of Old Town club, writes the song "City of New Orleans."

The 1,127-foot John Hancock Building opens.

Victor Aitay
Concert Master
Emeritus of the
Chicago Symphony
Orchestra

SYMPHONIC SUPERHEROES

In a celebration usually reserved for celebrities and sports figures, Chicago honored its musical heroes with a ticker-tape parade when the Chicago Symphony Orchestra returned from its first-ever European trip.

BY VICTOR AITAY

There have been ticker-tape parades in Chicago for astronauts, politicians and sports heroes.

But in October 1971, it was the Chicago Symphony Orchestra returning from our first European tour that drew thousands of cheering fans to watch us ride down State Street in a large trailer.

"This is wonderful and about time," I remember thinking as we moved towards Orchestra Hall and a welcoming luncheon. "Now, everybody recognizes we have the best symphony orchestra in the world."

For five weeks the orchestra led by music director Georg Solti and principal guest conductor Carlo Maria Giulini performed 25 concerts in nine countries and then spent another week recording Gustav Mahler's "Eighth Symphony" in Vienna.

Dignitaries and royalty attended many concerts. The applause was thundering, and the foreign reviews were almost all sensational. Sun-Times music critic Robert C. Marsh accompanied us and reported from London that the audience at our concert "went wild in a manner that rather disproves the myth of the unemotional Briton."

Sir Georg Solti

JANUARY

Chicago teachers end a week-long strike, agreeing to a two-year contract that makes them the highest-paid teachers of any large city in the nation.

U.S. Steel agrees to accept a court-ordered timetable to quit discharging toxic wastes into Lake Michigan.

MARCH

Workmen begin digging the foundation for the new Sears, Roebuck & Co. headquarters in a one-block section of Quincy Street between Wacker and Franklin. The architectural firm of Skidmore, Owings & Merrill was chosen to build what would be for many years the world's tallest building at 1,450 feet.

APRIL

Mayor Daley is elected to his fifth term with 70 percent of the vote.

MAY

Three Chicago policemen are shot and wounded by riflemen from a building used by the Black Panthers.

JULY

Some 150 police remove 100 Native Americans from an abandoned missile site they were occupying on Lake Michigan in protest of a lack of housing in the city.

Maestro Georg Solti (right) is joined by Louis Sudler (left) and Henry Mazer as thousands of Chicagoans cheer the symphony's triumphant return from Europe.

On our return here, even city officials acknowledged the significance of the tour. Mayor Richard J. Daley and the City Council awarded us with Certificates of Merit.

It was grueling traveling to so many cities—Paris, Berlin, Milan, Edinburgh, Brussels, Helsinki, Goteburg, Stockholm, Frankfurt, Hamburg, Munich, Hanover, London and Vienna. There were 130 of us, including wives, orchestra board members and staff, plus about 30,000 pounds of baggage.

But the physical strain was erased by the joyful receptions. When we were not rehearsing or performing, we would sightsee, have reunions with old friends and enjoy the European cuisine.

My wife, Eva, and I spent many of these non-performance hours in the company of Maestro Solti and his wife, Valerie, taking walks or playing bridge.

Georg and I were fellow Hungarians. We are both from Budapest, attended the same

school—the Franz Liszt Academy—and had many of the same teachers, even though he was several years ahead of me.

I was studying violin, and he was a pianist, but I knew of him. During the war, he was in Switzerland. I was in a labor camp, but escaped twice and was recaptured. On my third try, disguised as a priest, I made it back to Budapest, where I was taken into safety at the Swedish Embassy by Raoul Wallenberg.

I came to know Solti after the War. Our friendship really began after I joined the CSO in 1954, and he came to conduct at Ravinia.

We had great music directors before, such as Fritz Reiner, who imposed discipline on the orchestra. But Solti generated the excitement and brought international respect to us. He knew the orchestra needed foreign tours to build up its reputation, and he was right.

After 1971, the Chicago Symphony became a veritable national treasure. The whole world discovered there is something else besides Al Capone in Chicago. And it was all Solti's idea. He knew this was a gem of an orchestra. And I mark 1971 as the year when it all started happening.

Victor Aitay, Valerie Solti, Georg Solti and Eva Aitay enjoy their free time during the Symphony's European tour.

AUGUST

Fourteen law enforcement officials, including State's Attorney Edward Hanrahan, are charged with conspiring to obstruct justice in connection with a police raid on the Black Panthers.

Mike Royko publishes his book *Boss: Richard J. Daley of Chicago*, an account of big-city machine politics.

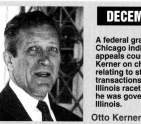

DECEMBER

A federal grand jury in Chicago indicts federal appeals court Judge Otto Kerner on charges relating to stock transactions involving Illinois racetracks while he was governor of Illinois.

Otto Kerner

ALSO IN 1971

Sylvester "Two-gun Pete" Washington, the deadliest cop in Chicago, who claimed to have killed 16 men and made 20,000 arrests in 18 years, dies at 65 of natural causes.

Woodfield Mall, then the world's largest shopping mall, opens in Schaumburg.

1972

MANGLED WRECKAGE

Wally Phillips
Former anchor of WGN-AM morning show, now host of Saturday morning program on WAIT-AM

Rescuers work to free victims after an Illinois Central commuter train rammed into the rear of another Loopbound train at the 27th Street station.

BY WALLY PHILLIPS

I've taken some unusual telephone calls in my years as a radio broadcaster.

But I'll never forget the man who called WGN-AM early Oct. 30, 1972, with the first news of Chicago's worst train disaster. His voice on the telephone and over the air quivered with emotion.

"Oh, it's so awful! I can't...I mean it just happened. It's...Oh God!" he exclaimed to a background of sirens and screaming.

Throughout my morning show, we listened to reports as rescuers tried to retrieve the injured and the dead from the mangled wreckage. Our hearts were particularly captivated by the ordeal of two 17-year-old girls, Lisa Tuttle and Patricia Wysmierski.

They were riding on an Illinois Central Railroad express commuter train on their way to part-time jobs downtown. As they approached the 27th Street station, the two friends had no idea that just minutes before, a local commuter train equipped with a new type of brake had overshot the station and then backed up to discharge passengers.

Lisa Tuttle is rushed to a waiting helicopter that ferried her to Billings Hospital.

JANUARY
An AWOL Army private who doubled as a psychologist is indicted for allegedly placing bombs in safe deposit boxes at eight branch banks in Chicago, San Francisco and New York.

MAY
Chicago Daily News columnist Mike Royko wins a Pulitzer Prize. Royko was selected for his humor and for taking the side of the underdog fighting the complexities of modern life.

Mike Royko

JULY
The city is shocked by the beating death of 7-year-old Johnny Lindquist. His parents are charged with slamming the boy's head into a door, prodding a broomstick into his back to force him to kneel, throwing him on the floor and beating him with a metal-lined leather belt.

OCTOBER
Cook County State's Attorney Edward V. Hanrahan is acquitted of conspiring to obstruct justice stemming from a controversial raid by his police on a Black Panther apartment in 1969. But Hanrahan was defeated in his bid for reelection by Republican Bernard Carey.

The crash of a United 737 engulfed the sky with smoke and flames and killed 45.

Their train slammed into the rear of the double-deck first train with a massive impact. Within seconds, 45 of Lisa and Pat's fellow passengers were crushed, and dozens more, including themselves, were trapped in the mangled wreckage for six hours.

Lisa and Pat, who lay side by side under twisted steel while being given morphine injections to dull their pain, were the last two victims extricated. Lisa's legs were both broken and Pat's left ankle crushed.

In the months to come, we followed their progress and medical treatment. I would frequently call them on the air to wish them well and even had them on the program many times in later years.

Dan Walker

The train crash wasn't the only transportation disaster that year. On Dec. 8, a United Airline Boeing 737 preparing for a stopover at Midway Airport slammed into a Southwest Side neighborhood and killed 45 people.

One of the victims was E. Howard Hunt's wife, Dorothy. She died with $10,000 cash in her purse, which was presumed to be Watergate hush money, but the hushee was never identified.

Then, on Dec. 21, a North Central Airlines plane departing O'Hare struck a taxiing Delta Air Lines craft, killing 10 people and injuring 15.

Also in 1972, Police Superintendent James Conlisk demoted two officers and suspended a captain and eight patrolmen for refusing to answer a grand jury's questions. Later, 40 officers were indicted for shaking down tavern owners, as a result of an investigation conducted by then-U.S. Attorney James Thompson and the Justice Department.

That same year, a group led by Alderman William Singer bumped Mayor Richard J. Daley and 58 others from the Democratic National Convention in Miami, and the aptly named Dan Walker hiked his way to the governor's mansion in Springfield.

And a promising young lawyer named Richard M. Daley married Margaret Ann Corbett. The bride wore ivory chiffon. The groom wore visions of a sojourn in paternal footsteps.

On the sports front, the Cubs, the White Sox and Blackhawks remained mired in mediocrity, St. Michael had not arrived yet to restore the Bulls, and the Bears were 14 years away from Super Bowl euphoria. But a ticket to watch them cost only $7. A dinner for two at Don Roth's Blackhawk restaurant, including wine, was $19. A Big Mac was 55 cents and a first-class stamp was 8 cents.

Come back, 1972. Some is forgiven.

OCTOBER

Hillside patrol officer Anthony Raymond is abducted and slain after stopping a car containing three men who had just robbed a restaurant of $5,000. Raymond was forced into the getaway car with a gun, then strangled with a guitar string. Silas Fletcher received 100 to 200 years in prison for the murder and a partner got up to 100 years. A third defendant was found shot to death before trial.

NOVEMBER

A U.S. appeals court voided the convictions of Chicago Seven defendants Abbie Hoffman, Tom Hayden and Jerry Rubin.

DECEMBER

Operation PUSH, an offshoot of the Southern Christian Leadership Conference, hosts the fourth annual Black Expo in Chicago. PUSH leader Jesse Jackson said the group's boycotts had obtained more than $100 million in concessions from major corporations and banks in the form of hiring and promotion, deposits in black banks and contracts with black supporters.

ALSO IN 1972

Eight Chicago area murders are attributed to a terrorist gang known as the "De Mau Mau." The murders include the Paul Corbett family of Barrington Hills, the Stephen D. Hawtree family of Monee and William Richter, a soldier on leave who was sleeping in his pickup truck on the Edens Expressway in Highland Park.

Leon M. Despres

A member of the
Chicago City
Council for 20 years

CRACKS IN THE DALEY MACHINE

Despite trouble
brewing in his
organization, Mayor
Daley was all smiles
as he welcomed four
new aldermen to the
City Council. From left
are John Madrzyk, Tim
Evans, Mayor Daley,
Tom Cullerton and
Gerald Jones.

BY LEON M. DESPRES

1973 promised to be a great year for Chicago.

Peace came in Vietnam, and the Sears Tower opened on Wacker Drive as the world's tallest building (for the next 23 years).

Faithful aldermen persistently praised the administration of Mayor Richard J. Daley, who had been in office for 18 years.

"You're the greatest mayor on earth," thundered Ald. Claude Holman in the City Council, adding "and in outer space too."

The mayor never ruled praise out of order.

Then, some cracks began developing in the great Daley organization. The federal Shakman decisions against patronage hiring and firing began to threaten the precinct worker army. And the press disclosed that the mayor had personally diverted city insurance business to his son's firm.

In March, the mayor lost his temper explosively and protractedly at a televised City Council meeting. Ald. Dick Simpson had contended that the mayor's appointment of an alderman's son to a city board was nepotism.

The mayor took offense. "I apologize for nothing," he shouted. "What's a father for?"

The Sears Tower opened on
Wacker Drive as the world's
tallest building.

JANUARY

Lynn Baer gives birth to quintuplets, three girls and two boys, at Highland Park Hospital on Jan. 5. "I lost track at about number three. When they [doctors] said, "My God, there's another one,' I knew we had more than the twins we were banking on."

Baer
quints

FEBRUARY

The U.S. Supreme Court upholds an Illinois law allowing taxation of personal property of corporations, but not individuals.

MARCH

U.S. Supreme Court upholds, 6-3, the Illinois tax on aviation fuel loaded on commercial jetliners within the state.

The Chicago Symphony's recording of Mahler's 8th Symphony in E Flat Major wins best classical album in the 15th annual Grammy awards.

Cook County clerk Edward J. Barrett is convicted of taking $180,000 in kickbacks from a voting machine company.

Just a year before his conviction, former Governor Otto Kerner testified before the U.S. Senate as chairman of the President's Commission on Civil Disorder.

He went on to make a public bid for his critics to kiss his "mistletoe," a term understood to refer to his posterior.

The year brought other calamities. Otto Kerner, who had been the Democratic organization's ornament as governor, was convicted of improperly receiving racetrack stock. Former Illinois revenue director Theodore J. Isaacs also was convicted in the scandal. Former county clerk Edward J. Barrett was convicted of taking bribes in connection with the purchase of voting machines.

Other politicians who did not think 1973 was a very good year were former

Melvyn Zahn hugs his wife, Judith, after escaping from his kidnappers.

aldermen Casimir J. Staszcuk, Joseph Potempa, Joseph Jambrone and Fred Hubbard. Their federal prosecutor, Jim Thompson, looked like a clear Republican win as the next governor!

Ald. Thomas Keane, the City Council floor leader on whom the mayor relied to control the aldermen, was acquitted on conflict-of-interest charges but indicted (and later convicted) in another case.

Worst of all, U.S. Rep. Ralph Metcalfe, a pillar of the organization, defected. Metcalfe could no longer tolerate administration indifference toward police mistreatment of African Americans.

He broke with the organization. This was a seismic shock. Metcalfe became a standard-bearer for protest. Later, when Daley decided to punish Metcalfe by running a blue-ribbon candidate against him and ousting him from Congress, Metcalfe got 85 percent of the vote and became stronger than ever.

As in every year in Chicago, 1973 brought innumerable extraordinary events. Melvyn Zahn, the 34-year-old president of Louis Zahn Drug company, was kidnapped and escaped after being held for $1.5 million ransom.

A little-noticed 1973 event was the presence in the General Assembly of a Chicago Democratic legislator named Harold Washington who was pursuing independent legislative programs without organization blessing.

Ten years later, he was mayor of Chicago.

MARCH	APRIL	MAY	AUGUST	OCTOBER	NOVEMBER
The Justice Department sues Chicago, charging that it discriminates against blacks and Hispanics in the hiring and promoting of firemen. In August, it alleges discrimination in the city's hiring of police officers.	Former Gov. Otto G. Kerner is sentenced to three years in prison for conspiracy, fraud, perjury, bribery and income tax evasion in connection with the sale of racetrack stock.	The Sears Tower tops out at 1,468 feet and 110 stories—it will be the world's tallest building until 1996. An explosion in a Southwest Side ink factory triggers an eight-block fire, the largest since a 1934 stock yards blaze, and does $50 million in damage.	Gov. Walker signs a bill outlawing the sale of cheap handguns in Illinois.	The Illinois Supreme Court rules unconstitutional two state programs that provide aid to low-income families sending their children to Catholic school. Police Supt. James B. Conlisk resigns after 35 police officers are convicted of shaking down nightclubs and bars.	The U.S. Supreme Court throws out an Illinois law barring people from switching parties from one primary to the next.

CHICAGO'S OUTDOOR MUSEUM

Michael L. Lash
Director of Public
Art for the City of
Chicago

**Alexander Calder at the
dedication ceremony of
his "Flamingo" in the
Federal Building Plaza**

BY MICHAEL L. LASH

At the September 27, 1974 unveiling of Marc Chagall's mosaic sculpture in the First National Bank Plaza, Mayor Richard J. Daley thanked the artist. As he returned to his chair, the usually composed mayor was startled to receive a thank-you of his own— a kiss from 87-year-old Marc Chagall.

Chagall had arrived in Chicago several weeks earlier from his studio in France to oversee final details of this massive five-sided mosaic, which depicts the changing seasons of Chicago. "The Four Seasons" was a gift to the city from the artist and his devoted friends, Chicago philanthropists William and Eleanor Wood Prince.

Chagall meticulously designed the 70-foot-long mosaic of countless thousands of tiles, which were then assembled by two assistants, shrouded beneath a protective canopy in the Dearborn Street plaza.

A month after Chagall was here, another of the 20th century's best-known artists— Alexander Calder—arrived at the Federal Center Plaza atop a white-and-gold circus wagon drawn by 40 horses to dedicate his bright red "Flamingo," a 35-ton steel sculpture.

"The Loop is now one of the world's largest outdoor museums for contemporary

**The 100-foot Batcolumn
sculpture by Claes Oldenburg
was commissioned by the
General Service
Administration's Art in
Architecture program.**

FEBRUARY	MARCH	APRIL	MAY
The U.S. Supreme Court declines to review lower court rulings allowing the Black Panther Party to sue Chicago and Cook County for damages arising out of the 1969 police raid on an apartment where two party members were killed. In a year when more than 70 current or former Chicago police officers are indicted or convicted, new police Supt. James Rochford shifts his top command personnel.	President Nixon, in a televised speech before the Chicago Executives Club, concedes that Watergate "has had a disturbing effect" on his administration, but stresses that he is determined not to resign.	The Chicago Sun-Times' Art Petacque and Hugh Hough win a Pulitzer Prize for uncovering evidence that led to a reopening of the case surrounding the murder of Illinois Sen. Charles Percy's daughter. Thousands of South Side residents are forced from their homes after a giant cloud of hydrochloric acid forms over the area, the result of a leak in a chemical storage tank.	Mayor Richard J. Daley suffers a mild stroke and undergoes surgery on his carotid artery. Wheaton native Bob Woodward and his Washington Post colleague Carl Bernstein sell the paperback rights to their book on Watergate, *All the President's Men*, for $1 million.

art," beamed Daley, releasing hundreds of celebratory balloons.

The Chagall and Calder works joined Pablo Picasso's huge Cor-Ten steel 1967 "Untitled" sculpture in what is now the Richard J. Daley Center. The Picassso launched an outdoor art Renaissance that had earlier seen such masterpieces as the 1893 Art Institute bronze lions by Edward Kemys, the 1897 Augustus Saint Gaudens statue of Gen. John Logan and the 1930 "Ceres" atop the Board of Trade Building.

The Picasso was followed by outdoor works including:

Henry Bertoia's 1975 metal sculpture on the side of the Amoco Building.

Joan Miro's 1981 "Chicago" at Brunswick Plaza.

Louise Nevelson's 30-foot steel 1983 sculpture, "Dawn Shadows," at 200 W. Madison.

Jean Dubuffet's 1989 "Monument with Standing Beast" in front of the State of Illinois Building.

Roger Brown's 1991 "Arts and Science of the Ancient World" mosaic over the entrance of 120 N. LaSalle.

Richard Hunt's 1993 free-form aluminum sculpture on the facade of the Illinois State Office Building.

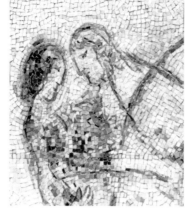

Marc Chagall's artwork at the First National Plaza, a five-sided mosaic, depicts the changing of seasons in Chicago.

The year was critical for public art in Chicago. Not only were the Chagall and Calder installed, but the federal government's General Services Administration commissioned a 20-ton, 100-foot-tall "Batcolumn" sculpture by Claes Oldenburg for outside the Social Security Administration Center.

In addition to these permanent sculptures, the Art Institute that year mounted a temporary exhibition in Grant Park featuring five artists: Hunt, Mark di Suvero, Michael Hall, Kenneth Snelson and John Henry.

The 1974 events helped inspire a city ordinance four years later that requires 1.33 percent of the construction budget for municipal buildings to be used for artwork. As a result, there are currently more than 400 art pieces displayed at City Hall, courthouses, libraries and police and fire stations.

Today, the Chicago Public Art Program continues the tradition of temporary sculpture exhibitions in Grant Park, begun in 1994 with the colossal bronze sculptures of Columbian artist Fernando Botero.

In 1999, we did not organize an exhibition for Grant Park due to the

Mayor Daley presents a medal to Marc Chagall who, in turn, surprises the mayor with a kiss on the cheek.

construction of the new Millennium Park. But because the Public Art Program is responsible for maintaining Chicago's legacy as THE city for public art, we came up with a different exhibition idea. Cows.

DR. STRIKE AT COUNTY HOSPITAL

Dr. Quentin D. Young

Past president of the American Public Health Association, clinical professor of preventive medicine at the University of Illinois College of Medicine

Striking doctors march past Cook County Hospital on their way to the Civic Center.

BY QUENTIN D. YOUNG

A flu outbreak hit Chicago the winter of 1975. Thankfully, the death toll remained low. But a more troubling medical issue confronted the city's health system that year.

Young doctors at Cook County Hospital walked off the job for 18 days in November. The strike by interns and residents at the city's largest public hospital resulted in contempt-of-court citations against seven doctors.

And because I sympathized with the physicians, I was fired as director of medicine by Dr. James Haughton, executive director of the Health and Hospitals Governing Commission.

I sued and eventually won my job back. I left five years later, but my concerns remained. How were we reaching our patients? I felt we had to treat people in their neighborhoods for chronic or preventable diseases of the poor, like hypertension, not wait for them to be admitted to the hospital as stroke and heart attack patients.

Yet, I was only able to set up three outlying clinics. In 1975 there were 1,800 beds in the outdated 60-year-old facility. A Committee to Save the Hospital called for a replacement. But nothing was done.

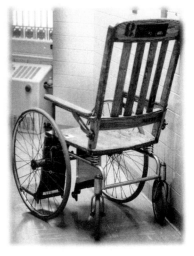

Outdated equipment like this wheelchair raised cries for more modern facilities at Cook County Hospital.

FEBRUARY

University of Chicago president Edward H. Levi is sworn in as President Ford's attorney general.

Elijah Muhammad, who led the Nation of Islam for more than 40 years, dies and is succeeded by his son Wallace.

MARCH

Trapped for 31 hours after falling into an 8-foot moat next to his Brookfield Zoo pen, Ziggy the Elephant walks to freedom up a 42-ton gravel ramp built by rescue workers.

Daily News breaks the story on a Chicago police undercover "Red Squad" infiltration of community and civil rights groups, including Operation PUSH, and of keeping intelligence files on State's Attorney Bernard Carey, former Bears star Gale Sayers and Notre Dame president Theodore Hesburgh.

Ziggy

APRIL

Mayor Richard J. Daley is elected to an unprecedented sixth term, defeating Republican John Hoellen by a margin of 5-1.

Cook County Hospital doctors and medical technicians rally outside Karl Meyer Hall following a march.

Nothing had been done in 1934, either, when the Chicago-based American College of Surgeons protested the facility was "too outmoded for the performance of modern surgery."

Ground was finally broken in 1999 for a state-of-the-art 450-bed hospital that will open to patients in 2002!

County Hospital has a special place in my affections. In addition to my 10 years as medical director, I had spent 5 years there training for internal medicine in the post-World War II years.

I was just one of thousands of doctors from around the world who flocked to the hospital for training. From 1914 until he retired in 1967, Dr. Karl A. Meyer led County through often-complicated political realities. Under his watch, training programs and medical research flourished, as Chicago's best doctors volunteered to teach and serve.

Some of County's medical advances include the world's first blood bank, first radiographic rooms for technical heart and brain exams, the nation's first cobalt-beam therapy unit and the first successful reattachment of severed fingers.

With six medical schools, Chicago is among the great medical centers. Quality of health care is possible, but access to it is problematic. In 1975, not everybody had medical insurance. Many poor people died or suffered needlessly from delays after transfers were ordered from other hospitals.

Strikes by medical personnel can be dangerous. But the massive 1975 walkout probably had a beneficial impact on County. My friend Dr. John Raba, who headed the house staff organization, spent a week in jail for contempt.

He later served as director of health services at the jail's Cermak Hospital and is now Cook County Hospital's co-medical director for ambulatory services, overseeing 30 clinics throughout the county.

"The strike started a process. It sensitized more than 500 doctors to take action for health care rather than just deliver it," Raba said.

There are now more than 320,000 visits each year to the hospital's outpatient clinics. The hospital has the largest burn unit and is the single largest provider of care to people with AIDS in the Midwest.

MAY		JUNE	AUGUST	DECEMBER	ALSO IN 1975
Sun-Times movie critic Roger Ebert wins a Pulitzer Prize for movie criticism, making him the first film critic to win the prize. **Roger Ebert**		Chicago mob boss Sam Giancana, who is linked to CIA assassination plots against Cuban premier Fidel Castro, is shot to death at his Oak Park home.	Northwestern University astronomer J. Allen Hynek, inventor of the term "close encounter" for contacts with extraterrestrial phenomena, gets a special phone line at his Center for UFO Studies so that police anywhere in the country can pass along UFO sightings.	John Paul Stevens joins the U.S. Supreme Court. He was Phi Beta Kappa at the University of Chicago, a Northwestern University Law School graduate and a U.S. Court of Appeals judge in Chicago.	The Grant Park Bandshell was named for James C. Petrillo. He was the musicians union leader for 20 years and started the first outdoor concert in the parks.

POLITICAL MAGIC

James R. Thompson

Chairman of Winston & Strawn law firm, former U.S. attorney and governor of Illinois

Jim Thompson celebrates his election as governor.

BY JAMES R. THOMPSON

For a rookie like me, the summer of 1976 unfolded like a piece of political magic. I walked in countless parades, shook hands at county fairs and railroad stations, spoke at Rotary Clubs and chambers of commerce and preached at black churches.

It was a remarkable year—one that changed forever my professional and personal life. I was married to Jayne Carr, the most wonderful woman in the world, and in the same year, millions of Illinois citizens placed their hope and trust in me by electing me as the 37th governor of the State of Illinois.

The story actually began in 1945. A Chicago radio show featuring a different Sunday school class interview each week came to my small Presbyterian church on the West Side.

The host went around to each kid asking, "And what do you want to be when you grow up?" The answers came quickly…"a fireman," "a policeman," "a railroad engineer." I was last, and in my most authoritative nine-year-old voice, said, "I want to be president of the United States."

Politics had a hook in me at an early age, and I became a lawyer, in part, as a steppingstone to a political career. Happily, I

Jim Thompson and his dog

FEBRUARY

"Beethoven: Symphonies" by the Chicago Symphony Orchestra, under Sir Georg Solti, wins a Grammy for best classical album.

APRIL

At Wrigley Field, the Cubs blow their biggest lead ever—13-2—after the Philadelphia Phillies' Mike Schmidt hits four consecutive homers. Final score: 18-16 in 10 innings.

MAY

Former governor Otto Kerner dies. At the time of his death, Kerner was on parole from a three-year sentence after being convicted of racetrack fraud in 1974. He was prosecuted by U.S. Attorney James R. Thompson.

The mother and father and 13-year-old brother of Patricia Columbo are murdered in their Elk Grove Villiage home. Columbo and her lover, Frank DeLuca, were found guilty of the murders.

Patricia Columbo

fell absolutely in love with the law, but politics took a backseat until 1975, when I left the U.S. Attorney's office to run as a Republican candidate for governor.

I had only one opponent in the March 1976 primary election—Richard Cooper, a wealthy and more conservative Chicago businessman. I first met Cooper the previous summer at a Republican picnic near Decatur.

Dick arrived in a long, black car and immaculate suit, and as the founder of Weight Watchers, he could not resist lecturing the farm wives in attendance about eating too much Swartz's pie—a local delicacy!

I doffed my jacket, loosened my tie, rolled up my sleeves and worked the crowd with no reference to the weight problems of the local folks. I carried Macon County (and all the others!). Dick, now a dear friend, went back to the business world.

Until the first polls were released in August, few believed that a political newcomer could beat an acomplished veteran like Mike Howlett, the Democratic Secretary of State who had the support of the mighty Democratic machine in Chicago and the backing and money of organized labor in a state that was Democratic by registration. At one point, declining contributions put us a week away from closing our

A doorman wipes away tears after learning of Mayor Richard J. Daley's death.

Jim and Jayne Thompson arrive at Mayor Daley's funeral mass.

headquarters and laying off our campaign staff.

We were saved by the renewed help of people whose optimism defied cold political logic. In August, the polls predicted a 20-point victory for me.

Election Day was almost anti-climactic. Jayne and I voted early, and later I got to the hotel just before the polls closed to watch returns. When the 6 p.m. TV news began with an announcement that I had been elected, I turned to "Gov," the young Irish Setter puppy I bought on the trail, and said quietly, "Hey, dog. We won."

And win we did, by a record 1,390,137 votes.

Six weeks later, political tragedy struck when Mayor Richard J. Daley died suddenly in his doctor's office. If Chicago was the "city of big shoulders," Richard Daley was the "mayor of big shoulders" who, through his wisdom, strength and political cunning, transformed a warring group of political fiefdoms into an unsurpassed political juggernaut.

Daley fashioned his beloved city into a colossus that could carry its people and their aspirations into the next century. Sitting with Jayne in the pew at his funeral mass, I was struck by the irony of one political career beginning while another had suddenly ended.

JUNE

The musical comedy "Chicago" marks a year on Broadway.

AUGUST

An acting ensemble including John Malkovich, Gary Sinise, Laurie Metcalf, Terry Kinney and Jeff Perry premiere as Steppenwolf Theatre Company with four one-act plays in a church basement in Highland Park.

OCTOBER

Two University of Chicago professors win Nobel Prizes—Saul Bellow for literature and Milton Friedman for economics.

Sun-Times editor James Hoge moderates the first campaign debate ever between vice presidential nominees. The candidates were Bob Dole and Walter Mondale.

Michael Bilandic
Illinois Supreme
Court justice and
former mayor of
Chicago

THE MARATHON MAYOR

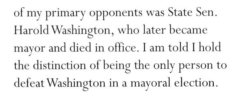

Mayor Bilandic not only helped organize the first Chicago Marathon, but he is the only Chicago mayor to have run the 26.2-mile race. Today, the Chicago Marathon attracts almost 30,000 runners and more than 750,000 spectators.

BY MICHAEL BILANDIC

From my perspective, the most important event of 1977 occurred on a hot, steamy day in July at Holy Name Cathedral, when Cardinal Cody pronounced Heather Morgan and myself husband and wife.

Six months earlier—a few weeks after the death of Mayor Richard J. Daley—found me acting mayor of Chicago. As a first-generation Croatian American, this was an unexpected honor. I had worked with Daley for many years, and my life has been enriched for having known him.

Special primary and general elections were held to fill his unexpired term. One

of my primary opponents was State Sen. Harold Washington, who later became mayor and died in office. I am told I hold the distinction of being the only person to defeat Washington in a mayoral election.

As mayor, I hosted and met many important people. A month after Jimmy Carter was inaugurated president, I visited him in the Oval Office with Rep. Dan Rostenkowski and Sen. Adlai Stevenson. A year later the president was an overnight guest at our home in Bridgeport.

Prince Charles was made an honorary citizen after a whirlwind visit to Chicago in 1977. As the most eligible bachelor in the

Mayor Bilandic and his bride, Heather Morgan

world, he not only stopped traffic, but also the hearts of mothers with daughters in search of a Prince Charming.

Although I was her husband and the mayor, my wife, being part Welsh, considered Charles to be her prince. Someday he may be king.

I had a hand with some "royal" events in Chicago, though. I helped Lee Flaherty and his associates get the Chicago Marathon under way. And I believe I am the only Chicago mayor to run a marathon. It took 4 hours to run 26 miles and 385 yards! And I was being followed by news reporters who expected me to collapse.

Running a city was more difficult. Within a month of my swearing-in, striking gravediggers and the cemetery owners arrived in my office. Bodies were stacked up, waiting to be buried. But a 12-hour negotiating session resulted in a new contract and resolution of that dispute.

Another labor squabble landed in the mayor's office on a February Sunday afternoon when members of the Lyric Opera orchestra threatened to withhold their services. The matter was resolved hours before the season was to be canceled. Heather and I later

Mayor Bilandic visits the site of one of Chicago's worst transit crashes.

Battered and bloodied, a victim of the L crash is taken from the accident scene to a local hospital.

attended opening night, starring tenor Luciano Pavarotti in "L'Elisir d'Amore."

We were soon tested again when the butcher's union prevented food stores from selling fresh meat after 6 p.m. This dispute was also resolved.

During rush hour on Feb. 4, one of the worst train crashes in Chicago transit history occurred. An elevated train rounded the curve at Lake and Wabash, striking the rear of a stopped train. The lead car jumped the rails, plunging 20 feet to the pavement of a busy intersection, dragging the next three cars with it. Twelve people died, and more than 180 persons were injured.

The Lakeview restaurant was converted into a hospital emergency room. Cardinal Cody and clergy of all denominations administered last rites. I raced over from City Hall and tried to comfort some of the victims. It was mass confusion and fear. But I witnessed many heroic acts by firefighters rescuing passengers from one car hanging precariously from the tracks.

No mayor before or since has been tested with so many significant crises in such a short time span.

JUNE

No one is hurt as an FALN bomb goes off in City Hall. Hours later, Puerto Rican Day festivities get out of hand in Humboldt Park, triggering two days of riots that leave three dead and more than 100 injured.

AUGUST

Col. Jacob Arvey, the former Democratic Party chairman (1946-53) who was instrumental in launching the careers of Gov. Adlai Stevenson II and U.S. Sen. Paul Douglas, dies at 81.

A Kenyan marabou stork, which escaped from the Brookfield Zoo, is recaptured in Lake Geneva, Wis. Its wings had been improperly clipped to prevent flight. The public reported more than 50 sightings of the bird, mostly of great blue herons.

NOVEMBER

Walter Payton sets an NFL record for most rushing yards in one game, gaining 275 yards against the Minnesota Vikings in a 10-7 Bears victory.

Walter Payton

DECEMBER

Hanna Holborn Gray, acting provost and Yale president, is named University of Chicago president. She held the post until 1994, when she was replaced by Hugo Sonnenschein.

LAST OF THE OLD YEARS

Scott Turow
Partner with the law firm of Sonnenschein Nath & Rosenthal and best-selling author

After modest beginnings at Navy Pier, Chicagofest has evolved into the weeklong "Taste of Chicago" extravaganza that annually attracts millions of people to Chicago's Grant Park.

BY SCOTT TUROW

In 1978, after many years away, my wife and I resumed life in Chicago, where we'd been raised.

I'd just finished law school, and I was apprehensive about coming back to Midwestern weather, uncertain family relations and a city which for years had seemed invulnerable to needed reforms.

The year's grimmest local story unfolded in December, with the discovery of the first of the more than 30 bodies of young men ultimately found buried beneath or near the home of John Wayne Gacy.

But for most Chicagoans, the dominating events were economic. OPEC's oil squeeze

had led to rampant inflation and wage-price controls. The prime rate ballooned by year's end to 11 percent.

Trying to catch the train, boomers like us—ready to start our families—were furiously bidding up the prices of suburban real estate. The crowds at Sunday open houses looked like an attraction at an amusement park.

Yet what was most significant about 1978, in retrospect, was that it was the last year of the old way. After the convulsions of the

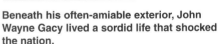

Beneath his often-amiable exterior, John Wayne Gacy lived a sordid life that shocked the nation.

JANUARY

Billionaire John D. MacArthur, who built one of the nation's largest fortunes by selling dollar-a-month insurance policies door to door, dies at 80. The bulk of his estate goes to the John D. and Catherine T. MacArthur Foundation, best known for its MacArthur Fellow "genius" grants.

Arlington Heights must rezone to allow a low- and middle-income housing development, the U.S. Supreme Court rules.

A blizzard closes O'Hare Airport for only the fourth time in its 23-year history. It reopens after 22 hours.

MARCH

The Chicago Daily News, recognized as one of the country's greatest newspapers, goes out of existence, leaving Chicago with only two major newspapers.

An EPA suit accuses Outboard Marine Corp. of dumping 2 million gallons of toxic PCB into Waukegan Harbor over an 18-year period.

The National Organization for Women says its boycott of states that haven't passed the Equal Rights Amendment has cost Chicago more than $20 million. Three months later, a ratification vote in the Illinois House falls two votes short.

greeting dissent with the warmth of a middle linebacker.

Worse, City Hall, like much of state government, maintained a Pompeian obliviousness to the smoldering volcano of race. There were riots in the prison at Pontiac, and continuing agitation as the beleaguered school board president, Joseph P. Hannon, chased the dream of a voluntary program to desegregate the city schools.

The American Nazi Party, after winning permission in the U.S. Supreme Court to march in Skokie, home of many Holocaust survivors, chose instead to parade through the changing Marquette Park neighborhood, leading to a melee and the arrest of 72 persons.

Yet, new winds were swirling, some ominous, others benign. U.S. Steel closed operations at the South Works. I remember being thrilled by the first Chicagofest that summer, a bigger forerunner of the Taste of Chicago, which was staged at Navy Pier and brought big-name musical acts and huge crowds to the lakefront.

It seemed to show that many shared my hunger for a more lively, diverse and welcoming Chicago, a place less afraid of fun.

After the death of Mayor Daley, Ald. Edward Vrdolyak assumed virtual control of the City Council.

'60s, the status quo seemed precious to Americans, and Chicagoans were holding on for dear life. Republican Charles Percy was reelected to the U.S. Senate, narrowly defeating Democrat Alex Seith, and Republican Jim Thompson coasted to a second term as governor.

Locally, we were in the doldrums that followed the death of Richard J. Daley, as the Democratic machine maintained its blinkered attempts to ensure that nothing changed.

The City Council was led by Ald. Edward "Fast Eddie" Vrdolyak, and city government was still characterized by party control, a tolerance for venality and a habit of

I did not know then that the storms of the winter ahead would ultimately whip those yearnings, and the city's growing racial and economic tensions, into a force that would topple the long-accepted political arrangements and finally open the pathways for change.

Governor Thompson was easily reelected in 1978.

JULY

The movie "Animal House," set in 1962 in a college fraternity and starring Second City graduate John Belushi, is released.

DECEMBER

In the biggest art theft in U.S. history at that time, three Paul Cezanne paintings valued at $4 million are discovered missing from the Art Institute. In May 1979, a former shipper-packer was arrested while trying to ransom the paintings for $250,000.

ALSO IN 1978

The house of John Wayne Gacy is ripped apart by local authorities in their search for bodies and skeletal remains of the murder victims buried under Gacy's house and garage.

BYRNE STORMS CITY HALL

Jane M. Byrne
Former Mayor of
Chicago

A lone man crosses the intersection of Randolph and Michigan after the blizzard of 1979.

BY JANE M. BYRNE

It began in the snow.

At a minute to midnight, I welcomed in the New Year of 1979 by kneeling at the open window of my Near North Side apartment for a moment of prayer and then expected to hear the shouts of merrymakers. But there were no sounds from the streets below. Chicago had been hit by a big storm.

Earlier that night, I had planned a birthday party for my daughter Kathy. But because of the near-record snowfall, none of the guests could make it. The same thing was happening all over the city. Yet as I looked out my window, the snow-covered city looked quite beautiful. More than two feet of snow fell before it was over.

As an underdog candidate for mayor, I had sensed for months that there was discontent in the neighborhoods. Even before the blizzard, it was clear to me that senior citizens, minorities and women were in the mood for change.

When it was clear that the city had failed in its snow-removal efforts, there were some indications that the blizzard might be a factor in the election. Then it became a mess.

More snow and the passage of plows made the task of digging out parked cars a difficult one.

FEBRUARY	MARCH	JUNE	JULY	SEPTEMBER
Federal drug agents raid the Chicago Board of Options Exchange just after the close of trading and arrest 10 brokers, market makers and clerks for selling and distributing cocaine on or near the floor of the exchange.	Businessman Louis Steinberg receives 10 years in prison and a $29,000 fine for his part in a $6.8 million swindle of Cosmopolitan National Bank. Steinberg had fled to Rhodesia in 1971 but returned to the U.S. in 1978. The DePaul Blue Demons, led by former Chicago prep star Mark Aguirre and Hall of Fame coach Ray Meyer, defeat UCLA and earn the school's first-ever trip to the NCAA Final Four.	Prosser Vocational High School graduates its first class with women. There were 74 women among the 262 graduates, many planning careers in auto mechanics and other male-dominated fields.	Disco Demolition, a promotional stunt by radio personality Steve Dahl between games of a White Sox doubleheader against the Detroit Tigers, turns sour. During the chaos, 37 people were arrested and the White Sox were forced to forfeit the second game.	The city loses its prestigious AA bond status. The lowered rating means that Chicago has to pay up to one-quarter of 1 percent more in interest.

Jane Byrne is sworn in as the new mayor of Chicago as outgoing mayor, Michael Bilandic, looks on.

As the temperature dropped way below freezing, the two feet of snow were turned into solid ice. Several weeks later, two more feet of snow fell, and our city was buried. The garbage couldn't be picked up. Trains came to a halt. The airport closed. The blizzard exposed the myth that Chicago was "the city that works."

By the middle of February, polls indicated that I was coming on strong, though still trailing Mayor Michael A. Bilandic. But on election night, Feb. 27, I did what the pundits and politicians said couldn't be done. My Democratic primary victory—and election as mayor a few months later—disproved the myth that "You can't fight City Hall." All across Chicago, people voted for change.

Crews survey the wreckage of a DC-10 near O'Hare.

It was the first time in Chicago's history that a woman had been elected mayor, and the first time since 1927 that the Regular Democratic organization's slated candidate had lost. If the blizzard of '79 helped to achieve this

result, my election was regarded as a second blizzard by the political establishment.

When I took office, I faced some tough decisions. I was told by bureau chiefs that the city's finances were in trouble, that mass transit workers were on the verge of a strike and that the school system was in chaos. All of these reports turned out to be true.

The CTA workers went on strike in the middle of the Christmas shopping season. The union had to give up its cost-of-living escalator. When the public and news media supported the city's position, the strike was short-lived.

In November, it was announced that the schools were deeply in debt. Teachers weren't going to be paid for the rest of the year. A bailout was eventually structured with the state's aid.

There was also great drama that year. Just before Memorial Day, Chicago witnessed one of the worst air disasters in history, as an American Airlines DC-10 went into a roll after losing an engine following takeoff from O'Hare and plunged to earth. All 271 aboard and two on the ground perished.

Then there was the memorable two-and-a-half-day visit of His Holiness Pope John Paul II in October. His goal was to get as close to "the little guy" as possible. More than half a million people turned out for his mass at Grant Park. It was very cold during the mass as the wind blew off the lake. But the warmth of the crowd filled the air that day.

OCTOBER

Bombs planted by the FALN Puerto Rican terrorist group explode at a downtown office building and at the Great Lakes Naval Training Center. A third bomb was defused before it exploded.

Two persons are killed and 43 injured when an Amtrak passenger train slams into the rear of a parked freight train about 30 miles south of Chicago.

Pope John Paul II visits Chicago.

NOVEMBER

A federal judge rules that the political patronage system in the city and county is unconstitutional in a lawsuit filed by Michael Shakman, an attorney defeated by the Democrats in a bid to become an independent delegate to the 1970 Illinois Constitutional Convention.

DECEMBER

The Bears, with a record of 10-6, win an NFC playoff spot on the final day of the season. Walter Payton leads the NFC in rushing for the fourth straight year and enjoys his fourth straight season of running for more than a thousand yards.

It seemed more than possible that the entire world financial system would collapse if our markets failed. The smell of fear mixed with the sweat of traders the following morning, even before the markets opened. But the Fed stepped in to assist financial institutions that backed the trading firms.

Within four months, the markets had rebounded—then the shortest bear market on record—setting a foundation for an uptrend that would within 12 years take the Dow over 10,000.

But very few would have put their money on that result during those terrifying days of the Stock Market Crash of 1997. For the next two years, Chicago's futures and options exchanges were investigated as the cause of the crash until it was revealed that keeping the futures markets open had actually mitigated the disaster.

from a stroke, but the Cubs had again to wait "one more year." Andre Dawson hit his final home run at Wrigley Field.

The most resounding memory of 1987 (for me, at least) was the incredible Oct. 19 stock market crash, that sent the Dow Jones Industrial Average nosediving an unbelievable 508 points.

At the time, I was the financial reporter for WBBM-TV, Channel 2 news. I watched with my camera crew on the floor of the Chicago Board of Options Exchange, where at times the silence was deafening and the panic palpable. When the New York Stock Exchange suspended trading because the electronic ticker and specialists' order books couldn't keep up, the Chicago options traders were left standing limply in the pits.

Only at the Chicago Mercantile Exchange did futures keep trading for most of the day, giving witness to the carnage.

While the New York Stock Exchange suspended trading on Oct. 19, 1987, the Chicago Mercantile Exchange kept trading futures for most of the day.

OCTOBER

The Sun-Times reveals that the cash-strapped CTA routinely gives new executives up to $4,500 for new office furnishings, wallpaper and carpets.

NOVEMBER

The Cubs Andre "Awesome" Dawson is named the National League's MVP. He's the first player from a last-place team to win the award.

Larry Heinemann, a Vietnam veteran and former CTA bus driver, wins the National Book Award for *Paco's Story*, about the Vietnam War. He is the third Chicagoan to win the award: Nelson Algren won once and Saul Bellow was honored twice.

Andre Dawson

ALSO IN 1987

Michael Jordan edges out Magic Johnson and Larry Bird as top sports hero in a poll of American teenagers. It's the first time basketball players take the top three spots. Jordan was runner-up to the Bears' William "Refrigerator" Perry in 1986.

SWEET HOME LOCATION

Roger Ebert
Sun-Times movie critic

John Belushi and Dan Aykroyd perform as Jake and Elwood Blues with The Blues Brothers Band.

BY ROGER EBERT

Chicago's modern history as a movie location begins in 1980 with a film that could not have been more native: "The Blues Brothers," big, loud, exuberant and brawling, the Sherman tank of musicals.

Jake and Elwood Blues (John Belushi and Dan Aykroyd), in their black suits, black hats and dark glasses, got out of Joliet Penitentiary and headed to sweet home Chicago, and the city was permanently on the movie map.

Movies had been filmed here before. Hiding from the patent holders who tried to shake down anyone using a movie camera, Charlie Chaplin made a brief stop at the Argyle Street Studios on the road to Southern California. Tom Mix westerns were even shot here.

But during the administration of the first Mayor Daley, the city didn't have the welcome mat out for visiting film crews. A few films were shot here, notably "Mickey One" (1965), a fantasy about a paranoid nightclub comic. It starred Warren Beatty, and sank without a trace (his next film: "Bonnie and Clyde").

More troublesome to City Hall was Haskell Wexler's "Medium Cool," filmed during the tumultuous 1968 Democratic Convention, with actors plugged into real-

Jake and Elwood size up the situation in "The Blues Brothers."

life events. Mayor Richard J. Daley, displeased with its portrait of the city, did not encourage filming here.

Not only did City Hall want script approval (it was sensitive about depictions of Chicago police), but a different form of police script approval was operating at street level. When Norman Jewison came to Chicago to shoot "Gaily, Gaily" (1969), he was shaken down for so many payoffs to cops and city agencies that after a week of filming, he yanked his movie out of Chicago and finished it in Milwaukee.

Daley died in 1976, and his successors, Michael Bilandic and Jane Byrne, were more hospitable to filmmakers. New state and city film offices rolled out a welcome mat, and Lucy Salenger, our new ambassador to Hollywood, explained that movies were the ideal industry: They brought in money, didn't pollute and enhanced the city's image.

"The Blues Brothers," shot when Byrne was in City Hall, wasn't the first movie to benefit from the new climate. Brian De Palma's thriller "The Fury" was made in 1978; "My Bodyguard" (1979) was about a kid who lived in the Ambassador East Hotel. But "Blues Brothers," with its local story and music and Second City heritage, was the big one that showcased Chicago locations.

Chicago has recently become the home for many high-profile productions such as "The Fugitive" (above) and "Chain Reaction" (below).

City Hall promised director John Landis: No kickbacks, no problems, anything you want. *Anything?* Landis asked, and Loop passersby were treated to the spectacle of police cars crashing through the glass of the Daley Center and speeding across its lobby. Hollywood was here to stay.

No mayor has welcomed it more enthusiastically than Richard M. Daley does. The current mayor belongs to a circle of film buffs who regularly discuss videos, and he slips into theaters incognito every week or two.

In the 20 years since "The Blues Brothers," hundreds of movies have used Chicago locations. Just last year, 50 productions spent $83 million.

"It's the most photogenic modern city in the world," says Chicago-born director Andy Davis, who shot "Code of Silence," "The Fugitive" and "Chain Reaction" in Chicago.

Two favorite Chicago shots have become familiar to the world's moviegoers: A helicopter shot zooming in low over the lake and tilting up to the glories of the skyline and the Chicago River; and a shot looking south from Lincoln Park, as lovers walk along the lakefront with the skyline in the background. Sweet location Chicago.

JUNE
Arthur Nielsen, market researcher who devised the TV rating system, dies in Chicago at 83.

Millionaire businessman Bruce Rouse and wife Darlene are found shotgunned and stabbed to death in their Libertyville home. The crime isn't solved for 16 years, when son Billy—31 and living the party lifestyle in Florida—confesses. Police had long suspected Billy and brother Kurt, who was never charged.

SEPTEMBER
Susan Getzendanner becomes Chicago's first female federal judge. She leaves the bench in 1987.

Susan Getzendanner

OCTOBER
Eleven uniformed Nazis are pelted with rocks, eggs and small pieces of metal when 2,500 protesters show up at a planned Nazi march in Evanston.

NOVEMBER
Police officers vote to unionize under the Fraternal Order of Police banner. New FOP chief John Dineen demands pay hikes, dental insurance, new grievance procedures and binding arbitration to resolve disputes.

Ray Meyer
Former DePaul
basketball coach

BLUE DEMON BLUES

Legendary DePaul coach Ray Meyer teamed with star Mark Aguirre for 79 wins and a 1979 Final Four appearance during Aguirre's three years on the team. But it was DePaul's one-point loss against St. Joseph's in the 1981 NCAA tournament that burns most deeply in the memories of all DePaul fans.

BY RAY MEYER

Ask a Chicago sports fan about the disappointments this city has seen. There are plenty—and I'll bet our 1981 DePaul basketball team is one of them.

I should know. I coached DePaul for 42 years, but the hardest loss I ever had came that year. And I think the city shared our feelings.

Ever since we reached the NCAA Final Four two years earlier, we had been riding high nationally with one of the best players I ever had, Mark Aguirre. He was only a junior, but I knew this probably would be his last year with us. A pro career was waiting, and Mark did go on to become the

first player selected in the NBA draft that year.

That happened after his and my biggest disappointment.

Mark was co-captain of our team, but what a supporting cast he had—Terry Cummings, Skip Dillard, Jerry McMillan and Clyde Bradshaw. We lost only twice that year, by two points to Texas on the road and by one point at home to Old Dominion. But we finished the regular season ranked No. 1 in the country and a favorite to win the national championship.

Mark Aguirre dominated the Chicago basketball scene before becoming the Dallas Mavericks' first overall pick in the 1981 NBA draft.

JANUARY

Jerry Reinsdorf heads a group that buys the White Sox from Bill Veeck. Veeck's original plan to sell the club to Ed DeBartolo was killed by the American League because of DeBartolo's racing holdings.

Jerry Reinsdorf

MARCH Jane Byrne

Mayor Jane Byrne moves temporarily to public housing in Cabrini-Green, saying she wants to highlight dangerous conditions in the North Side housing project. Critics say Byrne is trying to mollify the black community after dumping two black School Board members in favor of two white busing foes.

MAY

Clad in an orange-and-green Spiderman suit, actor and mountain climber Daniel Goodwin scales the Sears Tower—then the world's tallest building.

JUNE

First Deputy Police Supt. James Riordan, while off-duty, is shot to death outside a Marina City bar by a man he was trying to remove for harassing customers.

Ray Meyer with his wife, Marge; his son Joey (left), then a DePaul assistant; and his son Tom, then the coach at the University of Illinois at Chicago.

They nullified the basket, and St. Joe's came down to score again. Now we're ahead by one with seconds to play. We crossed mid-court and Skip Dillard got tackled from behind, but the referees didn't call an intentional foul. We didn't mind because Skip was an 80 percent free-throw shooter, and I was confident he'd make the one-and-one.

I called time out to set up our defense. If Skip made both baskets we would fall back into a zone. If he made just the first, we would play man-to-man.

But Skip missed the first. St. Joe's came down court with about six seconds to play. Our defense broke down and St. Joe's had an open man under the basket. He dropped it in at the buzzer, and we lost 49-48.

We had a bye in the first round of the NCAA tournament that year and our first opponent was St. Joseph's. I remember going to the local television studio in Dayton, Ohio, where we were playing, to watch a film of their team. They made 27 turnovers and looked terrible. Maybe the players sensed I wasn't worried because they started thinking more about Indiana, who would be our next opponent.

I still remember the St. Joe's game so vividly. We had the game won with a nine-point lead late when Clyde Bradshaw got into foul trouble. Then things started happening. We started turning the ball over, but we still had a three-point lead with less than a minute to play when Terry Cummings took a jump shot from the right corner. It went in, but one of the referees called him for an offensive foul. I couldn't believe it.

I remember how devastating it felt. I went to the press room to meet the media, and by the time I got to the locker room, everyone already had left. That's the only time I remember that happening.

Some of the players walked the two miles back to the hotel. When I got there, I called everyone into my room and I talked to them with a very heavy heart.

I've always felt sorry for Skip in that game. He was one of our best free-throw shooters, but sometimes even the best miss. I never blamed him, but I think a lot of people did, and I know how bad he felt.

It was a bad night for people who cheered for DePaul because we had a team that could have gone a long way. But we went from the penthouse to the outhouse in a few hours.

Together, Ray Meyer and son Joey coached the Blue Demons to 955 wins in 55 years.

AUGUST	SEPTEMBER	OCTOBER	NOVEMBER	ALSO IN 1981
The sale of the Cubs to the Tribune Co. is approved by the league. The family of William Wrigley had owned the club since 1915.	The gritty police drama, Hill Street Blues, makes its debut and begins its five-year run. The show helped cement Chicago's reputation on the TV- and movie-making map.	The Guardian Angels, a self-proclaimed crimefighting group from New York City, begins patrols in Chicago. Mayor Byrne and police Supt. Richard Brzeczek called the group "vigilantes."	Daniel Goodwin climbs the John Hancock Tower, despite firefighters' attempts to stop him with torrents of water. He was charged with criminal trespass, fined and placed on six months' court supervision.	The Rev. George Clements, pastor of Holy Angels Catholic Church, announces he will adopt a young boy and launches "One Church, One Child" to encourage adoption of African-American youngsters. The 1980 census figures show Chicago nudging out Los Angeles as the nation's second-largest city. Chicago has just over 3 million people; L.A. has 2.9 million.

DEMOCRATS: PUNCH 10

Edward R. Vrdolyak
Attorney

After taking over the leadership of the Democratic Party in 1982, Edward Vrdolyak set out to reestablish the dominance enjoyed by Democrats during Richard J. Daley's tenure as mayor.

BY EDWARD R. VRDOLYAK

I remember 1982 coming in like a bear, as we experienced record low temperatures of almost 30 degrees below zero. The year ended like Tyrannusaurus Rex, politically speaking, with Jane Byrne, Richard M. Daley and Harold Washington slugging it out to be the city's next mayor.

Early polling showed Daley enjoyed a big lead. But as the newly elected chairman of the Democratic Party, I received much criticism for predicting the non-party-endorsed Washington would win because most people would naturally, but wrongly, vote along racial lines.

We all know that Washington won and locked swords with me in what was to be known as the Council Wars. But not many people remember that in 1982 Washington was an ally in my effort to rejuvenate the Democratic Party.

When I became chairman in March 1982, the Democratic organization—once an important player in the making of presidents—was divided and faltering.

Since the death of Mayor Richard J. Daley, the party had lost its edge. It didn't

Governor Thompson's narrow victory over Adlai Stevenson III in 1982 is the closest gubernatorial election in Illinois history.

JANUARY

Chicago breaks a 109-year record when the temperature plummets to minus-26. The cold is blamed in 24 local deaths. Across the country, record lows contribute to 261 deaths.

FEBRUARY

A law banning handguns in Morton Grove goes into effect. The law, passed in June 1981, is the first of its kind in the country and survives several legal challenges.

MARCH

An Air National Guard jet tanker crashes into a ball of flames in McHenry County, killing four crew members and 23 guardsmen.

Dianne Masters, wife of prominent lawyer Alan Masters, disappears after a meeting of Moraine Valley Community College board members. Her body is found in the trunk of her yellow-and-white Cadillac, submerged in the Sanitary and Ship Canal in Willow Springs.

The U.S. Supreme Court rules unanimously that Hoffman Estates can restrict the sale of drug paraphernalia in so-called "head shops."

JUNE

A city plan to hold a lakefront world's fair in 1992 is approved in Paris by the Bureau of International Expositions, a 36-nation organization that regulates world's fairs.

Legislators refuse to ratify the Equal Rights Amendment despite protests in Springfield.

seem to stand for anything except losing elections. My predecessor's decision to endorse Teddy Kennedy in the 1980 presidential primary had been a disaster, and the organization lost two of its three most recent primaries.

I was raised a Democrat. My parents, immigrants from Croatia who had a tavern on the Southeast Side for more than 50 years, were Franklin D. Roosevelt Democrats. The party helped them and provided an opportunity to make a better life for themselves and their children.

My first priority as chairman was election of the Democratic ticket. Republican Gov. Jim Thompson was up for reelection, and the polls showed him leading Democratic rival Adlai Stevenson III by 20 percentage points. But the state's economy was hurting—especially in the Chicago area— and I thought that the Democrats had a chance.

So we launched an all-out voter-registration drive that added record numbers to the rolls. Then we came up with the "Punch 10" campaign for straight-ticket Democratic voting. This was done partly because Stevenson was unpopular with organized labor and other key Democratic voting blocs.

We sold the party instead of the candidate. Mayor Byrne and Congressman Washington did very effective commercials for the ticket.

The Democratic Party's "Punch 10" campaign was so effective that Governor Thompson called it the "Vrdolyak Express."

Joseph Bernardin (left) became Archbishop of Chicago after the death of Cardinal Cody in 1982.

In 1982 the "Punch 10" campaign wiped out Thompson's big lead. We had a 71 percent turnout in the city and a record number of straight-ticket votes, which helped get Mike Madigan his first speakership of the Illinois House.

It was the closest gubernatorial race in Illinois history. Stevenson was denied a recount, and Big Jim later referred to "Punch 10" as the "Vrdolyak Express." Thompson should have called it "The Miracle of DuPage," because it took almost four days for this upper-income, privileged county to tally the votes. DuPage kept counting until Stevenson lost.

The year also saw Joseph Bernardin installed as Archbishop of Chicago, following the death of Cardinal Cody, whose last year was plagued by a federal investigation into the alleged diversion of tax-exempt church funds to a lifelong friend.

And in September of that year, events in Chicago raised the fears of a nation, as the first of seven people died following consumption of Extra-Strength Tylenol capsules laced with cyanide. The crime was never solved, but it changed—for the better—the packaging of over-the-counter drugs.

And the city proved once again it can survive any political government no matter who is the leader.

AUGUST

Ernie "Mr. Cub" Banks becomes the first Cubs player to have his number—14—retired.

SEPTEMBER

Northwestern University ends the worst losing streak ever in major college football—40 games—by beating Northern Illinois.

Elk Grove Village-based United Airlines is found guilty of violating federal age-discrimination laws and is ordered to pay $18 million to 112 employees affected by the airline's policy of forcing flight engineers to retire at age 63.

The first Mike Royko Annual Rib Fest sponsored by the Chicago Sun-Times and the Chicago Park District pulls in some 5,000 people, including Mayor Jane Byrne (right).

OCTOBER

University of Chicago professor George G. Stigler wins the Nobel Prize in economics.

DECEMBER

A federal jury in Chicago convicts Teamster president Roy L. Williams and four others of conspiring to bribe a senator and defraud a union pension fund.

WASHINGTON'S BREAKTHROUGH

Laura S. Washington
Editor and publisher of The Chicago Reporter

Fueled by record voting numbers in the black community, and with the support of many white "lakefront liberals," Harold Washington made history in 1983 as Chicago's first black mayor.

BY LAURA S. WASHINGTON

In a city where elections are hammered out in the bitter winter and blustery spring, the 1983 campaign was perhaps the hottest ever, seared with no-holds-barred racial politics.

Harold Washington was a most reluctant candidate, drafted out of incendiary African-American anger over unfair treatment by incumbent Mayor Jane M. Byrne.

In some ways, Washington was also an unlikely candidate for a political crusade, born out of a career as a loyal Democratic soldier in the Illinois General Assembly and Congressman from the First Congressional District.

But he was black, and his mantra was reform. In the Democratic primary, his opponents never saw him coming. Byrne was not about to give up her office after a turbulent first term. And Cook County State's Attorney Richard M. Daley decided he was ready to assume what was, after all, his birthright—the office his father, Richard J. Daley, held for 21 years.

Blacks in Chicago and around the nation were cheering Washington on as he bested the opposition with unbounded energy, charisma and a voluble vocabulary. And in the primary they voted for "Harold" in record numbers, anointing him the Democratic nominee for mayor.

Black voters, who had helped elect Jane Byrne in 1979, voted en masse for Harold Washington in 1983.

JANUARY

Allen Dorfman, convicted in a Teamsters union bribery case, is shot to death gangland style outside the Lincolnwood Hyatt hotel.

FEBRUARY

Archbishop Joseph Bernardin is installed as a cardinal by Pope John Paul II.

Jeanine Nicarico, 10, stays home from school and disappears from her Naperville home. Her body, raped and beaten, is found two days later in a wooded area in DuPage County.

Mob gambling boss Ken "Tokyo Joe" Eto is shot three times in the head while sitting in his car outside a Northwest Side theater. He survives, demands to be placed in protective custody and turns government witness.

Archbishop Joseph Bernardin

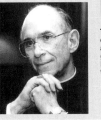

MAY

The National Conference of Catholic Bishops adopts a pastoral letter, guided by Cardinal Bernardin, condemning the nuclear arms race.

JUNE

Nuns from Mother Teresa's Missionaries of Charity order dedicate their mission at 115 N. Oakley, next to the Henry Horner housing project. The 18 nuns arrived in Chicago in May.

Bernard Epton

For decades, that assignation was virtual assurance the nominee would be the next mayor. Republicans in Chicago were few and far between. But suddenly, many white, lifelong Democratic politicians and voters fell in love with the white Republican nominee, a little-known state legislator named Bernard Epton.

They talked about Washington's lack of administrative experience and his convictions on tax charges, but whispered about blacks taking over and the city going to pot. Anyone but Harold, they said. And Epton's campaign slogan offered its own warning: "Epton: Before it's too late."

So once again, Chicago showed its ugliest side—its penchant for racial politics. One campaign button circulating on the North Side urged, "Say No To Washington." One depicted a slice of watermelon. Another was just plain white. The message was clear.

But Washington prevailed by a slim 40,000 votes. And with characteristic twinkle and grin, he reminded Chicagoans that his election did not cause the city to slide into Lake Michigan.

But in his April 29 inaugural speech, he declared the Democratic machine dead and called for white elected officials who had opposed him to get with his program.

To Aldermen Edward R. Vrdolyak and Edward M. Burke, that was a call to battle, and Council Wars was born. They forged the all-white City Council majority bloc, the "Vrdolyak 29," and spent the rest of 1983—and another three years—thwarting most every major Washington initiative.

The Windy City moniker got replaced by "Beirut on the Lake." An early casualty: Standard & Poor's rewarded

Former mayor Jane Byrne looks on as Harold Washington takes the oath of office at his 1983 inauguration.

Chicago with a lower bond rating. In full disclosure, I should note that I jumped into the fray myself when I went to work for Washington (no relation) in 1985 as his deputy press secretary.

As with racial politics, 1983 continued other dubious Chicago traditions: The public school teachers went on strike. And the city entered a new era of corruption, with indictments from Operation Greylord, a federal probe of the courts.

Although they were political allies before the 1983 mayoral election, Harold Washington and Edward Vrdolyak engaged in the bitter "Council Wars" during Washington's first term in office.

JULY	AUGUST	OCTOBER	NOVEMBER
Fermilab's high-energy particle accelerator becomes the world's most powerful atom-smasher. Chicago hosts Major League Baseball's 50th All-Star game at Comiskey Park. The American League wins for the first time since 1971, 13-3. Four elderly patients die at the Center for Human Development nursing home when the air conditioning fails during a heat wave.	Operation Greylord hits the news. The secret three-year federal investigation of corruption in the Cook County Circuit Courts eventually results in convictions of a host of judges and lawyers for "fixing" everything from traffic tickets to murder cases.	Judge Henry A. Gentile and lawyer James A. Piszczor are shot to death in a Daley Center courtroom by a divorce-case defendant. School teachers go on the longest strike in city history: 15 days. It ends when teachers win a pay raise and a one-time bonus. George "Papa Bear" Halas dies at 88.	Marshall and Frederick Field announce they will sell the Sun-Times to Australian media magnate Rupert Murdoch.

JUDGES ON THE TAKE

Thomas P. Sullivan
Retired lawyer, former U.S. attorney for the Northern District of Illinois

Among the judges caught in Operation Greylord were (top, left to right) John Murphy, Frank Salerno, Richard LeFevour, Reginald Holzer, John Reynolds; (bottom, left to right) Raymond Sodini, John Devine, James Oakey, Wayne Olson and John McCollum.

BY THOMAS P. SULLIVAN

As a litigator, I have spent decades in court making arguments and questioning witnesses. In 1984, however, it appeared I could be the one on the stand being grilled about controversial evidence-gathering techniques.

Federal prosecutors thought they might call me to testify about how proof was obtained that some Cook County judges were on the take. My appearance would have coincided with initial trials in the Operation Greylord corruption probe.

Luckily, my testimony was not needed for juries that spring to convict Judge John M. Murphy and court clerk Harold Conn of taking bribes. Over the next few years,

more than 15 judges, 4 court clerks, 13 police officers and 50 lawyers were convicted as a result of the most successful undercover sting operation by the U.S. Justice Department.

My involvement in Greylord began six years earlier when, as United States Attorney, I received reports of crooked judges, "miracle" defense lawyers and dishonest clerks and police.

Working in cooperation with the FBI, the Cook County state's attorney, Chief Criminal Court Judge Richard Fitzgerald and high-ranking police officials, we launched this highly secret investigation.

Terrence Hake, a young assistant state's attorney at the time, went undercover to assist the U.S. Justice Department in Operation Greylord.

JANUARY — Oprah Winfrey interviews Michael Jordan

Oprah Winfrey, a little-known television personality from Baltimore, debuts as host of "A.M. Chicago." Within two years, it expands to one hour, gets renamed "The Oprah Winfrey Show" and enters syndication, soon to become the most popular and lucrative show in television history.

David Mamet's "Glengarry Glen Ross" receives its American premiere in the Goodman Theatre studio. The production, starring Joe Mantegna, went to Broadway, where it earned numerous Tony Awards and the Pulitzer Prize.

MARCH

Walter Mondale defeats Gary Hart in the Illinois presidential primary.

MAY

Helen Brach, widow of candy magnate Frank Brach and heir to a $20 million fortune, is declared legally dead. She was last seen in February 1977.

Once the Greylord investigation became public, media scrutiny of the case was intense.

George Orwell put it in *1984,* that Big Brother was watching.

While the Greylord convictions shook the roots of the judiciary and public confidence in the courts, it led to many reforms and reassured Chicagoans that judges, lawyers and police are not above the law.

A few blocks from the Dirksen Federal Building, where the trials took place, adversarial proceedings of another sort were under way at City Hall. The so-called "Council Wars" raged between Chicago's first African-American mayor, Harold Washington, and 29 aldermen, led by Edward Vrdolyak and Edward Burke.

Because we did not want to risk the release of real criminals, we staged phony robbery, drunk driving and unlawful weapons cases, with FBI agents posing as perpetrators offering money to get charges dismissed.

Chicago public schools were also in the news when teachers walked out for 10 days in a dispute over pay and benefits and the Board of Education failed to renew Supt. Ruth Love's contract. Later, I defended the board against Love's lawsuit for alleged discrimination, which eventually was dismissed.

We targeted only persons we suspected were corrupt based on reliable information. Most readily took the bait, which was often offered by Terrence Hake, a young assistant state's attorney who wore a concealed microphone as he pretended to be a crooked prosecutor and later defense attorney.

The year 1984 saw Charles Percy's tenure as U.S. senator come to an end, while the Cubs' Ryne Sandberg rose to rare heights by winning league MVP honors.

That same year, Fred Rice was appointed Chicago's first African-American police superintendent, the Federal Deposit Insurance Corporation saved Continental Illinois National Bank and Trust Company and 4-year-old Jimmy Tontlewicz was rescued after falling through the ice of Lake Michigan and being underwater for 20 minutes. In a coma for 8 days, he recovered and is now 20, 6 feet tall and in good health.

Hake says now, "If I had known how corrupt the system really was, I would have been even more aggressive in my undercover role."

U.S. Sen. Charles Percy (R-Ill.) lost his seat to downstate Democrat Paul Simon. The Cubs won a divisional championship, the Bears won their first division title since 1963 and the Chicago Sting won their second North American Soccer League championship in 4 years.

The investigation continued after I left office under successors Dan K. Webb and Anton R. Valukas, and became public in 1983. The fact it remained secret was in part attributable to the arrogance of those involved, who thought they wouldn't be caught. Little did they know, as

JUNE	JULY	AUGUST	SEPTEMBER	NOVEMBER	DECEMBER	ALSO IN 1984
The Bulls, with the No. 3 pick, select Michael Jordan in the NBA draft. Thus begins Chicago's greatest sports dynasty.	Seventeen people are killed in two explosions at a Union Oil Co. refinery near southwest suburban Romeoville. The impact of the blasts could be felt 30 miles away.	House painter Larry Eyler is charged with the murder of Daniel Bridges, whose dismembered body was found in a dumpster near Eyler's apartment.

Bart Conner of Morton Grove earns two Olympic gold medals in men's gymnastics. | Deerfield-based Walgreens celebrates the opening of the chain's 1,000th store. | Ben Wilson, the No. 1 high school basketball player in the country, is gunned down while walking with a girlfriend near Simeon High School. | Eight elderly residents of a Waukegan hotel die in a fire on Christmas morning. The city's fire chief said smoke detectors could have saved their lives. | John Callaway launches Chicago Tonight on WTTW-TV. |

PUNK ROCKS THE SCENE

Jim DeRogatis
Sun-Times pop
music critic

**The Effigies broke
new ground in the
Chicago music
scene and paved
the way for many
Chicago talents in
the 1990s.**

BY JIM DEROGATIS

Though it isn't remembered with anywhere near the reverence of the seminal blues scene or the early Chess Records years three decades earlier, 1985 was one of the most important eras in the history of the Chicago rock scene.

Although our town produced a few stray chart-topper groups in the '60s (the Buckinghams, the Shadows of Knight), as well as a handful of acts capable of filling arenas in the '70s (Chicago, Styx, and Cheap Trick from neighboring Rockford), the Windy City's contributions to the roster of great American rock bands were vastly

out of proportion to its size or the influence it exerted on the worlds of jazz and blues.

Punk rock emerged in the late '70s as a reaction against the right-wing politics of Ronald Reagan and Margaret Thatcher, and as a musical alternative to the bloated, soulless sounds that had come to dominate the pop charts. By the mid-'80s, a second generation of Midwestern punks was introducing a new sophistication to the music while continuing to voice their anger at the status quo.

Steve Albini founded the trio Big Black.

JANUARY

Eight current and former Chicago police officers are indicted for allegedly shaking down motorists suspected in minor hit-and-run accidents. The officers told the drivers they could avoid being charged by paying $20 to $300.

FEBRUARY

Chicago real estate developer Lee Miglin becomes head of Bitter Automobiles of America, headquartered at 200 W. Madison. The sleek Bitter sports sedan was made in West Germany.

APRIL

Studs Terkel wins the Pulitzer Prize for nonfiction for his book *The Good War: An Oral History of World War II.*

Studs Terkel

MAY

Gary Dotson is freed after born-again Christian Cathleen Crowell Webb recants her rape accusation against him. Webb said she lied to cover up the fact that she had sex with her boyfriend. DNA tests later prove Dotson's innocence.

The State of Illinois Center and the first phase of Deep Tunnel open. Helmut Jahn designed the blue-glass and salmon-colored steel building nicknamed "Starship Chicago." Deep Tunnel is meant to keep stormwater from flooding rivers and basements.

Naked Raygun

Leading the charge in Chicago: Naked Raygun, the Effigies and Big Black, all of whom were at the height of their powers in '85.

Naked Raygun used ringing, metallic guitars, a stampeding beat and massive singalong choruses to deliver their message, which included ironic homages to militarism ("Rat Patrol," "Surf Combat," "Managua") and a generational update of Bob Dylan's "Don't follow leaders."

"Listen now to what I say/About the kids of today/Subscribe them all your fears/'Til they become like you/What poor gods we do make," Jeff Pezzati sang in the anthemic "I Don't Know."

Led by singer John Kezdy, the Effigies issued their "Fly on a Wire" album, a spare punk assault that summarized the pessimistic outlook of a group that had not yet been pegged "Generation X." Even more abrasive

musically and lyrically was the trio Big Black, the brainchild of former Northwestern University journalism student Steve Albini.

Albini's group was in between two strong recordings in '85, "Racer X" and "Atomizer," and it was honing its craft onstage, effectively utilizing two extremely noisy guitars and bass over the relentless rhythms of a drum machine. The sound would inspire countless industrial/noise bands later in the decade.

The headlines out of Chicago in '85 were about politics—the so-called Vrdolyak 29, led by Ald. Edward R. Vrdolyak, continued their battle with the 21 aldermen who remained loyal to Mayor Harold Washington—or about other cultural institutions like the Chicago Symphony Orchestra naming Henry Fogel executive director (and beginning the struggle to erase a $710,000 deficit) and the Steppenwolf Theatre (John Mahoney starred in "Orphans") company winning a Tony for outstanding regional theater.

Chicago politics in 1985 continued with "Council Wars," led by Ed Vrdolyak's majority of 29 aldermen facing off against the 21 aldermen loyal to Mayor Washington (left).

The punk bands of '85 were celebrated only on the underground level, and they never broke through to widespread acceptance. But Big Black's Albini would later produce bands Nirvana, Bush, Plant and Page, and other major rock acts.

And the ground that Naked Raygun and the Effigies broke would help pave the way for the alternative explosion of the mid-'90s, which saw homegrown talents such as the Smashing Pumpkins, Urge Overkill, Liz Phair and Veruca Salt win major national success.

AUGUST	SEPTEMBER		OCTOBER	NOVEMBER	ALSO IN 1985
The city is sued because the written exam for police officers had been limited to applicants 34 and under. In two months, another exam for applicants up to 70 is given.	Ryne Sandberg steals his 46th base, the most by a Cub since 1907, when second baseman Johnny Evers also stole 46.		Vito Marzullo, 25th Ward alderman for 32 years, announces he'll retire. A court-ordered ward remap put Marzullo's home into a neighboring black ward and made the 25th predominantly Latino.	Drug dealer Flukey Stokes' flamboyant funeral draws hundreds. He was buried in a $9,000 mahogany casket with a white telephone in his hand. His son's 1984 funeral was even more garish: Willie "The Wimp" was laid to rest in a replica Cadillac coffin with $1,000 bills stuffed between his fingers.	The first Air Jordan basketball shoes—red, white and black—debut in the spring. "The Breakfast Club" movie is filmed in Des Plaines; "About Last Night" is filmed in Chicago.

Vito Marzullo

THE BEARS' GREATEST SEASON

Mike Ditka

Former Chicago
Bears coach 1982-
1993, now coach of
the New Orleans
Saints

**Bears' coach Mike Ditka
waves to fans during the
victory parade that drew
800,000 people out into the
bitter cold to cheer their
Super Bowl champions.**

BY MIKE DITKA

We won the Super Bowl on Sunday, and on Tuesday the Challenger blew up. It put everything in perspective. Hey! It took all the glamour off winning. That's how it was to me.

But I still think the Bears' historic 46-10 win over the New England Patriots was the greatest moment in sports in Chicago.

Sure, the Bulls won six championships, but you have to picture what it was like after the Bears became world champions.

Challenger explosion

It was bone cold out there, but there were 800,000 people standing on the streets of Chicago to welcome us home that January Monday after the game.

They threw tons of shredded paper. They were playing the Super Bowl Shuffle. There were big banners for us, and even the Sears Tower became the Bears Tower after we decimated the Patriots.

**Bears fans cheer their Super Bowl
heroes from all angles.**

JANUARY	APRIL	JUNE	JULY	AUGUST
American League President Bobby Brown sends a letter to White Sox owners Jerry Reinsdorf and Eddie Einhorn urging them to leave aging Comiskey Park. The pair threaten to leave town but eventually get a new park.	The state files suit against two former executives of Goodwill Industries after a Sun-Times investigation reveals that the pair diverted cash, real estate and other assets to themselves through dummy charities and deceptive land deals.	They came with wives and children, sporting short hair and long hair, dressed in fatigues and uniforms: 200,000 Vietnam veterans, cheered by 300,000 onlookers, march to Grant Park.	Sun-Times President and Publisher Robert Page and a group of investors buy the paper for $145 million from Rupert Murdoch.	The New Regal Theater, heir to the old Regal from the '20s through the '60s, opens at 1645 E. 79th. Soul group Gladys Knight and the Pips play after a black-tie gala.

I was so proud of the team. I can't think of any one highlight moment, but I would have to say one high point of it all was the domination of our defense as the game went on. They got better and better. Sure our offense was good. After all, we had Jim McMahon and Walter Payton.

But it was our defense that became such a force. We had great players, good coaches and it worked. The chemistry was there.

In 1963, when I was a Bears tight end, we won the world championship. As coach 23 years later, we won the Super Bowl and the NFL championship. I have to say it is much more fulfilling as a coach because it makes you feel like you had something to do with blueprinting it. You are part of what's making it happen.

I have one regret, though. Probably, I think the biggest thing that came out of the game that I didn't realize at the time was not giving Walter the chance to score a touchdown—and we could have. All you think about is the game and winning. Yeah, you talk to him, but you can't undo it. That's like the guy who killed someone and then says, "I'm sorry."

Walter Payton was the best football player I've ever seen. I'm not trying to slight any of the rest of them, but he was the best.

He was not selfish. He was a team player. He raised people to another level and played that game heart and

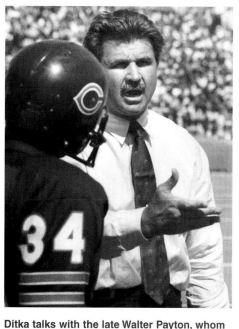

Ditka talks with the late Walter Payton, whom Ditka called "the best football player I've ever seen."

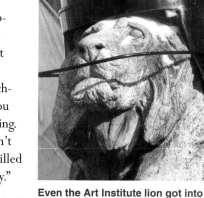

Even the Art Institute lion got into the Super Bowl spirit.

soul. He played every game heart and soul. Sure, he fumbled on the second play, but that was because the quarterback called the formation wrong, but that can happen to anyone in the heat of the game.

I keep in touch with some of the people from that year, but not all. I haven't seen William "Refrigerator" Perry, although we have talked. Many other guys are in different places. McMahon lives in Northbrook. Mike Singletary lives in Barrington, Richard Dent lives in Chicago, Mike Hartenstine lives in Lake Forest. They have reunions, but we haven't had one in a long time, not since I went back to work as a coach.

It's ironic that I now live in New Orleans, where I had three big wins. I played in the city as a tight end for the Dallas Cowboys in the 1972 Super Bowl against the Miami Dolphins, in 1978 against Denver when I was assistant coach for the Cowboys and then coaching the Bears in the 1986 Super Bowl. I guess God puts people in places for a reason.

I like New Orleans a lot. But I spent a majority of my life in Chicago, living, playing and coaching. It was 21 years. It's the city that works. It's clean. It has so many neat things. I love the people. I love the fans and even those who criticize me. Chicago is the city of my heart.

SEPTEMBER

Mayor Harold Washington snipped a ribbon, floodlights scanned the sky and men in black tie and women in sequins entered the refurbished Chicago Theater for the first time in 31 years. Frank Sinatra plays to sellout crowds for five nights.

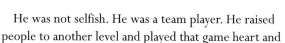

Chicago Theater

NOVEMBER

The Illinois Supreme Court bars newly elected Judge Joseph McDermott from taking the bench while he is a target of the ongoing Operation Greylord investigation. McDermott later gives up the new seat.

ALSO IN 1986

Death claims the lives of three legendary Sun-Times journalists: distinguished columnist Sydney J. Harris and two top rewritemen, Pulitzer Prize winner Hugh Hough and Chip Magnus.

Jeff Fort, leader of Chicago's El Rukn street gang, is convicted of conspiring to commit terrorist acts in the U.S. for Lybian leader Moamer Qaddafi. Fort is sent to prison and remained there at the century's end.

MAYOR DIES—MARKET CRASHES

Terry Savage
Sun-Times financial columnist

Crowds line the Daley Center Plaza to remember Harold Washington.

BY TERRY SAVAGE

Chicago was presented with two shocking headline events in 1987—one political and one financial. Each shook the city to its core and had long-lasting repercussions.

The political year started off smoothly. Harold Washington was reelected in April. He also gained a majority in the City Council. But just when politics in City Hall seemed to have settled down after several turbulent years, the unthinkable happened.

Washington was rushed to Northwestern Hospital, where he died on Nov. 25 from a heart attack. Despite shock and mourning, Council Wars began anew. Competing factions finally agreed to install Eugene

Sawyer as mayor in a special 10 ½-hour session that ended after midnight.

Other politicians also made the headlines in 1987. Ald. Ed Vrdolyak became a Republican. Ald. Clifford Kelly pleaded guilty to taking cash and Super Bowl tickets as bribes. And former governor Dan Walker pleaded guilty to federal fraud charges related to a savings & loan he ran.

That same year the Chicago Bears returned to the gridiron as reigning Super Bowl champs, but pro football began the fall season with a 24-day strike. Earlier in the summer Harry Caray resumed his place in the WGN broadcast booth after recovering

A mourner holds two candles and wipes away a tear as she watches the funeral procession for Mayor Washington.

JANUARY	MARCH	MAY	AUGUST	SEPTEMBER
Home plate at Comiskey Park is covered with snow as Gov. Thompson signs a bill creating the Illinois Sports Facility Authority to sell $120 million in bonds for a new stadium. Six Chicago-area people—all over 60—die of apparent heart attacks while shoveling snow after the season's first major storm dumps 7 to 9 inches on the city and suburbs.	James Moffat, principal of Kelvyn Park High, is convicted of sexually abusing five teens in his office at the school. Moffat at one time was the No. 2 man in the school system. He later got 15 years in prison.	Nine people, including two former aldermen and a former aide to Harold Washington, Clarence McClain, join seven already indicted in the ongoing Operation Incubator investigation. The scandal involved bribe-taking by city officials to help a New York firm get $100 million in contracts to collect overdue parking fines.	Sandra Fabiano, the owner of two Palos Hill child care centers, insists she's innocent of allegedly molesting four young girls in her care. Neighbors and clients rally to her support. Fabiano was acquitted in one case in 1989; prosecutors dropped the remaining charges.	Nearly a century after its founding by pioneering black surgeon Daniel Hale Williams, the bankrupt Provident Hospital shuts down. It's eventually sold for $1 to Cook County.

Rosalind Rossi
Sun-Times
education reporter

TRAUMA AND REFORM HIT SCHOOLS

Linda Corwin shows the granite marker honoring her son, Nick, who was killed by Laurie Dann. The marker was placed in Nick Corwin Park in Winnetka.

NICHOLAS BRENT CORWIN
1980 ——— 1988

NICK CORWIN'S YEARS WERE FULL OF LIFE AND ENTHUSIASM. HIS KINDNESS, WILLINGNESS TO HELP OTHERS AND SENSE OF HUMOR MADE HIM A CHERISHED MEMBER OF OUR COMMUNITY.
WINNETKA PLACES GREAT VALUE ON ITS CHILDREN AND THE LOSS OF ANY ONE OF THEM IS A LOSS TO US ALL. NICK CORWIN PARK IS DEDICATED TO ALL THE CHILDREN OF THE COMMUNITY—PAST, PRESENT AND FUTURE.

BY ROSALIND ROSSI

Many Chicago area schools—and parents—were never the same after 1988.

On May 20, a mentally unstable Glencoe babysitter named Laurie Dann opened fire on a second-grade classroom in Winnetka's Hubbard Woods School. One child was killed and five were injured. Blood puddled the floor of Classroom 7, but Dann killed herself before explaining why.

4756

Laurie Dann

Bonnie Agnew will never forget that day. Hearing of the shooting, she ran to Hubbard Woods to check on her two sons, then in third and fifth grade.

As anxious parents milled outside, the principal emerged, covered in blood. He pointed in Agnew's direction. "I need to see you," he said. Agnew froze.

"Me?" a terror-striken Agnew said. It turned out, however, that he was pointing to another mom, whose daughter was among those shot. "Both our knees, I know, were shaking," Agnew said.

The nation shook as well; murder had pierced the sanctity of the classroom. And it happened in the well-manicured, stately North Shore suburb of Winnetka.

Family members cling together before entering a counseling session at Hubbard Woods School.

MARCH	APRIL	MAY	JUNE	JULY
The Rat Pack reunites—Frank Sinatra, Dean Martin and Sammy Davis Jr. appear at the Chicago Theater for a three-night engagement.	Former Willow Springs Police Chief Michael Corbitt admits his role in the 1982 murder of Dianne Masters, the wife of lawyer Alan Masters. Masters, Corbitt and Cook County Sheriff James Keating are later convicted of conspiracy in the crime.	Harry Golden Jr., the longtime Sun-Times City Hall reporter, dies and is memorialized at a City Council ceremony. City Hall's pressroom is renamed in Golden's memory.	For seven days, temperatures soar to 100 and above. More than 40 people die of heat-related causes. "Global warming" becomes part of the public lexicon as scientists try to link it to a national drought.	Two Wheaton College students surface after a four-month disappearance that triggered national headlines. They said they had been secretly married and were inspired to vanish by a book about a couple in search of "perfect love." The White Sox seem on the verge of moving to St. Petersburg, Fla., until lawmakers, in a "midnight miracle," sweeten the deal for a new, publicly funded stadium.

Ald. Allan Streeter (center) and Ernest Jones (right), escorted by police, leave the Art Institute with the impounded painting of Mayor Washington.

The incident was the first of a string of fatal school shootings that stunned the country through the end of the 1990s. But in its immediate aftermath, Agnew recalled, "All of a sudden, doors were locked" at Chicago area schools. Visitors were screened. Three suburbs passed handgun bans that year. The shooting prompted gun debates nationwide.

Meanwhile, drastic change was brewing for the Chicago public school system—the nation's third-largest.

Parental anger had boiled over the year before when schools were idled by a 19-day teachers' strike—the ninth since 1970—and U.S. Education Secretary William Bennett labeled Chicago schools the "worst in the nation." Nearly half the students who entered Chicago high schools were not graduating.

That spring, as city parents and businessmen joined forces to demand school reform, nine outraged Chicago

Mayor Daley looks on as Governor Thompson signs the Chicago school reform bill.

aldermen helped "arrest" a painting of the late Mayor Harold Washington donned in women's undergarments. That summer, the city sweltered through 100-degree heat. By summer's end, on the North Side, the Chicago Cubs got lights—only to be rained out on their inaugural night.

By fall, Gov. James R. Thompson signed the Chicago school reform law, giving parents more power than anywhere in the nation. They had a majority-vote on local school councils that hired and fired principals and oversaw what grew to be $450,000 a year in spending in the average elementary school.

In 1988, Natividad Hernandez' daughter had classes in a rat-infested mobile trailer at Chicago's severely over-crowded Hammond School. Other classes met in the basement. "I remember a special education class in a closet…with no windows at all," Hernandez said. Kids were using 25-year-old books.

But after the 1988 legislation passed, Hernandez was among more than 5,000 residents elected to local school councils. She even was named president of her LSC. Like three-quarters of the schools in the first four years of reform, Hammond changed princi-pals—but only after a fight.

The new principal brought in new books, new teachers and new programs for kids. Flexing new political muscle, Hernandez and other LSC members lobbied for another school. It opened in 1995—the year lawmakers amended the reform law to solve nagging financial and academic problems. LSCs stayed, but Mayor Richard M. Daley was given control of the city's schools in reform's "second wave."

By then, reform had changed not only Hammond, but also Hernandez, a native of Mexico, and many like her. She learned English through a new Hammond program for parents. She got a job. Reform, said Hernandez, "changed my whole life."

AUGUST

It's lights on at Wrigley Field for the first time for night games. Thousands of flashbulbs pop as Rick Sutcliffe throws the first pitch for a game against the New York Mets.

A ban on smoking in most public buildings goes into effect.

SEPTEMBER

David and Cynthia Dowaliby of Midlothian report their daughter Jaclyn, 7, missing. The girl's body is found four days later in a wooded area of a neighboring suburb's apartment complex.

NOVEMBER

Christie Hefner, daughter of Playboy founder Hugh M. Hefner, is elected Chairman and Chief Executive Officer of Playboy Enterprises.

Christie Hefner

DECEMBER

Fermilab Director Leon Lederman of the University of Chicago wins the Nobel Prize with two other physicists. In 1961, the trio discovered a subatomic particle believed to be one of the key building blocks of matter.

A national coalition of black leaders emerges from a meeting at the Hyatt Regency O'Hare and says blacks no longer want to be called blacks. The term African American "has cultural integrity," said the Rev. Jesse Jackson.

FUTURES AND A NEW DALEY

Leo Melamed
Chairman emeritus and senior policy advisor to the Chicago Mercantile Exchange and CEO of Sakura Dellsher Inc. commodities firm

Cleared of all major charges by federal investigators, the Chicago Board of Trade and the Chicago Mercantile Exchange emerged in the 1990s as two of the city's most important financial institutions.

BY LEO MELAMED

For Chicago and arguably for its primary economic engine—the futures exchanges—1989 began with the winter of despair.

No question about it. Chicago's winter storms are world class, and 1989 was no exception. But that year, January also brought a storm of federal agents with subpoenas in hand upon the homes of futures traders.

This culminated a two-year investigation of trading on the floors of the Chicago Board of Trade and the Chicago Mercantile Exchange. FBI agents, posing as traders with hidden tape recorders, had penetrated the trading pits of both exchanges and allegedly found evidence of major wrongdoing.

Both the local and national media had a field day reporting on the so-called Operations Hedgeclipper and Sourmash.

This sad chapter in media coverage caused the spread of baseless accusations, rumors and innuendoes. Our traders were presumed guilty even before a shred of credible evidence was available for scrutiny.

In April, Chicagoans turned their back on the winter of despair and overwhelmingly elected Richard M. Daley mayor of the city that had become synonymous with his family name.

Daley, with his family, takes his oath of office.

JANUARY	FEBRUARY	MARCH	JUNE
Daniel Barenboim is named successor to Georg Solti as music director of the Chicago Symphony.	The city's new human rights ordinance goes into effect. It bars discrimination on the basis of race, color, sex, age, religion, disability, national origin or sexual orientation.	Sun-Times editorial cartoonist Jack Higgins wins the Pulitzer Prize.	New York sports agent Norby Walters and associate Lloyd Bloom are sentenced to federal prison after being convicted in Chicago of luring college athletes to sign improper contracts and threatening harm if they reneged.

Richard M. Daley is shown with his wife, Maggie, and (left to right) Governor Thompson, Cardinal Bernardin, Robert Healy and Congressman Martin Russo after being sworn in as mayor.

The investigation turned out to be a colossal government fiasco and a huge waste of taxpayers' money. By the end of 1989, the integrity of Chicago futures traders was vindicated, the eminence of our markets was restored and our membership values resumed their record climb.

Not only was the FBI sting rebuffed, the brutal attack on our markets in the aftermath of the 1987 stock market crash was equally discredited. The myriad of academic and government studies that probed the cause of the crash unequivocally proved to the financial world that the Chicago futures exchanges were exemplary in providing an indispensable modern risk-management mechanism for hedging and trading, especially during moments of crisis and upheaval.

At the age of 46, the eldest son of the former mayor, Richard J. Daley, having completed three successful terms as Cook County State's Attorney, became the city's fifth chief executive in a decade. He and his wife, Maggie, told their supporters that to thank the citizens of Chicago, they would do their very best in the years ahead. They have done just that.

Daley's election signaled a rejection of the age of foolishness and a return to the age of wisdom. As the strife at City Hall of previous years became a distant memory, as Chicago resumed its role as the city that works, so ceased the unwarranted attacks on Chicago futures exchanges.

After two years of intense investigation of more than 6,000 brokers and traders, after the disruption of a nationally vital industry for almost a year, after months of media blitz, after some 500 subpoenas were issued and as many interviews held and after the review of more than a million documents, a mere handful of traders was indicted, mostly for misdemeanors.

As a result, Chicago—and its exchanges—rose in prominence and importance. Indeed, the Chicago Mercantile Exchange, home of the world's most liquid stock-index instrument, the Standard & Poors 500 contract, for the first time in its history equaled the prestige of the New York Stock Exchange.

After rebuffing an FBI sting, the Chicago Mercantile Exchange catches baseball fever.

JULY	Phil Jackson	SEPTEMBER	DECEMBER	ALSO IN 1989

JULY

Clarence McClain and former Circuit Court Clerk Morgan Finley, a protégé of the late Mayor Richard J. Daley, are convicted in the Operation Incubator scandal. McClain later gets eight years in prison, Finley 10.

Popular Bulls coach Doug Collins is fired and Phil Jackson is tapped for the job. A disgruntled fan pens a letter saying that the "dream of a basketball dynasty in Chicago has been spoiled."

SEPTEMBER

Thousands of revelers celebrate at Clark and Addison after the Cubs win the National League East title. The Cubs lose the pennant to the San Francisco Giants.

DECEMBER

Mourners pack the church and 500 more stand outside in the cold to remember firefighter Kevin Anderson, 27, the first fireman in more than two years to die while fighting a blaze. It took 18 hours for Anderson's colleagues to find his body in the rubble of Rose of Sharon Community Baptist Church, 2950 W. Warren.

ALSO IN 1989

Two former aldermen become radio talk show hosts. Clifford Kelley, convicted in the Operation Incubator scandal, signs on with WGCI-FM. Ed Vrdolyak becomes a co-host on WLS-AM with veteran radio personality Ty Wansley.

ON THE TOWN IN THE NINETIES

John Carpenter
Sun-Times staff
reporter

Demolition progresses at the old
Comiskey Park.

BY JOHN CARPENTER

The last decade of the 20th century dawned on a Chicago headed in two different directions.

For the first time in 70 years, the city was officially home to less than 3 million people, continuing a decades-long migration of residents to the ever-sprawling suburbs.

But many of the people sticking around—increasingly time-strapped but affluent professional couples—were fueling a revitalized city dining and nightlife scene that was offering the first evidence of a restaurant revival that has put Chicago on the culinary map.

We said good-bye to our Palace of Baseball, the crumbling grandstands of old Comiskey Park, where generations of baseball fans watched their venerable, albeit only occasionally good, White Sox. More than a few tears were shed on Sept. 30, when fans packed the old ballpark for her last game, even as the new Comiskey was looming, partially constructed, across 35th Street.

There was tragedy in Plainfield, where 29 people were killed by a tornado. But we were comforted in knowing the death toll could have been far worse had quick-thinking high school coaches not rushed their teams to safety. The school was destroyed.

NA-NA-NA-NA, NA-NA-NA-NA...
HEY, HEY, GOODBYE

JANUARY

Illinois state legislators approve riverboat gambling in the state, foreshadowing a cash windfall for state and local coffers, as well as politically connected investors.

FEBRUARY

After a three-month grace period, Chicago's first new area code is now required. Callers to the suburbs must dial 708 in the first of four area code splits in the '90s to accommodate the rapid growth of cellular phones and computer modems.

APRIL

Nancy and Richard Langert are murdered in their Winnetka town house. Although initial speculation pegged the killing on everything from the mob to the Irish Republican Army, Langert neighbor and New Trier High School student David Biro, 17, was arrested and convicted of the killings.

AUGUST

A tornado cuts a 700-foot-wide swath across subdivisions and farm fields in and around Plainfield, a far Southwest suburb. The tornado kills 29 and injures more than 350. Dozens of buildings, including Plainfield High School, are destroyed.

During the Plainfield tornado, four-week-old Danielle Friedl was thrown into the debris of the family's home, but survived without a scratch.

More than anything, though, it was a year in which we saw a renewal of city living. Neighborhoods like Bucktown, Wicker Park, River North, Roscoe Village, to name a few, saw old homes restored and real estate values soar.

Some people were fed up with the long commutes to and from the suburbs. Others refused to give up the proximity to nightlife and culture the city offers.

And, said Chicago magazine Dining Out editor Penny Pollack, people were eating out in droves. In the always trend-heavy restaurant business, two were emerging in 1990—comfort food and bistros.

"More people were happy to keep living in the city, and they were going out, but they didn't want heavy meals every night," Pollack said. "The bistro and the trattoria became the casual, chic way of eating."

But it wasn't all Cobb salads and cous cous. Homey foods like bread and mashed potatoes were poised for a comeback, as diners were either looking for straight-up, retro, just-like-mom-used-to-make themes or funky variations on same, Pollack said.

At the same time a Randolph Street fixture, Barney's Market Club, was poised to close, another restaurant on the street, Vivo, was ready to open. By the end of the decade, Randolph Street would be one of the hottest dining districts in the city, if not the country, Pollack said.

February, meanwhile, brought the first whiff of a very '90s phenomenon. Chicago's new area code—708— became required dialing as of Feb. 1. Phone company officials said they needed the new code because of the increase in phones. Little did we know then that the explosion in cellular phones, home fax machines, and pagers and computer modems would require three more new area codes—for a total of five in a city that had but one before 1990—by the end of the millennium.

There was also a grim foreshadowing in the ledger books of the Chicago Police Department, where officials added a new category, "drive-by shooting" to the list of murder motives recorded. The increasing proliferation of illegal drugs backed by growing street gangs was blamed

Oprah Winfrey stands with Rich Melman (middle) during a preview party for their new Eccentric restaurant.

for the murder rate reaching a nine-year high in 1990, with 854 people killed. Murders would not drop below that figure for another five years, when a steady drop began that continues as the century comes to a close.

SEPTEMBER

The last baseball game is played at the old Comiskey Park after 80 mostly mediocre years. More than a few tears were shed at the sellout farewell game. Although officials prepared for trouble, expecting fans might ransack the stadium to collect souvenirs, the game and festivities afterward went off without incident.

OCTOBER

Tension in the Persian Gulf mounts as the United States and other countries protest the Iraqi invasion of Kuwait. Eventually, more than 1,000 reservists form Illinois will be sent to the Middle East as part of Operation Desert Storm.

ALSO IN 1990

Joseph "Pops" Panczko, dean of trunk poppers and lock pickers, "retires" at 72 after serving time for his 200th arrest. He began his career at 12 by stealing coats from the cloakroom at Humboldt Park Elementary School. He and his brothers Paul "Peanuts" and Edward "Butch" once worked together, but the brothers later branched out in their crime careers. "Pops" managed at least one more arrest, in 1994, for allegedly passing a counterfeit $20 bill.

Vito Marzullo, legendary Chicago alderman, dies at the age of 92, a year after an erroneous report of his death. Franz Benteler and his violinists played at the City Council memorial service for Marzullo.

Maggie Daley
First Lady of
Chicago and Chair
of Gallery 37

YOUNG ARTISTS BLOOM

Former apprentice artist Kadrena
Cunningham (left) and Maggie
Daley reminisce about Gallery 37.

BY MAGGIE DALEY

August 16, 1991, was the closing ceremony of the first Gallery 37, Chicago's job training initiative that pays young people to apprentice with professional artists.

Kadrena Cunningham, who turned 18 that day, remembers snapping photos with dozens of friends in front of the sculptures, painted furniture and murals they created over the six-week program.

"That summer, I met some of my best friends," Kadrena remembers. "We were from all over the city, and for many of us, it was our first time riding the L downtown. We learned about music, movies and art from our teachers and each other. It was a great summer job!"

Conceptualized only six months earlier, Gallery 37 had taken root and, indeed, blossomed. This beautiful garden of Chicago youth creating art had evolved from a number of seeds.

Initially, as a mother with two teenagers at home, I realized that, although there were many cultural programs available for young children, those geared for teenagers were slim to none.

Lois Weisberg, a dear friend as well as Commissioner of Cultural Affairs, agreed and began organizing brainstorming sessions

Brian Malone, 14, concentrates on
his work during a clay class at
Gallery 37.

JANUARY		FEBRUARY	MARCH	JUNE
University of Illinois and Chicago Bears running back Harold "Red" Grange, who was nicknamed in the 1920s the "Galloping Ghost" by famed sportswriter Grantland Rice, dies in Florida.	Harold "Red" Grange	Jeanne McHough is appointed commander of the Chicago Police Department's Belmont District, becoming the city's first female district commander.	A picture that for years had hung in the living room of a suburban Milwaukee couple is sold at auction in Chicago for $1.3 million—well over twice the Chicago-area record of $504,000 paid in 1989 for an 18th-century secretary-bookcase. The couple had recently learned that the picture, "Still Life with Flowers," was painted by Vincent Van Gogh around 1886.	The McAuley School in West Chicago, the last one-room schoolhouse in DuPage County and dating from 1914, shuts down. All six students either graduated or moved away.

to impact this vital age group. At the same time, my husband, Richard, asked all the city commissioners to come up with ideas for using Block 37, a vacant lot in the heart of the Loop.

I still smile today when I recall that several weeks after Richard's April 1991 inauguration, he asked Chief of Staff David Mosena about the ideas.

"Well, one is to employ high school kids to create art under circus-like tents," David answered.

"What are you talking about?" Richard asked, incredulously. "Whose idea is that?"

"Well, actually, it's Maggie's idea," David answered.

There was a pause.

"Oh, well, that's a wonderful idea."

This double-take response echoed among city officials and private funders. When we insisted Gallery 37 begin that summer, people told us it was ludicrous. Nonetheless, they helped. And they have continued to help to this day building a program that has been replicated 18 times in the U.S. and abroad and last year was awarded the "Innovations in American Government" Award from the Ford Foundation and Harvard University's Kennedy School of Government.

"We realized that there had never been a program like this before,"

Harold Washington Library

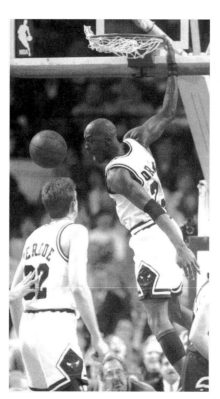
Michael Jordan and the Bulls won their first NBA championship in 1991.

recalls Kadrena, now a graphic designer, who valued that first opportunity to work with people from different backgrounds and neighborhoods.

The apprentices who represented the full spectrum of ethnicities and family incomes shared a common dedication and creative talent that spawned mutual respect and unprecedented friendships.

Demonstrating a maturity and idealism not often attributed to teens, the apprentices voted to sell their artwork at the end of the summer—not to keep the profits, but to use the money to help more teens experience Gallery 37.

In 1991, Chicagoans experienced a range of wonderfully noteworthy events. On a personal note, I was proud of my husband, who had been elected mayor with 71 percent of the vote. The Chicago Public Library found a permanent home in an awesome structure named for Mayor Harold Washington. The Shedd Aquarium opened its Oceanarium, bringing dolphins and beluga whales to Chicago. The Bulls won their first NBA championship.

And that first group of Gallery 37 apprentice artists inspired us to take a closer look at the City's most precious natural resource—its youth.

AUGUST	OCTOBER		NOVEMBER
Chicago's murder total hits a monthly high of 121.	Shanti, the first Asian elephant born in Illinois, celebrates her first birthday at the Lincoln Park Zoo.		Chicago ranks 48th among 50 major American cities in "fiscal strength," according to Crain's City & State magazine.
	Ronald H. Coase, a professor emeritus at the University of Chicago Law School, wins the Nobel Prize in economics. He's the university's 62nd Nobel winner.	 **Ronald H. Coase**	David Dowaliby is freed from prison after his conviction for the 1988 murder of his seven-year-old daughter is reversed. His wife, Cynthia, was acquitted a year earlier.

CHICAGO'S SOGGY SPRING

Bill Zwecker
Sun-Times staff
columnist

Huge hoses are used to
pump dehumidified air
into a DePaul University
building after the flood.

BY BILL ZWECKER

A lot of water passed under the bridge in 1992—literally.

It was the year of the Big Flood. But it was also a big year for women, a year of big disappointments for Mayor Richard M. Daley and the end of the "Big Tuna"— Chicago mob boss Tony Accardo.

Without question, the top story of 1992 started at 5:30 a.m., April 13, when a slow leak—bubbling for an estimated seven months—blew open Chicago's little-known, 63-mile-long downtown freight tunnel system.

A bridge protection piling had been pounded into the side of the tunnel where it crossed under the Chicago River's North Branch near the Kinzie Street Bridge. About 250 million gallons of water flooded the basements of most Loop buildings, including Marshall Field's State Street store.

The event knocked out electricity, evacuated the Loop, closed two CTA subway tunnels and cost the city $40 million—the price tag for the 5 ½ weeks it took to pump out all the water. It also cost nine top city workers their jobs for not reacting quickly months earlier, when they learned the tunnel was leaking.

Dubbed the "Flood Stud" by the press, John Kenny Jr. of the Kenny Construction

The death of Tony Accardo (left),
with Sam Giancana, signaled the
end of an era for Chicago
mobsters.

Co. was tapped by the mayor to spearhead the city's efforts to plug the leaks.

Though besieged with a variety of ideas—from filling the flooded tunnel with Jell-O to using mattresses to stop the flow—Kenny and his team solved the crisis by first plugging shafts east and west of the river and filling them with cement. Later, bulkheads were created to ensure what the mayor termed a "permanent solution."

Though testy with reporters during much of the crisis, Daley today calls it "one of the most dramatic chapters in the city's history." The mayor says he's proud of how everyone reacted after the floodgates opened.

"Look. No one was killed or seriously injured. We evacuated the downtown so smoothly…even the federal authorities were impressed we did it so quickly," he said.

On the heels of the flood, an engineering failure caused the Michigan Avenue Bridge to snap open, nearly threat-

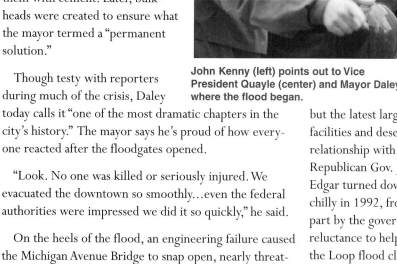

John Kenny (left) points out to Vice President Quayle (center) and Mayor Daley where the flood began.

Workers survey the flooded pedway near the Daley Center.

ening the important holiday shopping season on the Magnificent Mile.

Then negative national publicity flared about the serious rioting and looting on the West Side following the Bulls' second consecutive championship. And in a year with a soaring murder rate, the murder of 7-year-old Dantrell Davis, en route to school near his Cabrini-Green home, served as another signal of street gangs' power in the inner city.

Spiegel and Oscar Mayer were but the latest large businesses to close headquarter facilities and desert Chicago. Never warm, Daley's relationship with Republican Gov. Jim Edgar turned downright chilly in 1992, frosted in part by the governor's reluctance to help fund the Loop flood cleanup.

Tagged "The Year of the Woman," Illinois voters proved it by electing to the U.S. Senate the relatively unknown Cook County Recorder of Deeds, Carol Moseley-Braun—making her the first African-American female senator.

Carol Moseley-Braun

The year also marked the end of an era for organized crime, when reputed Chicago mob boss Accardo, 86, once Al Capone's bodyguard, died peacefully in his bed at St. Mary of Nazareth Hospital on May 27.

AUGUST	SEPTEMBER	OCTOBER	DECEMBER	ALSO IN 1992
U.S. District Judge Ilana D. Rovner becomes the first woman on the U.S. Court of Appeals in Chicago.	A leaf of the Michigan Avenue drawbridge snaps open, flipping a huge crane, showering the street with debris and causing nearly $5 million in damage. No one is seriously injured.	Alarm clocks given to guests at a pre-concert party by the Chicago Symphony Orchestra beep persistently during a performance of the Tchaikovsky piano concerto No. 1 performed by Daniel Barenboim under the direction of Georg Solti.	Catholic priest Robert E. Mayer, former pastor of a Berwyn parish, is convicted of criminal sexual abuse for fondling a 13-year-old girl in the church rectory. He is later sentenced to three years.	Oprah Winfrey announces her engagement to Stedman Graham. At the century's end, they were still engaged.

MICHAEL'S FIRST RETIREMENT

Jerry Reinsdorf
Chairman of the
Chicago White Sox
and the Chicago
Bulls

After leading the Chicago
Bulls to three straight
NBA championships,
Michael Jordan stunned
the sports world with the
announcement of his
retirement, which was
covered by media from all
around the globe.

BY JERRY REINSDORF

Two images—both clinching moments in Chicago sports history—flash through my memory when I recall 1993.

The first came in late June when guard John Paxson gave the Chicago Bulls their third consecutive NBA title when his Game 6 shot seconds before the buzzer sealed the victory over the Suns in Phoenix.

The second came in late September, when Bo Jackson clinched the American League West title for the Chicago White Sox with a three-run home run in a 4-2 victory over Seattle. It was the Sox' first division title in a decade.

I couldn't have been sitting in a better spot to see Paxson's game-winning jumper. From where I sat, you could draw a straight line from me, through Paxson, to the basket. As he went up to shoot, a single thought raced through my mind: "It's Dallas all over again."

Two or three years before, the Bulls had trailed the Mavericks by two in Dallas. We brought the ball the length of the court with Michael Jordan passing off to Paxson.

John's shot cut through the net just as the buzzer sounded, and the Bulls escaped with a win. The same image repeated itself in my mind.

Paxson for three, YES! And the Bulls win their third straight NBA crown.

JANUARY		FEBRUARY	MARCH	APRIL	MAY
Chicago Bears coach Mike Ditka is fired. Seven people are found shot to death in a Brown's Chicken and Pasta restaurant in Palatine. The crime has not been solved. Mike Ditka		Former Chicago Heights mayor Charles Panici is convicted of pocketing kickbacks for inflated sweetheart city contracts. He is later sentenced to 10 years in prison and ordered to pay the city $1.1 million restitution.	Twenty are killed in a fire at the Paxton Hotel, 1432 N. La Salle. The tragedy prompted changes in the fire code, including a requirement that so-called Single Room Occupany hotels have fire alarms.	Former Cook County judge Thomas J. Maloney is found guilty of fixing three murder trials. He is later sentenced to 15 years in federal prison.	Motorists scoop up tens of thousands of dollars that fall from an armored car on Stevenson Expy.

While still in his prime, but rocked by the murder of his father, James (right), and with his growing interest in baseball, Jordan announced an early retirement from basketball.

This time, Paxson's shot meant a third straight NBA championship as the Jordan-led team became the NBA's first since the Boston Celtics' dynasty of the 1960s to boast back-to-back-to-back rings.

As the ball shot off Bo's bat on that September evening, all I could think was: "He did it. What a wonderful, fantastic story." Bo had come back from that serious injury—he had hip replacement surgery in April 1991 and missed all of the 1992 season—to help us to a division title.

When the ball landed just beyond the left-field fence, Comiskey Park erupted in celebration.

Not long after the basketball season ended, Michael and White Sox General Manager Ron Schueler were talking in my Comiskey Park suite during a Sox game.

They called me over. Michael wanted to play a few games for our Class A club in Hickory, N.C. He wanted

Bo Jackson

to know if that was OK with me.

I knew he had taken batting practice at Old Comiskey Park in 1990 and enjoyed the experience. This way he could be near his home in North Carolina and give playing baseball a shot.

"Yeah, go ahead, it's OK with me," I said. What we didn't know that day was that his father was already dead, killed in a highway robbery.

That September, I saw Michael at his annual gala charity event. Considering the summer he had gone through, he seemed very upbeat and happy.

I invited him out to Comiskey Park to throw out a first pitch during the playoffs. Soon after, Michael's agent, David Falk, called to say, "I don't know how serious he is, but MJ might not want to play basketball this year."

I was stunned.

On Oct. 2, I met with Michael and David. Michael said he wanted to retire. I didn't try to talk him out of it, but I told him, "We can't announce it until you talk to [Bulls coach] Phil [Jackson]."

"I don't want to talk to Phil," Michael said. "He might talk me out of it."

"Then you have to talk to Phil," I said.

We held a press conference in Deerfield on Oct. 6 to announce Michael's retirement. Michael wanted to say he was never coming back.

I told him, "Never say never."

JUNE	JULY		AUGUST	OCTOBER
Downpours flood much of the South Side.	President Clinton approves the closings of Glenview Naval Air Station and Air Force Reserve Station at O'Hare Airport.	 Bill Clinton	Dr. Martin R. Sullivan, 68, a prominent plastic surgeon, is shot to death in his Wilmette office. Police charge Jonathan Preston Haynes, 34, who says he hates people who create "fake Aryan beauty."	University of Chicago economist Robert Fogel wins the Nobel Prize in economics. His keystone work was an analysis of slavery that concluded the system was profitable and probably would have continued had the Civil War and the empancipation of slaves not occurred.

TRAGEDY UPON TRAGEDY

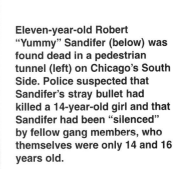

Della de Lafuente
Former Sun-Times
reporter

Eleven-year-old Robert "Yummy" Sandifer (below) was found dead in a pedestrian tunnel (left) on Chicago's South Side. Police suspected that Sandifer's stray bullet had killed a 14-year-old girl and that Sandifer had been "silenced" by fellow gang members, who themselves were only 14 and 16 years old.

BY DELLA DE LAFUENTE

Children killing children, a year without a World Series and World Cup Soccer defined 1994 for many Chicagoans.

First, on a cold February day, the discovery of 19 children, ages 1 to 14, crowded into a squalid apartment at 219 N. Keystone shocked the nation.

Five sisters—mothers of 23 children—and a brother initially were charged with misdemeanor child neglect. Denise Turner, then 20, and the mother of three of the children, was charged with felony cruelty to a child.

But headlines about the so-called "Keystone Kids" were soon replaced by others on

horrific crimes committed by youngsters. The increase in young murderers shocked even police. At least 10 youths 12 years old or younger were charged with murder in Chicago in 1993 and 1994.

"It's tragedy upon tragedy upon tragedy," said then-Cook County State's Attorney Jack O'Malley when he announced the arrests of two young suspects in the death of Robert "Yummy" Sandifer, 11.

Sandifer, the chief suspect in the murder of 14-year-old Shavon Dean, who was cut down Aug. 28 by a stray bullet while playing outside her home in the Roseland neighborhood, spent three days as a fugitive and later

MARCH	APRIL	MAY	JUNE
The Chicago Sun-Times is purchased by American Publishing Company, a subsidiary of Hollanger Inc., which also owns The Daily Telegraph (London) and the Jerusalem Post. The investment group which sold the Sun-Times was headed by Leonard Shaykin.	A federal judge bars warrantless weapons sweeps in CHA public housing projects.	John Wayne Gacy, 52, is executed by lethal injection. Thus ends one of the most gruesome chapters in the annals of criminal justice.	U.S. Rep. Dan Rostenkowski pleads innocent to charges he misused more than $600,000 in federal funds since the early 1970s and steps down as chairman of the House Ways and Means Committee.

Five first-round World Cup games are played at Soldier Field, bringing in soccer fans to Chicago from throughout the country.

U.S. Representative Dan Rostenkowski

This fan held a candlelight vigil outside Wrigley Field to protest the strike that canceled the second half of the 1994 baseball season.

was found slain in a pedestrian tunnel about a mile from his home.

Police said fellow gang members wanted to silence him. Cragg Hardaway, 16, and his brother, Derrick, 14, were charged with the murder.

Then just days after Sandifer was killed, an 11-year-old boy was charged with murdering an 84-year-old neighbor the previous year. And just as it appeared the news could not be more grim, 5-year-old Eric Morse was dropped to his death from the 14th floor of a vacant apartment in the Ida B. Wells public housing complex on Oct. 13.

Two boys, 10 and 11, were charged with dropping him as Eric's 8-year-old brother struggled to save his life. The motive: the brothers refused to steal candy for the older boys.

Perhaps the sad stories of child murderers gripped Chicagoans even tighter because they were divested of lighter diversions as baseball players held their sport hostage.

The baseball strike that canceled the World Series, depriving the White Sox of a run at the pennant, was considered no less than a national tragedy by many diehard fans.

"The whole season was wiped out. The strike hurt a lot," says Jay Schaller, who's tended bar at his family's South Side tavern, Schaller Pump, since 1984.

"It was like the Super Bowl, or the Academy Awards, was cancelled. There was no baseball," recalls Jimmy Jones, owner of the Wrigleyville Tap, one of hundreds of sports bar owners who endured a business decline during the strike.

The strike put beer and food vendors out of work, and many of baseball's die-hard fans vowed never to return to the city's major league ballparks.

While the boys of summer took the season off, World Cup Soccer brought a new sport to Soldier Field, boosting the city's image around the globe. The 1,800 journalists who covered the five World Cup games here transmitted glowing accounts of the city around the world. This translated into a steady rise in visitors and a 75 percent hotel occupancy rate, up from 60 percent.

"It was an unprecedented opportunity to make Chicago an international destination," said Leslie Fox, director of the Chicago Host Committee for the World Cup.

Not all the news in '94 was bad. When the World Cup came to Chicago, the city shone brightly to millions around the world.

World Cup Soccer at Soldier Field

JULY

Horse trainer Richard Bailey is charged with soliciting the murder of vanished candy heiress Helen Vorhees Brach in 1977 because she caught on to his insurance scam.

OCTOBER

American Eagle Flight 4184, on its way to Chicago from Indianapolis, crashes in an Indiana soybean field during a storm, killing 68.

NOVEMBER

Sears transfers ownership of the Sears Tower to a trust overseen by its mortgage lenders in order to eliminate $850 million in debt.

1995

DEATH PENALTY DANGER

Thomas Frisbie
Sun-Times staff reporter and co-author of *Victims of Justice*

Rolando Cruz, freed in 1995, leaves the DuPage County Courthouse with his wife, Dora, after a subsequent court proceeding.

Michael Jordan, who had retired in 1993, returned to the Chicago Bulls in 1995.

BY THOMAS FRISBIE

The year 1995 was a year of turnarounds so surprising that, even after they happened, some people couldn't quite believe them.

In March, Michael Jordan, whose career statistics already had been carved in black marble at the base of a bronze statue at the new United Center on West Madison, came out of retirement. He would lead the Chicago Bulls to three more NBA championships on top of the three his teams had won in 1991-1993.

In the fall, Northwestern University's lowly football team, a perennial habitué of the Big Ten's cellar, beat gridiron titans Notre Dame, Michigan and Penn State en

route to a 10-1 regular season and the Wildcats' first Rose Bowl appearance in 47 years.

But perhaps the most remarkable turnaround was in Illinois' criminal justice system. In a year when the rest of the nation was focused on the O. J. Simpson trial, the long-running Jeanine Nicarico murder case culminated in a dramatic and unexpected acquittal.

On Nov. 3, in the DuPage County courthouse in west suburban Wheaton, Rolando Cruz was found not guilty of the 10-year-old Naperville girl's 1983 rape and

JANUARY

Violinist Rachel Barton loses her left leg after she is caught beneath a rolling Metra train. She later sues Metra and Chicago & North Western Ry. and, in 1999, is awarded $29.6 million.

FEBRUARY

The demolition of Chicago Stadium begins.

MARCH

Ald. Shirley Coleman discloses during her reelection campaign that she was once married to and had a daughter with Hernando Williams, who was on Death Row for a 1978 rape and murder. Williams is executed five days later. Coleman's opponent, Hal Baskin, reacts to the disclosure by saying that Williams committed the crimes because Coleman was not a good wife. Baskin later publicly apologizes; Coleman wins reelection.

Steinmetz High School's Academic Decathlon team is stripped of its state title in what a Board of Education officer calls the Chicago public schools' biggest cheating scandal in 20 years. Some of the team members admit cheating, saying that they were given stolen copies of tests.

Alejandro Hernandez, whose cause was taken up by Scott Turow, also had his conviction reversed.

murder. Two weeks later, Cruz's former co-defendant Alejandro Hernandez was freed.

Cruz and Hernandez each had spent more than a decade in prison, much of it on Death Row. Both had proclaimed their innocence from the start. Many people, however, were confident that the criminal justice system would never sentence innocent people to die.

A common reaction was summed up by Chicago lawyer and best-selling author Scott Turow, who—describing his own initial viewpoint—said, "Here are two defendants beefing, as usual."

As Turow learned more about the case, however, his skepticism turned into outrage. He agreed to represent Hernandez. And as serious flaws in the cases against Cruz

and Hernandez emerged, many citizens came to share Turow's point of view.

Prior to Rolando Cruz, no Illinois defendant ever had won a reversal of a second murder conviction. Only three men had been freed from Death Row since the death penalty was reinstated in 1977.

After Cruz's acquittal, many people no longer could take the fairness of the Illinois criminal justice system for granted. The result was a parade of innocent men leaving Death Row. As the end of the century neared, 12 men had been set free—a total equal to the number who had been executed since 1977.

After Cruz and Hernandez were freed, Death Row inmates Verneal Jimerson, Dennis Williams, Gary Gauger and Carl Lawson were released in 1996, followed by Anthony Porter, Ronald Jones and Steven Smith in 1999.

Attention then turned to the so-called Death Row 10—men whose confessions allegedly had been obtained through systematic abuse by Chicago Police Cmdr. Jon Burge and his detectives at Area 2. An investigation wound up in Burge's 1993 firing, but the Death Row 10 remained condemned men. In 1999, their appeals were still being debated.

"Each of these cases, beginning with Cruz, has had an impact on everyone involved in the criminal justice system," said Locke Bowman, legal director of the University of Chicago Law School's MacArthur Justice Center. "It has an impact on the way potential jurors think, on the way defense attorneys react to a client's protestations of innocence and hopefully on prosecutors and judges as well."

The 1983 murder of 10-year-old Jeanine Nicarico of Naperville led to the charges against Cruz and Hernandez.

APRIL

A four-year old boy known as Baby Richard is transferred to his biological father Otakar Kirchner from his adoptive parents Kim and Robert "Jay" Warburton as a crowd of media and neighbors watch. The dramatic turnover came after the Illinois Supreme Court voided the adoption and ruled the child belonged with Kirchner, who had been estranged from the boy's mother, Daniella, when he was born. The couple later wed and now have three children.

Baby Richard

JULY

Two fatal heat waves lead to an estimated 733 deaths and tens of thousands of people becoming seriously ill. Cooling centers are opened around the city.

AUGUST

U.S. Rep. Mel Reynolds is convicted of sexual misconduct, child pornography and trying to block an investigation. Later, he is sentenced to five years in prison.

OCTOBER

Seven teenagers are killed and nearly two dozen are injured when a Metra train slams into a school bus in northwest suburban Fox River Grove. The accident prompts a massive federal review of railroad crossing safety.

TINY PARTICLES—BIG DISCOVERY

Leon M. Lederman
Nobel Prize winner, former director of Fermilab and University of Chicago professor

Leon M. Lederman points to the sign on his door at Fermilab that identifies him as a Nobel Prize winner.

BY LEON M. LEDERMAN

It was a banner year for particle physics, an exotic subject that simply seeks to know how the Universe works and engages some of the most brilliant physicists in the Chicago area.

They are residents at the University of Chicago, University of Illinois at Chicago, Northwestern University and the Illinois Institute of Technology, but the focus of activities is Fermilab, home of the world's most powerful particle accelerator.

In 1996, a series of experiments on this big machine finally paid off in the discovery of "top"—the affectionate name for the top quark, the missing piece in a puzzle of primordial constituents of matter.

So what does this mean to the Chicagoans lining up at Wrigley Field, strangling in an Eisenhower traffic jam, or exiting the Lyric in a trance of satisfaction? If I had another thousand words, I know I could convince Mayor Daley, Studs Terkel, Sammy Sosa and Sun-Times readers that, in 1996, we learned something profound about our universe.

For 17 years, laboratories around the world raced to find "top," but one by one they dropped out of the quest because their machines were not powerful enough.

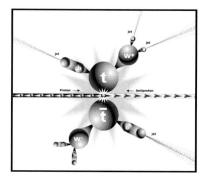

In the above illustration, the proton and antiproton are colliding at nearly the speed of light, which produces a top Quark (t) and the antitop Quark ($\bar{t}$).

In 1996, Chicago was the site of the Democratic National Convention, the first held in the city since the riotous 1968 convention.

electric charge, mass, spin and others, but with no internal structure. Physics had tracked matter from molecules to atoms to nuclei to protons to quarks, but there is a belief that quarks are the bottom-line basic building blocks.

However, the top quark was a curious object, a point particle more massive than a gold atom, which is precisely why it was so hard to find. We know from Einstein that mass is equivalent to energy, and only Fermilab had enough energy to produce a particle as massive as top.

We were successful in mastering the awesome technology of machines and instruments. These are having a major influence on our economy, on medical advances.

In 1994, only Fermilab was left to screen the millions of head-on-collisions of protons and antiprotons at the unprecedented energy of almost 2 trillion electron volts. By 1995, research data hinted the big discovery was near.

It was also an eventful year for Chicago. First, there was the Democratic convention, which in its very tranquility, recalled its traumatic predecessor, the convention of 1968, also the year Fermilab was founded.

The death of Cardinal Joseph Bernardin was another event that shook the physicists and moved them, temporarily, from their computers to the TV. Bernardin had visited Fermilab, and his concerns for nuclear disarmament strongly resonated with the physicists.

But now we had the top emerging as the result of two independent experiments. The data were solid, but the properties of top were astonishing. Quarks, to the best of our knowledge, are point particles, rich in properties like

However, what moved us in our 1996 euphoria was that our research for top was both satisfying and suggestive. What we did at Fermilab was to move us closer to the place where the workings of our universe—in which humanity is embedded—will be understood. If history is a guide, the new laws of nature will be transcendentally beautiful. By the designs, we will know how the world evolved to accommodate us. And perhaps—perhaps—we will also learn a deeper purpose to our lives.

Cardinal Joseph Bernardin

JUNE

The Chicago Bulls complete the greatest season in NBA history with a 72-10 regular-season record and their fourth NBA championship in six years.

SEPTEMBER

Gov. Jim Edgar threatens to have the state take over Meigs Field if Mayor Daley proceeds with his plan to close the airfield. Daley proposed developing the site on Northerly Island into a $27 million nature preserve and recreational complex. Edgar and Daley later settled on a compromise to close the airport in 2002.

Governor Jim Edgar

DECEMBER

Mystery writer Eugene Izzi is found hanged outside the 14th-floor window of an office building at 6 N. Michigan. Police spent weeks trying to learn whether Izzi was murdered or tried to make his suicide look like murder. They eventually concluded there was no foul play.

DOWNTOWN RENAISSANCE

Avis L. Weathersbee

Sun-Times assistant features editor

In its heyday, the Empire Room at the Palmer House (left) drew people from all around the Chicago area. Today, with the renovations of many theaters and music halls, Chicago once again is an entertainment destination for many.

BY AVIS L. WEATHERSBEE

In the latter half of the century, Chicago's glorious downtown—like those of other major cities—fell into decline. Gone were the movie palaces, nightclubs, concert and dance halls that once gave the area its cultural cachet.

But 1997 marked a turning point for the city, as projects aimed at revitalizing the once-flourishing entertainment mecca got under way.

One major shot in the arm that year was the start of the $32 million renovation of the Oriental Theater, an ornate former movie palace with an exotic Far East motif.

The refurbished Ford Center for the Performing Arts/Oriental Theater opened the following year with "Ragtime," a play that appropriately captured the spirit of Chicago's diverse population.

The Oriental restoration was an important cog in plans to fashion a thriving legitimate theater district in the heart of the city. That district will include a new home for the Goodman Theatre, the reborn Palace Theatre (formerly the Bismarck) and the already operational Chicago and Shubert theaters.

Interior of the refurbished Oriental Theater

MARCH

Lenard Clark, a 13-year-old African-American youth, is beaten into a coma in Armour Square Park in the Bridgeport neighborhood. The racially motivated attack eventually sent Frank Caruso Jr. to prison for eight years. Michael Kwidzinski and Victor Jasas received two years and 30 months probation, respectively.

MAY

Developer Lee Miglin is found brutally slain in his Gold Coast garage. The suspect, Andrew Cunanan, also is wanted in the killings of two men in Minnesota. Soon another victim is found in New Jersey—a cemetery caretaker apparently killed for his truck. The final victim, before the manhunt ended with Cunanan's suicide, was fashion designer Gianni Versace in Miami Beach.

JUNE

The Bulls win their fifth championship in seven years. Michael Jordan is once again named MVP of the NBA Finals, the fifth time in his career.

AUGUST

Flowers, notes, pictures, stuffed animals and religious cards are left at the Wrigley Building, where people line up to sign the British Consulate's condolence book after the death of Princess Diana, who a year earlier paid a royal visit to Chicago.

Gov. Jim Edgar announces he will not seek a third term in Illinois' highest office, nor would he be a candidate for the U.S. Senate, as had been speculated.

"It's a magnificent coalescence of cultural energies in one remarkable place—ground zero of the Loop," says Frank Galati, who directed "Ragtime" and often works with the Goodman and the renowned off-Loop Steppenwolf Theatre Company. "It is the revitalization of a splendid dimension of urban life."

At one time Chicagoans would get dressed up to come downtown and enjoy stars like Gertrude Lawrence at the Civic Theatre, Katherine Hepburn at the Selwyn-Harris theaters, Danny Thomas and Sophie Tucker at the Chez Paree and George Shearing at the London House.

They'd listen to Fats Waller at the College Inn, Billie Holiday at the Blue Note Club and Maurice Chevalier at the Empire Room. And they would admire the footwork of the Merriel Abbott dancers at the elegant Empire Room or swing dance to Art Tatum at Three Deuces.

"The Empire Room was gorgeous. People really enjoyed nightlife in those days," recalled Sherry Wynn, 79, a former Abbott singer and dancer.

In 1999, people were flocking back to urban Chicago. Besides theater, downtown offers music clubs like the Plaza Tavern, Buddy Guy's Legends, Koko Taylor's Celebrity, the House of Blues and the Jazz Showcase. And now our town is second city to none in the area of dance, as well.

Sophie Tucker

Billie Holiday

Art Tatum

The Joffrey Ballet, which moved here from New York, and other Chicago troupes such as the popular Hubbard Street Dance Company will soon leap and pirouette in a 1,500-seat, recessed theater being built in the new Millennium Park at Randolph Street and Michigan Avenue.

And stage arts will have another city home at the just-completed Shakespeare Theater—the plan was first unveiled in '97—which will keep the Bard's musings ever on the lips of all who visit Navy Pier.

About 12 blocks west of the pier, 95-year-old Orchestra Hall dressed up for the new century during 1997 after a $112.7 million remodeling.

Rechristened Symphony Center, the larger facility gave the Chicago Symphony Orchestra badly needed rehearsal and administrative space and allowed more pop and jazz to take their place alongside the world-class CSO.

Opera has been an icon in Chicago for decades, and as the century turns, remains so. In 1997 at the renovated Civic Opera House, Lyric Opera of Chicago produced the ambitious "Amistad," a new opera by Anthony Davis recounting the saga of an 1839 revolt aboard a Spanish slave ship.

"Amistad" demonstrated that opera, like the vibrant downtown area and Chicago itself, builds on its past and looks forward to its future with daring.

Princess Diana in Chicago

OCTOBER

The Sun-Times reports that Mayor Richard M. Daley's floor leader, Ald. Patrick Huels, had received a $1.25 million bailout loan for his private security company from a city contractor. Huels, a boyhood friend of Daley's, later resigns.

NOVEMBER

Northwestern professor Leon Forrest, a modernist writer whose 1,135-page novel *Divine Days* has been described as the *War and Peace* of African-American literature, dies at 60 of cancer. Forrest, who taught English and African-American studies on the Evanston campus for 24 years, is eulogized by novelist Toni Morrison, who edited his first three books.

Roger Brown, 55, one of the most celebrated practitioners of the Chicago school of painting called the Imagists, dies in Alabama. During the 1960s, Brown developed a signature style in which urban scenes were peopled by many silhouettes—on the streets and in windows—all making some large gesture. Major retrospectives of his work have been hung in the Art Institute, the Museum of Contemporary Art, the National Museum of American Art and the Whitney Museum of American Art.

MJ, THE CARDINAL AND SAMMY

Ernest Tucker
Sun-Times staff
reporter

Francis George, head of the
Archdiocese of Chicago, was
elevated to cardinal by Pope
John Paul II in 1998.

BY ERNEST TUCKER

An unexpected trio illuminated Chicago in 1998. One came from Brooklyn, N.Y., by way of North Carolina, another from the Northwest Side of Chicago, and the third from an impoverished island in the Caribbean.

One black, one white and one Hispanic. Each reached a different point on his arc that year. For Chicago-born Francis George, it was the start. Installed head of the Archdiocese of Chicago less than a year before, his elevation on February 21 by Pope John Paul II to the second-highest rank in the Roman Catholic church was a recognition of the city, not just his own achievements.

"Once you're archbishop of Chicago you kind of know eventually—unless you really, really foul up—you'll probably become a cardinal," he joked to reporters at his residence a month before the Rome ceremonies.

For Sammy Sosa, a player of sometimes suspect habits while with the White Sox and even the Cubs the year before, the Dominican Republican native exploded into a hemispheric hero. Although he lost the homer battle with slugger Mark McGwire, falling four short of the St. Louis lumberjack's single-season record of 70,

Sammy Sosa's historic home run duel
with Mark McGwire captivated all of
Chicago, as well as Sosa's Dominican
Republic homeland.

JANUARY

More than 1 million Hostess Ho-Hos, Twinkies and other snacks are recalled after asbestos is discovered in a Schiller Park plant that produced the goods.

APRIL

To carry on the tradition of Hall of Fame broadcaster Harry Caray, who died in February, Caray's widow, Dutchie, led the seventh-inning Wrigley Field rendition of "Take Me Out to the Ball Game."

Harry Caray

MAY

Cubs rookie Kerry Wood ties the major-league record by striking out 20 Astros in a game won by the Cubs, 2-0. Wood was later named the National League's Rookie of the Year.

Kerry Wood

JULY

The Chicago-based American Medical Association, harshly criticized for endorsing a commercial product, agrees to pay Sunbeam $9.9 million in compensation for backing out of a deal to endorse Sunbeam products.

Sosa earned the National League's Most Valuable Player award.

He led the Cubs into the playoffs for only the third time since 1945 by winning a one-game wild-card playoff over the San Francisco Giants, and then, even after losing two to Atlanta, found the courage to predict a victory at home.

"If we win tonight, I think things are going to change," he said.

They didn't, and the near-century-long championship drought continued.

What the Cubs couldn't do, the Bulls—with Michael Jordan—did one last time.

Despite a subpar performance in Jordan's final home game with the Bulls on June 12 at the United Center, when his 9-of-26 shooting helped the Utah Jazz to victory, Air Jordan concluded a career that helped push the National Basketball Association into global prominence, and in the process, kill off the old image of Chicago as Al Capone's home.

The image of Jordan, all sinew and sweat, spread into a billion-dollar worldwide franchise, with Bulls emblems sprouting wherever clothing was worn.

While some held out hope the hero wearing number 23 would return for the 1998-99 season—and somehow convince Bulls coach Phil Jackson and

Sosa salutes the crowd at Wrigley Field.

sidekick Scottie Pippen to stay—it was not to be.

"It's time for me to go," Jackson said merely a week after some 300,000 jammed Grant Park for the traditional victory rally. Six gleaming NBA trophies were on display.

"I do know that no matter what happens, my heart, my soul, my love will still be in the City of Chicago," Jordan said.

The bitter parting had been ordained since North Carolina's Michael Jeffrey Jordan arrived here for his 1984-85 rookie season and began the Herculean job of lifting Chicago from the murky depths of the basketball world. The fine print was there: the 6-foot-6 superman had actually been born on February 17, 1963, which meant at some point, improbable as it seemed, age would catch up and deflate His Airness.

Jordan had prepared everyone with a dress rehearsal when he retired on October 6, 1993, to pursue his dream of playing pro baseball. A statue was erected on the east side of the arena at 1901 W. Madison, depicting a soaring Jordan stomping over a claylike opponent. Once, like a Greek myth, it came to life after 17 months.

But except for a brief glimpse of Jordan throwing out the first pitch at the Cubs' playoff to his friend Sosa, the statue remains frozen, encasing a gold of the rarest kind, which dazzled in 1998.

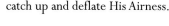

Michael Jordan announces his second retirement from basketball.

AUGUST
A second voice of Chicago fandom, Jack Brickhouse, dies. The Hall of Famer was 82.

SEPTEMBER
Goodman Theatre Artistic Director Robert Falls directs "Death of a Salesman" by Arthur Miller, starring Brian Dennehy. The production went on to Broadway, where it won four Tony Awards.

Brian Dennehy (right) and Kevin Anderson

NOVEMBER
Steppenwolf Theatre is awarded the National Medal of Arts at the White House, becoming the only theater company ever to receive the award.

Steppenwolf artistic director Martha Lavey with President and Mrs. Clinton

DECEMBER
The Bears sack coach Dave Wannstedt after five years. The hiring of Wannstedt's successor, Dick Jauron, was so poorly handled that Mike McCaskey lost his job as head of football operations for the Bears.

209

A SONG OF CHICAGO

Ramsey Lewis
Jazz pianist and
composer

Even as Chicago
celebrated Mayor Daley's
reelection to a fourth term
and the enormous
success of the Cows on
Parade exhibit, the city
mourned the senseless
slaying of Ricky Byrdsong
(below).

BY RAMSEY LEWIS

Imagine trying to write a jazz composition interpreting this last year of this last century in this first-class city.

It would require notes both high and low, plenty of familiar riffs, equal measures of cool phrasing and hot intensity and—since this is Chicago and a jazz piece—plenty of room for improvisation.

But throughout, one theme would emerge: Despite deviations and dark passages, strength and optimism would triumph.

Take one of 1999's darkest moments, when white supremacist Benjamin Smith went on a hate-filled July 4 weekend shooting spree, killing two and wounding nine.

Slain was former Northwestern University basketball coach Ricky Byrdsong, whose work with young people made him the opposite of everything Smith stood for.

But even as they grappled with their grief, Byrdsong's family forged ahead with his legacy. A month after the tragedy, Byrdsong's widow, Sherialyn, opened a basketball camp her husband had organized for inner-city kids by singing R. Kelly's inspirational anthem "I Believe I Can Fly."

It's a song Chicago has been playing for decades.

MARCH

Eleven people die and more than 100 are injured when the Amtrak City of New Orleans train from Chicago plows into a semi-trailer truck just north of Kankakee. The train was carrying about 215 passengers.

Marilyn Lemak of Naperville is charged with murdering her three children in their home. Police say she killed them and planned to kill herself after she and her husband, David, separated.

JUNE

The largest crowd to see a soccer game at Soldier Field, 65,080, cheers wildly as the U.S. women's team defeats Nigeria 7-1 in the first round of the Women's World Cup. The U.S. team would go on to capture the World Cup title a few weeks later.

Chicago saxophonist Ken Vandermark is awarded a $265,000 genius grant by the MacArthur Foundation.

AUGUST

McDonald's opens its 25,000th restaurant in the world, in the Bronzeville neighborhood of Chicago.

SEPTEMBER

More than 76,000 Illinois motorists choose a blue-and-white license plate with red lettering, Lincoln's image and the familiar Land of Lincoln slogan for new plates to be issued in 2001.

The century began with a Herculean effort to reverse the Chicago River. It ended with less auspicious projects—a techno scramble to avoid the Y2K computer glitch and Commonwealth Edison trying to keep the lights from going out.

And it was more than darkened TVs and spoiled food. One string of outages came during a heat wave that claimed at least 69 lives.

Mayor Daley won another term, moving closer to his father's long tenure. City Treasurer Miriam Santos lost her corruption trial, continuing a sadder Chicago tradition.

But the year had its lighter moments.

Chicago fell in love with the 327 fiberglass cows that turned downtown into a wild and whimsical pasture of people's art. Tourists and locals alike stopped, studied, snickered and snapped pictures and enjoyed some udderly uninihibited art appreciation.

And of course there was music. All kinds. The Rolling Stones and Bruce Springsteen made separate visits to give their Baby Boomer fans a chance to feel like kids again—if only for a night.

The Irish Tenors' mix of Celtic joy and yearning brought smiles and tears to the United Center in July. And on a starry night a few weeks later, Ravinia presented its last concert of the millennium—a benefit dubbed "the Ultimate Gala."

It featured the Chicago Symphony Orchestra and a feast of musical stars, including violinists Isaac Stern and Midori, mezzo-soprano Frederica von Stade, pianist Alicia de Larrocha—yours truly at the piano and my trio, dishing out some smooth jazz.

That's what is so great about Chicago as the millennium comes to a close.

Benjamin Smith

We have a jazz culture. We have real blues—brought up by the people who came here from the South. We have the greatest symphony orchestra, the Lyric Opera, dance companies, art, theater, world-class architecture.

And we have our children.

I was lucky. I had two parents. They both worked but still found time to spend with my two sisters and myself. I tried to do the same with my seven children, and they followed suit with their kids.

Other families are fighting that same battle daily.

That's because this town is a lot like a virtuoso jazz combo. It's a multicultural mix that takes the pain, the pleasure, the suffering, the joy, the smiles and the tears and tries to turn them into something beautiful.

It's improvisation Chicago style.

Ramsey Lewis shares his legendary jazz talents with the next generation of pianists and composers.

WALTER PAYTON 1954-1999
Bears great dies

LOOKING BACK: THE BARK OF THE UNDERDOG

Don Hayner
Sun-Times metropolitan editor and co-author with Tom McNamee of the *Metro Chicago Almanac*

BY DON HAYNER

Chicago began the century in pure Chicago fashion. It acted like God.

On Jan. 2, 1900, it reversed the flow of the river running through the center of town. In one bold swoop, it changed the course of its geography along with the course of its sewage.

And it didn't stop there. For the next 100 years Chicago kept rearranging its landscape like a giant playing in a sandbox.

In the opening decades, Chicago constructed a dazzling lakefront 29 miles long, almost all of it beaches and parks. In the closing decades, Chicago began burrowing beneath the city to build the mighty Deep Tunnel, a 131-mile stretch of sewers as wide as 36 feet and as deep as 320.

The century saw boulevards built, forests grown and massive expressways carved from the city's core and out to the suburbs like spokes on a huge wheel.

And year by year the skyline soared.

And while Carl Sandburg was right about the city's brawny shoulders, he failed to mention the chip on top.

Chicago always wanted to show the world who was boss. And in case you haven't heard, it ain't New York. No matter what it achieved, Chicago saw itself as the underdog with the "second city" syndrome. But its insecurity gave the city its power.

Chicago wanted to be better than the best, but never felt like it was. So it kept challenging New York and L.A. like a kid picking a fight with the toughest punk on the corner. Sometimes it even took on Paris.

Why else would we obsess over having the world's busiest airport, tallest building and biggest convention center— not to mention one of the best collections of Impressionist paintings this side of France?

My God, we even bragged about having the world's biggest sewage treatment plant. Pick a subject, any subject, and a Chicagoan can find some bragging rights. Who's the world's best-known gangster, greatest basketball player and most famous TV star? That's right, all made in Chicago— Big Al, Michael and Oprah.

And while this little attitude was annoying, it was also inspiring.

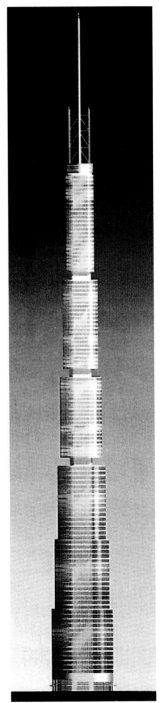

For the last 100 years, Chicago truly believed anything was possible. The city mantra came with a nod from architect Daniel Burnham: "Make no little plans, they have no magic to stir men's blood."

It seemed to apply to any Chicagoan—if you could solve the problem, step right up. And if an idea came from somebody nobody heard of, like Edward P. Brennan, hey, there was always a shot. Especially if your cousin was an alderman.

Brennan, a building superintendent for a downtown music store, came up with an incredible idea in the early 1900s to renumber all the city streets with a starting point at State and Madison. Aldermen scratched their heads over this preposterous idea. Then, led by Brennan's cousin, they passed it.

With that, Chicago was given a grid system as easy to read as lines on a sheet of graph paper. And since this is Chicago, Brennan also got something—a street named in his honor.

Chicago ran hard in the 20th century, always trying to outpace New York or any other place that felt it could outbuild, outdo or outhustle the rising prince of the prairie. With a chip that never fell from its shoulder, Chicago punched through the century like a fist through a paper bag. It controlled the country's food with its commodity markets, and as the birthplace of the skyscraper, it wrote its signature on the nation's skyline.

City boosters pointed to efficiency as a virtue on a par with motherhood. Meat packers bragged of making use of every part of the pig but the squeal. And billing became easier with the Chicago invention of the window envelope. But some of that, like the stockyards and the steel mills, came and went in the 20th Century. Yet, the city kept coming back.

If Burnham provided the mantra for the century, the 1893 Columbian World's Fair provided the motto: "I Will." Chicago union organizers and social activists here changed the way the nation lived and worked. With labor strife and child labor woes straining the country, Chicago saw itself as the great fixer.

Even if it meant fixing the way people act.

Indeed, sociology was largely invented here in the gray Gothic buildings of the University of Chicago. And with that came social work and immigrant settlement houses like the fabled Jane Addams Hull House. In Chicago, national reforms began to improve the lives of workers while removing 6-year-olds from sweatshops.

And on that same ivy-covered campus, the world was changed forever. There, a handful of scientists produced the world's first sustained nuclear chain reaction, making Chicago the birthplace of the atom bomb.

Sure, our troubled race relations have always been an embarrassment, but in the first decades of the century, Chicago still showed itself to be the city of possibilities, as it became the capital of black capitalism.

Here came self-made men like Jesse Binga, a barber from Detroit who arrived with $10 in his pocket and rose to become a millionaire as the Midwest's first black banker.

And here, Robert Sengstacke Abbott handed out a couple sheets of printed paper on the South Side in 1905 that became the Chicago Defender newspaper and eventually the largest African-American-owned business in the country.

And others who would follow also prospered. At the end of the century, Hispanic, Polish and Asian immigrants became Chicago's fastest-growing pool of newcomers.

Largest, biggest, first and fastest. That's the vocabulary of the city. Throughout the 1900s, Chicago talked, breathed and ate in superlatives of achievement. Except, of course, in the case of the Cubs. And even in the waning days of 1999, the front page of the Chicago Sun-Times once again sang a familiar song of the century.

"World's tallest building returns?" it said. "City may reclaim title with developer's plan."

Chicago, always the contender. Its chip was its strength.

Here was yet another incredible plan, an astonishing 108-story building rising more than 1,500 feet above street level. The idea was brought before the City Council in September 1999. Aldermen scratched their heads over this audacious idea, that would radically alter the skyline of the city.

And then they passed it.

Richard M. Daley
Mayor of Chicago

LOOKING FORWARD: THE YEAR 2000 AND BEYOND

The health, safety and education of the city's children are top priorities for strengthening and building the future of Chicago.

BY RICHARD M. DALEY

As we look to the first year of the new century, Chicago is well on its way to solidifying its position as one of the world's great centers of commerce and culture.

But for all of us who make our home here, the quality of life in our neighborhoods is of foremost concern. Strong neighborhoods anchored by good schools are the foundation of our city and our best hope for ensuring a proud and prosperous future.

While much progress has been made in improving school performance in the last four years, we have a long way to go before we can honestly say that all our schools meet—if not set—the standards required to compete in the next century.

Beyond that, however, I see our schools continuing a trend to be community centers where children can engage in safe, constructive activities during afternoons,

evenings and weekends, where families can gather for community events, and where local businesses, senior citizens and others can participate in a shared mission to improve the schools.

Investing over $5 billion in local money in our neighborhoods over the past 10 years has brought us closer to making them clean, safe, attractive and affordable, but here as well, there is more to be done.

I hope to see retail areas with storefronts meeting the sidewalk, not strip malls that put cars and pedestrians in conflict; and we hope to keep greening the city to offset the brick and concrete that goes along with urban life.

Mayor Daley assists with the reading program at a Chicago elementary school.

As we move into the next century, Chicago's financial district (above), along with the technology industry, retailing, health care services and tourism and convention business, will play a key role in continuing the city's prominence as a center of commerce.

Chicago in the next century will continue our traditional role as America's crossroad, and the nation's nexus of art, road, rail and inland shipping. We are already working hard to improve our airports and roads in order to ease the movement of people and freight.

Financial services, health care and retailing will all be major job sectors in the coming century, along with the technology industry, which has established a strong beachhead in the Chicago area, thanks to Motorola, Ameritech and several other companies. Now, the city is seeding start-ups and funding high-tech incubator projects to link the fast-paced technology industry with the thriving academic community in the South Loop.

Meanwhile, the visitor industry holds out the greatest promise for growth in Chicago. We already dominate the nation's convention trade, and recent improvements in labor, transportation and hotel costs will further strengthen this industry.

While we are seen today as the prime destination for midwesterners seeking a taste of a big city, Chicago will emerge tomorrow as the "quintessential American City"

for free-spending foreign tourists in search of a distinctly American experience.

The Chicago of tomorrow will be very much like the Chicago of today, only better. More and more young families will choose to stay in the city as the schools improve. More and more empty-nesters will move back in order to enjoy the amenities we have to offer.

And like today, Chicago tomorrow will both celebrate its diversity in parades, ethnic neighborhoods and multi-cultural activities, while pursuing our common aspirations for a good quality of life, a decent, attractive and affordable place to live, a good job that can support a family and good schools that offer our children real opportunities for a bright and productive future.

That is our vision. That is our promise. And if we continue to work together, that will be our future.

Ringing in the New Year with a huge fireworks display is a Chicago tradition.

All photos courtesy of the Chicago Sun-Times library except as noted below.